# NEW VOCAL REPERTORY

## An Introduction

# NEW VOCAL REPERTORY

## An Introduction

by

# Jane Manning

**A CRESCENDO BOOK**
*Taplinger Publishing Company*
NEW YORK

First paperback edition published in the United States in 1987 by
TAPLINGER PUBLISHING CO., INC.
New York, New York

ISBN 0-8008-5557-4 [pbk]

First published in 1986 by
The Macmillan Press Ltd
London
England

Typeset by Rowland Phototypesetting Ltd
Bury St Edmunds, Suffolk
in 11/12pt Sabon

Music examples drawn by Michael Finnissy

Printed in Hong Kong

# Contents

**Technical VI**

# CONTENTS

# Preface

It has long been my impression that the quality of the 'English-language group' in a traditional song recital has been a little disappointing, especially when compared with the richness of the German and French repertory. The same few songs, often culled from some examination syllabus many years ago, turn up constantly, and it appears that the available resources are not being used to best advantage. Our present century continues to provide us with the widest variety of styles imaginable, and works for voice and piano in English reflect this diversity. Recital items can range from weighty song cycles by British and American composers at their full maturity, to a wealth of more lighthearted fare.

This book represents a highly personal selection of suggestions for extending an English-language repertory right up to the present day. It is not intended as a comprehensive catalogue, and doubtless contains some idiosyncrasies. There are bound to be omissions because of the wide-ranging nature of the task; some are conscious, however, as I felt these composers were perhaps well enough exposed for the time being. I had to cast my bread upon the waters in obtaining scores, especially those from sources abroad, and I am well aware that for all the many fine composers I have managed to include, there are as many more that should have had a place. However, it is a special pleasure to find myself in the position of being able to promote the cause of some lesser-known music of the highest quality, most of it by living composers.

It became clear early on in the project that I could fill several volumes with eminently suitable material. I therefore had to limit myself by way of a few basic guidelines. It must be stressed that the book is not aimed at specialist virtuoso singers of new music or their audiences. Those of us who work in the new music world must beware the dangers of an élitism which may alienate others. Potential newcomers to the field are understandably put off if they are made to feel like outsiders, particularly when they may have to negotiate an obstacle course to find the music and information they require.

Prospective performers and vocal teachers, bewildered by the maze of available material and diffusion of publishers, may need positive encouragement and practical help to find the treasures that exist. Unpublished songs present further problems as many composers do not successfully promote their own music.

Prejudice against the unfamiliar is unfortunately inevitable. I find it depressing when visiting institutions in this country and abroad to be told by singing teachers that their pupils will not be attending my master class because they are 'not advanced enough to sing modern music'. So perhaps the most important reason for my writing this book is that the breaking down of stylistic barriers in vocal music is long overdue. Of all performing artists, singers have sometimes tended to be the least inclined to question accepted patterns or to indulge in intellectual or philosophical argument about their repertory.

It is unfortunate that an advanced musical idiom has tended to lead the faint-hearted to believe that new music is beyond their capabilities. In fact, many contemporary composers write as mellifluously for the voice as did Handel or Mozart; others may need more concentrated technical work before they lie easily, but are rarely more vocally taxing than Bach. The simplest avant-garde notation may look dauntingly modern on the page but turn out to be the most suitable of all for beginners. Executing so-called 'extended vocal techniques' may be less problematic than spinning a series of long legato notes with perfect control. Many new works can make the most modest demands vocally and musically yet give audiences a refreshing surprise.

A crucial distinction must be made between the standard of vocal technique (including interpretation) and the standard of musicianship required. I aim to clarify the situation by grading all works in these two separate categories – *technical* and *musical* – ranging from I to VI in progressive difficulty. Difficulties of technique invariably present the greater barrier, since they inhibit musical interpretation; the songs have therefore been ordered by degree of technical difficulty and then subdivided by musical difficulty.

I have a particular fondness for the many fine songs in 'English traditional' vein which are already familiar to all of us, but it does seem worth pointing out that some composers may have been over-performed at the expense of others equally worthy; this may explain why some obvious names are missing from this selection. I have also assumed (perhaps dangerously!) that people will not need reminding of the existence of works by established figures that are already classics in the field – the major cycles of Britten, Tippett, Walton and Copland, for instance, and the distinguished and varied vocal output of Charles Ives and Samuel Barber. Some admirable songs by Bliss, Lennox Berkeley, Milner, Rawsthorne, Rubbra and Tate, and the Americans Rorem and Argento appear, happily, to have already reached a wider audience. Stephen Banfield's excellent and comprehensive two volumes *Sensibility and English Song* (Cambridge University Press, 1985) are essential reading for those requiring a full knowledge of the field, especially of early 20th-century repertory. British readers are also urged to visit the indispensable British Music Information Centre in Stratford Place, London, to view scores at leisure.

It is my belief that every piece in this volume can take its place in a standard recital, and will appeal, for a variety of reasons, to a general, non-specialist audience, particularly if placed carefully in the programme. A short paragraph with a few suggestions on this aspect comes at the end of each feature.

Performance impact and entertainment value have been high priorities when making my choice. (Music is for performing after all, and competition Reading Panels ought always to keep this uppermost in their minds.) For this reason I have excluded any work, despite its distinction, which I feel to be so awkwardly set as to be impossible to sing with comfort, even after long practice. Singer and audience do not have to 'take their medicine', and the hedonistic side of performing is often overlooked! To be merely 'interesting' is not enough: a song should move and sensitise the listener. Songs for all moods and occasions are to be found. The range of styles has far exceeded even my own expectations and will, I firmly hope, prove stimulating to all those singers of reasonable competence for whom this book is meant.

Finding the songs is of course only the beginning. More practical guidance is often needed to help newcomers over the inevitable technical and interpretative hurdles that occur when tackling something unfamiliar. The treatment of the selected works is extremely detailed and covers specific problems from the point of view of both performer and teacher. A review of the works from a musicological standpoint is not intended, although I have attempted to describe basic features; the piano accompaniments are also discussed. I think it fair to say that skilled pianists able to cope with difficult accompaniments seem to be in plentiful supply nowadays, and some piano parts require more virtuosity than do the vocal lines.

Amongst those works which I was unable to include because of their exceptional vocal or musical requirements, I warmly recommend the following to singers of special expertise:

Milton Babbitt: *Phenomena* (Peters Edition)
George Crumb: *Apparition* (Peters Edition)
Michael Finnissy: *Anninia* (UMP)
Peter-Paul Nash: *Five Poems of Wallace Stevens*
George Perle: *Thirteen Dickinson Songs* (Theodore Presser)
Michael Rosenzweig: *Song Cycle for High Voice and Piano*
David Rowland: *Nashe Songs* (Donemus)

Joseph Schwantner: *Two Poems of Agueda Pizarro* (Helicon-
European-American)
Gillian Whitehead: *Riddles*
Peter Wiegold: *Songs from Grimm*
Charles Wuorinen: *A Song to the Lute in Musicke* (Peters Edition)

The fact that all are for high voice highlights a situation that seems to
have developed during the last 30 years or so. The principle of 'supply
and demand' has meant that repertory has tended to be weighted
heavily in favour of a handful of specialists.

I am much indebted to a great number of friends, colleagues and
well-wishers who have provided valuable advice, information and
practical help, amongst whom I must particularly mention John
Potter, who introduced me to some superb songs which would not
otherwise have come my way. I must also thank the representatives of
the Music Information Centres in Canada, Finland, Iceland, Australia
and the United States of America for their kind co-operation, and most
especially Roger Wright of the British Music Information Centre who
may be contacted by anyone experiencing difficulty in obtaining
scores.

All in all, I would like to think that the suggestions and observations
I have made prove a real help and encouragement to young and old,
and – most importantly – awaken new enthusiasms and adventurous
spirits at a time when 'playing safe' seems to be more prevalent than
ever.

Jane Manning
London, 1986

4

# Three Theatrical Songs
## (1946)

## Milton Babbitt (born 1916)

T I; M II
Any voice
Duration *c.*5′

These delightfully simple and original show songs are a real pleasure to sing. They are especially welcome from this distinguished composer whose impressive vocal output is otherwise too difficult to be included in this book (but is to be warmly recommended to singers of outstanding musicianship). As Babbitt says in the introductory note, the songs come from an entirely different side of his musical life and represent his prodigious knowledge, love and understanding of the great American show-song tradition, symbolised by such figures as Rodgers, Kern, Porter, Berlin and Gershwin. The *Three Theatrical Songs* come from the musical play *Fabulous Voyage*, an adaptation of Homer's *Odyssey* which has yet to be staged. An operatic style must be avoided at all costs; a fresh, seemingly untutored mode of delivery is desirable. The performance must be effortlessly rhythmic and straightforward, without mannerisms or exaggeration. All three songs are in *alla breve* time; the third one is the quickest. The musical idiom is tonal. Even a complete beginner will master the music and derive enormous enjoyment from it. The vocal range is set comfortably in the middle and the phrases flow with ease.

The songs would obviously be more appropriately sung by a woman as three different female characters are represented. This distinction is not, however, specified. The intention is to convey contrasting sides of the whole female personality rather than to present three separate characters. In the original the roles are meant to be played by the same person to emphasise the unity of this concept. The absence of dynamics in all the songs allows for sensitive variations of intensity to follow the texts.

## 1. As long as it isn't Love (Milton Babbitt)

The singer impersonates the nymph Calypso, who is nonchalant, uninvolved and very knowing. Good diction ensures that the message is conveyed without being underlined by too arch a demeanour. The more unexpected words, such as 'shove', must be delivered immaculately. The syncopations move naturally and idiomatically. Occasional subtle sliding between notes to keep a smooth legato is certainly permissible.

### 2. Penelope's Night Song (Richard S. Childs)

As the heroine unravels her handiwork she wishes she could have similar control over Time and put back the clock. This gentle piece should be sung with sweet simplicity and nostalgia. A clear, pure tone ensures that the fast-flowing words come across. Short notes, such as the quavers before bar-lines on 'world', 'that' and 'once' must be given their full value; rests should be observed scrupulously but with seeming casualness. There is a natural opportunity for a crescendo on 'the wondrous radiant glow', which should continue up to 'won' and then subside a little with some regret on the singer's part.

### 3. Now you see it (Milton Babbitt and Richard Koch)

The final song moves much more briskly. It is sung by the witch Circe and is truly enchanting with an infectious, dance-like quality. A slightly racy delivery seems appropriate here. Low chest notes (for example the B flats) can be exaggerated, and the singer must shed all inhibitions. The words are suitably outrageous and the whole effect is very jolly and rousing. It is enjoyable to end as if vanishing suddenly by falling away on 'Now you see it, now you don't'.

Babbitt's *Theatrical Songs* instantly appeal to audiences. A performer with the right manner, style and aplomb will enjoy drawing together a programme of similar cabaret songs with contrasting songs by other American composers such as Ives, Copland, Lou Harrison, Barber and Bernstein. They would also work well juxtaposed with more established show and film songs, for example groups from *Showboat* (Kern) and *Roberta* (Kern), *An American in Paris* (Gershwin) and, perhaps best of all, *Kiss Me Kate* (Porter).

# Chamber Music Book I
## (1981)

### Barry Seaman (born 1946)
### Text by James Joyce

T I; M II
Any voice
Duration *c.*9'35"

Barry Seaman belongs to the group of young composers who, mindful of the fact that much contemporary music falls outside the scope of the layman, aim to rectify this by quite deliberately writing music that is essentially simple, modest in its demands and capable of being sung and appreciated by keen amateurs. This is not to say that a professional performance is any less desirable: the added technical smoothness and efficiency of a well-trained voice will always prove an advantage in such clean-cut and graceful vocal lines as these. Seaman's music is minimalist, a most appealing and pleasant idiom which is based on constant reiteration of rhythmic and melodic cells. The resultant *perpetuum mobile* is immediately attractive to the listener. It takes a scrupulous composer of taste to prevent the music from sounding superficial, as commercially orientated works on a larger scale sometimes show.

This cycle is an ideal piece for a complete beginner. (The piano parts too are simple and are not virtuosic.) The vocal range lies comfortably in the middle of most voices, although there are some low As and Bs. By adopting the poised, clear tone that is suitable for the pieces the singer ought to ensure that there is no strain or intrusive vibrato. High-voiced singers should ease themselves down the gentle steps without losing the continuous thread of light sound. A heavy voice would be most inappropriate. If a singer has difficulty with such supple phrases, he or she should seek expert advice to try to correct any tendencies towards unwieldiness.

Such works ought to be cherished items in publishers' catalogues. It is to be hoped that the composer will soon be given the chance to promulgate his works to the general public for which they are clearly intended. Songs which ally such fine quality with simplicity deserve wider recognition.

7

### 1. My dove, my beautiful one

The first song is a model of clarity. The word-setting is ideally judged and any hazards in the enunciation are eliminated by the fact that the voice's range is centred around low E. A comfortable start is ensured, and, once the voice is flowing easily, the singer will have no trouble reaching the upper E in the legato span of the phrase. In such music, rhythms need careful attention as the time signature and phrase lengths constantly fluctuate. There must be nothing in the performance to suggest that the singer is rigidly counting out beats. Bar-lines should be blurred in the general stream of music and this means that breaths must be taken deftly, when there is no danger of a hiatus.

### 2. At that hour when all things have repose

The opening bars on the keyboard are particularly reminiscent of Baroque music. When the singer enters, the tempo steadies. A gentle series of 3rds underpins the vocal line which, in spite of being unadorned, contains nice details of accent and syncopation. At the cadence towards the middle of the piece there is a *ritenuto*, after which the music starts up again as if nothing had happened. The chromatic intervals are made much easier by the doublings in the accompaniment. The voice moves lower into a more warmly sonorous range for the closing section. A fuller tone should work well, as the lines are unhurried, except for the sudden flurry of short notes on 'invisible harps' which does however obey the natural speech rhythm and therefore should not disturb the reassuringly secure tread of the music. It is precisely such special moments as the delicate and syncopated imitations of a harp which heighten the musical interest and serve to throw into relief the serene quality of the whole song.

### 3. Love came to us in time gone by

For this brief and hypnotic song the piano part is written for one hand only; the use of the una corda pedal creates a slightly blurred texture of major 2nds. This piece probably needs more control than any of the others: the tempo must not be allowed to rush and some of the middle-range notes (for example the long A flats) have to be sustained with an even gradation of tone. The opening note in particular will benefit from careful practice (Example 1). The word is 'Love' and the 'l' helps the singer to prolong the sound until he or she is absolutely sure that the ensuing vowel is securely placed well forward, almost as if humming; the long crescendo can then be managed more easily. Proving that he is unusually aware of all the devices a composer may use to help the vocalist, Seaman places a low A flat immediately after this long opening phrase when support muscles have already been fully

Ex.1.

employed to carry through the line and will therefore be automatically and immediately responsive before the moment is lost. Any hesitation will lose the advantage at once. The first sentence should ideally be sung in one breath. Another breath may be taken after 'twilight'. Tuning of intervals is crucial as this tessitura can provide a few traps. The G flats in particular should be kept high. The very last sentence should also be sung as one phrase if at all possible and it lies so smoothly that singers should not be daunted at this prospect. The raptly concentrated lift up a minor 6th to G flat would otherwise be spoiled.

### 4. Rain has fallen all the day

After the subtle but undeniable demands of the third song, the fourth brings complete relief. The beautifully swaying vocal line is accompanied by gently drumming chords which depict the falling rain. Absolute clarity of tone is necessary throughout. The sudden *mezzo-piano* just before the end must be carefully placed. Consonants must be correspondingly more vividly projected as the tone becomes softer and the sound fades to *pianissimo*. The word 'speak' on B flat in the middle of a phrase may cause an awkward bump at first. Making the preceding note as long as possible helps to ensure that there is no break in the line.

## 5. Bid Adieu

To launch convincingly into the fifth and most fleeting song, the singer must remember the last pitch of the preceding song. 'Bid Adieu' consists of just one paragraph and it is an unadorned folksong in unashamedly traditional English vein. Strict tempo is essential, and breathing should be imperceptible. The composer marks a comma after the two short opening phrases, indicating that if a breath is taken here (easily concealed by the 'h' of 'happy' which follows), it would be a good idea not to breathe again until after the next two fragments. A suitably light, dancing effect should be easy to achieve.

## 6. The Last Song (Strings in the earth and air)

Seaman's setting of this familiar poem is also swift. Gently repeated major 2nds in the right-hand piano part create the continuous murmuring of the text's imagery, while the left hand complements (and sometimes doubles) the smooth vocal phrases. There is considerable subtlety of rhythmic nuance and the end result must be natural and effortless. The vocal range is exceptionally comfortable, ensuring a poised ending to the cycle.

Barry Seaman's work is to be recommended most highly to teachers and pupils. It is as attractive as it is undemanding and proves how much can be achieved by a simple approach as long as innate musicality and a clear compositional purpose are evident. Concert audiences will thoroughly enjoy the music at first hearing. Other settings of James Joyce (for example those by Moeran, Ireland and Bax) could be performed as a contrast. The set would make an admirable end to a concert. It could be used to provide welcome relief from more complex works, or the whole programme could be made up of songs of a similarly simple nature. As the overall mood of Seaman's cycle is contemplative, a bright and sparkling piece – perhaps a simple Baroque aria – should be included, or some cheerful folksongs.

# *Four Songs*
## (1958)

### George Newson (born 1932)
### Text by L. T. Smith

T I; M III
High voice
Duration 7'

There is much to admire in Newson's gift for writing lyrically, even romantically, and yet simply for the voice, and in his special awareness of the subtle resonances that give bloom and radiance to specific vowels at certain pitches. The composer clearly has a sensitive ear as well as a natural feeling for the vocal mechanism. The result is an unerring judgment in the creation of lines which never cause strain. The strong alliterative element in the texts evokes an appropriate response with music of instant appeal. Newson fully exploits the text and his word-setting is exemplary. Even if sung by a soprano, there are no uncomfortable moments where clear enunciation could result in too much pinching and smothering of the tone or where constantly high vibrations might obscure details of the text.

In general, the medium range of the voice is used; it is always the most rewarding, as the voice can cover the widest variety of vocal colours and dynamics without stress. High notes are saved for key moments. (As a soprano, I have often found it depressing to be confronted with lines which constantly place the voice at the extremes of register; the singer tries in vain to clarify a welter of sounds and syllables without becoming exhausted. This kind of vocal writing also puts a strain on the listener.) It is comparatively rare to find a composer with such an understanding for the voice as Newson has, and it is a great pity that his work is not known to a much wider public.

All four songs are straightforward and balance well with each other. The piano accompaniment is tailored to vocal and verbal needs; it provides many pitch cues so that the singer may seem effortlessly to enjoy the whole experience.

## 1. The River

The wonderful opportunities offered by the alliteration and sibilant syllables of the text are eagerly seized on. The dynamically interesting and characteristically attractive melodic vocal lines with their flowing cross-rhythms fall naturally in the voice. When singing the delicate, fragmentary repetitions the voice should stop and start again without taking extra breaths (Example 1). The 'oo' at the beginning of 'wet'

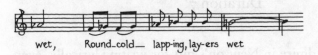

can be used to shape the sound and poise it exactly with the lips. The same is true of the tongue movement on the 'l' sounds, and the gently percussive 'm' of 'millings'. The comfortably low tessitura makes for a simple and clear tone. The singer should bring out such attractive rhymings as 'trebles' with 'pebbles'. A steadying of tempo brings more detail and there is ample time to make every note tell. The sensuality of the word images should be enjoyed, especially where the sibilants heighten the poetic atmosphere. Plays on words, as in 'sky-belly blue, blue-belly sky', can be deftly emphasised. No singer should have the least difficulty: a simple lyrical style is all that is needed and the song almost sings itself.

## 2. Be Vigilant

This extremely brief song powerfully mixes practicality with irony. The piano has a nervous pulsation of short repeated notes in the right hand while the voice keeps up a relentless march-like tread with a gradual crescendo to *fortissimo* on 'sky' and a sudden drop in volume for the bitter close. With each phrase the singer has to fit in an increasing number of words and rhythms become increasingly complex; a steady beat must be maintained throughout. A great deal of passion has to be conveyed in a short time. The singer needs tremendous concentration to control the tone and gauge the crescendo exactly.

## 3. I Love a Small Earth

The composer's marking is 'Playful and light'; the texture is suitably rhythmic and airy, allowing the voice to speak naturally. Throughout the song the voice is set in medium range and thus able to place notes perfectly and easily; the lines can be tossed out almost casually while the singer ensures that rhythms are accurate. Consonants must be well timed and crisply placed in the rests. The intonation must be unfailing and the tone kept pure and clear. It is more difficult to get across the words of the slower section. The singer must not seem hurried before the sudden *accelerando* into the original tempo, signalling the gentle coda that evokes raindrops. The detached notes will come out precisely if very little breath is used.

### 4. I Smiled and Turned Away

The final song starts most movingly and shows the composer at his most poetic, but there is no time for sentimentality. Again, the lines are beautifully placed in the voice (with a lovely melisma on 'falling'), so that the tone can glow. The vocal line does stray once into dangerous, potentially constricting territory around the upper reaches (Example 2), but this, appropriately, is when a sense of strain pervades the text.

Ex. 2.

I strained at the de-cay-ing street,     Wait-ing u – pon the ri-gor in my throat...

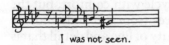

I was not seen.

A slight tightening of tone will be exactly what the composer intended, showing how his vocal writing responds acutely to the text.

The drama is conveyed through gentle understatement of poignant words for the first part of the song until the intensity rises at the question 'Could I escape?' The final stretch brings a more violent mood and starkly horrifying images which need a cutting tone, helped by percussive words. Only a very quick breath can be taken after 'nail' otherwise the pulse may be lost; the dramatic momentum rises to a frenzy, climaxing on a *fortissimo* high A on 'retch' (with a strongly rolled 'r'). A bleak, rather callous line ends the song: it must be delivered in an almost matter-of-fact manner but deep with irony and resignation.

This most concise and impressive cycle contains a range of emotion within a very short space. The vocal lines are a joy to sing and a young or inexperienced performer will be happy and comfortable throughout. The cycle makes its point simply and effectively without bombast and in a highly accessible style. A fine example of modern lieder writing, the pieces would go well in a Classical setting (Haydn, Mozart or Beethoven). Any contemporary works in the programme should be kept in the other half of the recital and should be of an entirely different character.

## *One and All*
### (1975)
### Karl Aage Rasmussen (born 1947)
### Text by Paul Borum

T I; M III
Any voice
Duration 7′

The beautiful understatement of Rasmussen's elegant style has a charm all its own. Any voice will sing the cycle with comfort, but the lightness of touch found in the higher voices (soprano and tenor) is perhaps most suitable for the purity and clarity of line and detail that is so important here. As is typical of this composer, there are elements of pastiche in the music. He imitates a wide variety of styles including conventional lieder (especially those of Mahler) and ragtime. In fact, *One and All* is the perfect modern equivalent of a group of German lieder: each one of the six songs is a deft miniature and together they make a homogenous but varied whole. There are few difficulties in the vocal part, but diction must be neat and well timed; the singer's main problem lies in dovetailing effortlessly with the piano part. Some entries are quite foxing at first, but the singer must remain calm. Some uneven rhythms need to be strictly defined and intonation must be exact. The whole impression is cool, detached and extremely touching despite the economy of expression. The piano part is generally more elaborate than the vocal line and fills in the gaps left by the enigmatic and inwardly passionate texts.

### 1. 'When I'm stretching'
The piano part's appealing, slightly off-beat phrases are suddenly interrupted as the music seems to stop in its tracks and then swings

nonchalantly on again. The voice part is extremely simple and straightforward and the only requirements are perfect timing and clear delivery.

## 2. 'In my body'

The piano introduces and closes the song very firmly. The vocal lines are even shorter in this song. The singer makes two forceful *fortissimo* statements; the notes should be separated but 'quasi legato' as the composer indicates. The 'stop-and-start' characteristic of the writing is again evident; its effect is fascinating and rather quaint.

## 3. 'On the trees'

This rag is delightfully catchy and requires a pianist with a good command of the idiom. The singer's quaver triplets sound above semiquavers in the piano and increase the languid air of the music. Once again clarity is an essential ingredient. The rather unexpected rhythmic twists test the singer for the song must be coolly poised and delivered without affectation. The fragmentary nature of the phrases gives an opportunity to practise the discipline of not breathing at every rest and using as little air as possible. In this way dynamics and accents are better controlled and notes spring out exactly as planned.

## 4. 'I remember her hands'

The rhythmic flow of this slow waltz is interrupted by passages in 5/8. The vocal lines are again direct and unadorned and the piano carries most of the action. The vocal phrases fall gently over the piano texture and it is important that the singer does not project the tone too strongly and thereby spoil the atmosphere.

## 5. 'At the distance of light'

The second half of this song is subtitled 'Intermezzo'. The voice is more overtly expressive; strongly accented fragments of music alternate with gentler passages. The dynamics must be judged precisely as the phrases are so short and their impact must be immediate.

## 6. 'And greatest of all is all'

The cycle ends with a rapt and emotive slow movement which is deeply felt and maintains the simplicity found throughout. Resonant repeated chords on the piano add fullness and warmth to the texture. The poignant final statement is especially telling in its sincerity; this aspect is enhanced by the plainness of the setting.

Although Rasmussen's most unusual cycle is not vocally taxing, it demands deftness and panache from the performer. It requires a singer with a fresh, direct manner and the intuition to identify with the songs at a deeper level, despite their apparent blandness. It is a most refreshing item with which to lighten a programme of weightier pieces. It must be tactfully placed so that its originality is not swamped by more virtuosic works. It is ideally suited to German lieder, in particular those of Mahler or Schumann.

# *May Rain*
## (1941)

### Lou Harrison (born 1917)
### Text by Elsa Gidlow

T II; M I
Any voice
Duration 2′

This enchanting piece by one of the senior figures of American music forms an ideal introduction for a newcomer to a more experimental idiom without posing any musical problems. The piano is prepared by inserting a screw between two of the three strings attached to each of six specified pitches to produce 'harmonics and a gong-like resonance'. (Veterans of contemporary music concerts will know that this means that the piano cannot be a hired Steinway, since they adhere very strictly to their policy of not allowing anyone else to tamper with the inside of their instruments. No harm is done, however, and it is worth taking the trouble to book a different piano if necessary.) The pianist plays an extremely simple part with one hand only, so that the other can be employed to strike (seven times at comfortable intervals) a deep-pitched tam-tam. Alternatively the singer could do this, or, as in some rare cases, a percussion player may already be available for the concert.

A fresh, unforced style of delivery is essential for the singer, who should almost sound 'untrained'. It is not easy for a trained classical singer to control vibrato perfectly in the middle range, but otherwise the musical and vocal demands are very modest and should not trouble a complete beginner; only a very small compass is used. There is a continual oscillation between major and minor 3rds in both piano and voice. The piece grows in a crescendo towards the middle and dies away again at the end. Care should be taken to avoid an anglicised overemphasis of diction; rolled 'r's for example, would be inappropriate. The total effect should be one of undisturbed serenity and contemplation, thus allowing the listener to be caught in the spell of this most unusual and haunting song, which already shows the composer's great interest in the music of the Far East, especially the Indonesian gamelan.

The song would form a perfect foil for an energetic and full-blooded Romantic song cycle, and would also go particularly well after some florid Baroque arias. It could make a captivating start to one half of a recital, or serve as an encore if the singer has enough strength to maintain a poised and steady tone.

# The Wonderful Widow of Eighteen Springs/A Flower
## (1942/1950)

### John Cage (born 1912)
Text by James Joyce/no text

T II; M I–II
Any voice and closed piano
Durations 2'/c.3'

These beautiful and simple songs belong in the 'contemporary classic' category, but they may not be as well known to the general music public as they deserve. Partly through ignorance and partly because of the wide range of styles that Cage employs, those not familiar with Cage's work may not appreciate the purely musical virtues which have always distinguished this visionary figure from his many imitators.

The composer stipulates that the vocal tone quality should be unaffected and without vibrato, as in folksinging. This may not be easy for some voices, but it does train the singer to place the tone securely. The choice of key is left to the singer, and it is wise to opt for a low-lying one. There are some very long phrases which should lie in the singer's most secure range on those notes least inclined to wobble under stress. In the rapt silence invariably engendered by these gentle songs, the slightest untoward jerk or bubble in the voice would be most disturbing.

The piano part is to be played on a closed instrument, thus making it into a delicate percussion accompaniment. The pianist plays with fingers or knuckles, as specified in the composer's extremely clear instructions in the score; diagrams of the profile of the piano are given to indicate the exact places on the instrument which are to be played. The pianist needs skill and patience but the pieces are within the scope of the average, well-co-ordinated player. Rhythms must be projected with exceptional clarity to differentiate the various types of attack and to make the groupings clear, as they are the singer's only guide. The singer must in turn show consideration to the accompanist, for the vocal lines are simpler than the piano parts; it is unreasonable to expect too much indulgence from the pianist if the voice fails to keep a disciplined beat. Good ensemble is almost impossible if the singer is not familiar with the piano part.

The songs are enormous fun to perform. A crooning style is appropriate, but with clean pitch. Slow glissandos are a feature of both songs, and these need good control. In *The Wonderful Widow* the enunciation should be gentle and the consonants should not be severe; if possible, a suspicion of an Irish accent could be incorporated. Dynamic markings must be scrupulously observed, for every detail tells in these pieces and the smallest change is of great significance. A still, unassuming platform manner is essential. A singer with a large voice may find the songs difficult and an almost untrained, slightly breathy voice would be more suitable. The songs are ideal for young, inexperienced singers who are not selfconscious and have steady nerves.

## 1. The Wonderful Widow of Eighteen Springs

A lovely series of melodic lines is woven out of three notes, with a great variety of nuance and phrase length, but virtually no exact repetition. This considerable feat of invention sounds effortless and has a subtly hypnotic effect. The voice begins unaccompanied; the first note must have a firm centre as the whole song pivots around it. The piano then sets up percussive patterns, some of which are quite complex. The words are beautifully set. A subtle acceleration on the words 'Win me, woo me, wed me' works towards a climax on 'Ah! weary me' (Example 1), after which the pace relaxes. The final section is the most

difficult to control. The voice is cruelly exposed on the word 'night' which is set low in the voice and sung unaccompanied; it carries a crescendo from *pianissimo* to *mezzo-forte*. The accompanist comes to the rescue, however, with repeated quintuplets in a gradual *accelerando*. The voice part's dynamic markings become more detailed. The lines then wind down again, ending in a very slow and difficult glissando which has to be timed to coincide exactly with the final soft 'le' of 'belle'. It helps to keep the tip of the tongue forward in readiness during the long vowel sound. The whole song is rendered more comfortable if poised on a fine thread of tone and sung with almost vibrating lips, as if humming. A well-placed but gentle and continuous legato is thus made possible. If the sound slips back it is harder to make the voice float because vibrato may obtrude; the intonation might also suffer. The apparent simplicity of this song is deceptive and the singer will need good technical control.

## 2. A Flower

One of the most delightful aspects of this song is its extremely delicate and unusual evocation of bird calls in an otherwise wordless vocalise. The rather long first phrase is the most difficult. It is wise to maintain a good sense of pulse from the outset to avoid loss of confidence. There is a welcome crescendo in the middle. At the end of a very long breath, after negotiating a diminuendo to *ppp*, the singer can take hold of the sound before it disappears; the lips should be used, rather as in playing a brass instrument, to make the staccato ending on 'wah'. There are many more prolonged soft sounds which require both control and naturalness. The piano rhythms become more complicated, but not quite as intricate as those in *The Wonderful Widow*. The dynamics are so soft that *piano* seems quite strong and the opportunity should be taken to relax and shake off any suspicion of tentativeness which may be induced by the inhibiting effect of so much quiet singing and the concentration needed to maintain it. A sudden *mezzo-forte* seems quite forceful in this context. The pitch rises with the dynamics but remains within a 4th until the end.

The understated bird imitations create a beautiful effect. The first is a pigeon: the composer instructs that the singer must articulate a fast one-note trill on an 'o' vowel with partly closed lips. The result does uncannily resemble the bird in question. There is an endearing and unmistakeable contribution from a wild duck and, with the composer's approval, I have always repeated the 'wah' sound on every note as this seems more realistic. A completely unaccompanied passage contains more pigeon calls, this time incorporating subtle glissandos in varied rhythms. The final phrase drops unexpectedly down a 5th. This must be prepared in advance to hold the pitch and the volume. The pianist gives gentle support which dies out in the last bar. The unaffected charm and acute detail of this song is a tribute to the exceptional judgment and unerring taste of its composer.

These two songs make a perfect introduction for a beginner to some of the best and most straightforward aspects of contemporary music. The style is fresh and appealing and will make people sit up and take notice. Audiences of all types should be thoroughly disarmed by its originality and accessibility.

The songs make an ideal foil for late Romantic vocal items. They should be centrally placed so that the singer is vocally poised but not tired. They would make a delightful surprise item in a standard programme. It could be interesting to set them in a mixed group of American music, including songs by Charles Ives and some classic show songs (Gershwin, Kern or Rodgers) or perhaps some Stephen Foster. They would also sound well beside early Webern, Stravinsky or Eisler. Lute songs or some other types of early music would form a pleasant contrast. It is worth noting that the composer has a special fondness for the songs of Erik Satie and these make particularly suitable companions; both Cage and Satie show striking originality and deceptive simplicity.

## *Two Songs*
### (1977)

#### Peter Racine Fricker (born 1920)
#### Text by T. E. Hulme

T II; M II
Baritone
Duration *c*.4'

The songs show the expertise that is typical of this fine and unjustly neglected composer. No singer should find them either musically or technically difficult and the piano part is equally undemanding. The vocal writing is smooth and shows Fricker's sensitivity to timbre. The musical idiom is fairly traditional with neo-classical elements. With great economy of means, the songs come across strongly and clearly and are beautifully integrated. The steady movement of the first, shorter song is contrasted with a more extended second song which is mainly in waltz rhythm with fluctuating tempos. The songs are an ideal choice for a comparative beginner.

## 1. Above the Dock

The right-hand piano part features repeated oscillations on a perfect 5th while the left hand plays a recurrent descending motif. The weaving and supple vocal line is soft and legato. The phrases are luxuriant and wide ranging and comfortable to sing; in Fricker's truly idiomatic vocal writing each syllable is perfectly judged. Only a few crescendos and diminuendos disturb the general air of tranquillity. The singer should sustain a continuous stream of sound which stretches seamlessly across the wide and graceful leaps that characterise this song (Example 1).

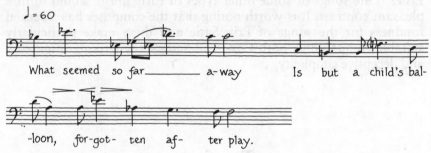

What seemed so far——— a-way    Is but a child's bal-loon, for-got- ten af- ter play.

## 2. The Embankment

The phrase written at the start of this song gives a clear indication of its general feeling and mood: 'The fantasia of a fallen gentleman on a cold, bitter night'. The piano opens with a lilting waltz of 8 bars which is continued by the singer. The counterpoint is shared between the three voices: each hand of the piano and the voice. As in the first song the voice part is so straightforward, except for some problems of pitch, that it is easy to sing it straight through at sight. The phrases are a perfect length for comfort. It is essential to keep a swinging, dancing feeling within a continuous legato. The dynamics rise to *forte* on 'hard pavement' and the piano then leads a slow diminuendo into a slower tempo for a simple 5/4 passage which makes the central message clear. The rubato marking gives the singer freedom to emphasise the words and thus command the listener's full attention. The opening waltz returns at a slower tempo and in a contemplative mood. In this long phrase, the only obvious opportunity for taking a breath is after 'Oh God' (Example 2). The left-hand piano part creates a restless movement with an *accelerando* and then a *ritenuto* before the slow waltz resumes for the last paragraph. The speed must not slacken for the music peters out 'a tempo', as if the waltz were still hanging in the air. A feeling of thoughts left unspoken lingers behind after the music.

Ex.2.

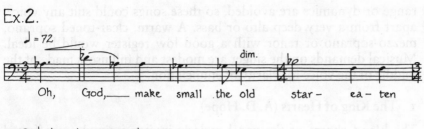

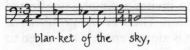

Fricker's beautifully written pieces are enjoyable to sing and perfect for a young baritone. The singer should take care not to cancel out their haunting delicacy and refinement by setting them beside songs that are too heavy: French music would be appropriate, as would brief and contrasting English songs, for example those of Britten.

# Five Cabaret Songs
## (1985)

### Keith Humble (born 1927)

T II; M II
Any voice
Duration *c*.10′

These songs represent the lighter side of one of Australia's most distinguished musicians, and they make an attractive recital item. They are immensely subtle and full of unexpected twists; they show an innate and effortless sensitivity, together with the exceptional musical polish and flair that would be expected from someone with such a broad knowledge and experience of the 20th century's rich resources. The two more ironic and satirical texts by A. D. Hope are well contrasted to the deeper philosophical enigmas of Yeats. These are by no means frivolous songs; they leave a curiously equivocal and slightly disturbing feeling in the air. Humble has achieved an admirably unembellished simplicity of style, and there is no danger of the aptly written piano parts overwhelming the singer's words. Extremes of

23

range or dynamics are avoided, so these songs could suit any voice, apart from a very deep alto or bass. A warm, clear-toned soprano, mezzo-soprano or tenor with a good low register would be ideal. Musical demands on the singer are modest and full use is made of the middle of the voice for clarity of enunciation.

### 1. The King of Hearts (A. D. Hope)

The bland charm of the vocal melody invites a simple, unaffected delivery without emphasis or exaggeration. There are no problems of any kind for the singer. The piano part is almost entirely restricted to repeated chords in the right hand only. Time signatures swing naturally between 3/4 and 2/4 at a leisurely speed.

### 2. The Lady's First Song (W. B. Yeats)

This waltz movement is marked 'Tempo rubato' and the performers are therefore free to take advantage of the one-in-a-bar feeling; they may linger on upbeats where appropriate, keeping the piano quavers flowing easily and allowing the singer room to poise special notes and highlight musical corners of particular piquancy. A *rallentando molto* in the piano leads to a crucial phrase in an anguished outcry. Dynamic markings are absent, but it is to be assumed that this line should be projected firmly. The pianist should make a strong contribution throughout, providing counter-melodies and leading the rubato at key moments. The very subdued ending paragraph is low and of a contrastingly heavy tone; the singer can employ darker vocal colours.

### 3. Girl's Song (W. B. Yeats)

This marvellously subtle, concise poem inspires music of poignant simplicity in three modified strophic verses. Each detail of the text is expertly handled. The slight chromatic variations on the basic melody must be well tuned, and the final, almost parenthetical fragment of each verse must be timed very carefully within the slackening of speed. The singer should linger on those notes marked with *tenuto* or pause signs, and articulate the words softly but separately with special clarity. Once again, no vocal problems occur. A final *piano* statement underlines the enigma.

### 4. The Bed (A. D. Hope)

This is the most lighthearted of the songs. It will be great fun for performers and audience and should elicit a ready response. A little exaggeration of cabaret mannerisms may be permissible here, but a poker-faced performance could be even funnier. The composer puts 'Ploddingly' as an indication of style. The piano maintains a steady tread of 'oompah' chords with sly harmonic twists. The voice part is deliciously simple, except for sudden swoops down to long, low B naturals at the end of the first two verses; the second, on 'agony', is more difficult to sustain. Words are of the utmost importance and notes can be shortened for extra crispness.

## 5. Her Anxiety (W. B. Yeats)

Yeats's deeply felt, somewhat elliptical verse is a challenge to the sensitive interpreter. The music fluctuates between a slow *alla breve* time and a faster, syncopated 3/4 rhythm which is wistful and elusive. The solemn, almost funereal tread of the *alla breve* cuts into the more sinewy progress of the *piu mosso* sections and has the final say in the two-edged last statement which ends the cycle on a note of profound reflection. The vocal lines here are wide ranging and tone quality must be evenly gauged. On the word 'touch' on a high G the singer should produce a tender, glowing sound. Throughout the piece there is every chance for the singer to remain comfortable and concentrate on such refinements of tone and verbal nuance.

The absence of dynamics perhaps indicates an unwillingness to encourage any form of overt expressionism. It is a most appealing and fascinating work and much more substantial than it might at first appear. It would go well in a concert of French music or with something in a totally different idiom, perhaps songs by Webern or Schoenberg. Late Romantic songs (Strauss or Mahler) or early Berg songs would provide an appropriate contrast.

*A Suite o' Bairnsangs*
(1953)

**Thea Musgrave (born 1928)**
**Text by Maurice Lindsay**

T II; M II
Medium/high voice
Duration 7′

These witty and vivacious settings of Scottish nursery rhymes are a delightful introduction to the work of this fine composer. The poems are aptly characterised in music of a most approachable style with rhythmic twists in an unmistakably Scottish folk tradition. A young singer would feel happy and comfortable performing these songs and should enjoy the challenge of the syllables of the Scottish dialect. For the faint-hearted, the author has made a straight English translation, but this diminishes the lively and bracing effect of the words. As always, when the composer has taken such care to set the Scottish syllables meticulously, one or two words will not roll out quite as smoothly in the adapted English version. A light, clear voice is needed for the springing lines of infectious vitality. The songs are ideally contrasted in mood and tempo, forming a beautifully balanced group of perfect proportions for a recital item.

### 1. The Man-in-the-Mune

This song looks simple at first, but some skill and practice is needed to make the decorative passages sound smooth, flexible and shapely without any apparent effort. Rhythms must be precise; breathing must be carefully worked out as the singer cannot afford to snatch breaths in the wrong place and lose rhythmic impetus. The cross-rhythms should bounce along naturally without showing any trace of the trouble they may have caused in the practice stages. The most simple, unaffected performance is often the result of long and detailed study. The glissando between 'say' and 'but' is most helpful, making the crescendo and sudden *piano* easy to negotiate (Example 1). It is always possible to sneak in a quick breath after a staccato note, having been denied the opportunity of breathing in the obvious place by the glissando and crescendo through the gap between the verses. The setting of 'but' is ideal; the final consonant can be cut off smartly, and the next word is 'his'. Under extreme pressure it is almost impossible to

Ex. 1.

An hears whit the star___nies say, But his cheeks gae black,

And hears what the stars___ say, But his cheeks go black,

distinguish between an inhalation or an exhalation on 'h'. The composer's own markings of accents, stresses and dynamic nuances are to be closely observed. No singer should be afraid of truly soft dynamics: the people in the audience should be made to sit up and concentrate fully.

## 2. Daffins (Daffodils)

Gentle arpeggios in the piano softly support a very smooth vocal line containing rhythmic subtleties within the seamless stream of sound. Some practice may be needed to keep the line as undisturbed as possible through the more percussive consonants. A rapt atmosphere must be sustained through the song, even in the warmer, louder phrase in the middle. It may be difficult to maintain the *pianissimo* asked for in the final phrase 'cool lauchan pools' because of the sudden upward leap; the liquid consonants – 'l', 'n' and 's' ('z') – help considerably.

## 3. Willie Wabster

This very jolly, sparkling song is marked 'allegro deciso'. The text is a real tongue-twister and should be practised by itself so that the tongue, lips, teeth and palate work quickly without pushing out too much air. The tempo must not be allowed to run away and in fact the piece sounds faster if perfectly controlled. The quicker line at the end of each verse ought to cause wry amusement if delivered with suppressed humour in a confidential manner. The contrast between loud and soft is crucial and cannot be overemphasised.

## 4. A Bairn's Prayer at Night

The music of this exquisite and enchanting song stays within a very small melodic range. Dynamic variations have to be judged carefully. The vocal tone must be sweet and clear without a hint of sentimentality.

## 5. The Gean (The Cherry Tree)

Like the opening song, 'The Gean' requires skill, dexterity and a clean attack with a light vocal touch. There should be no need to take a

27

breath other than in the given rests. The irrepressibly cheerful mood neatly finishes the cycle. The ringing high G on 'clood' is beautifully placed; the *pianissimo* start to the paragraph, however, may be a little uncomfortable because of the register break and the fast-changing syllables. It is best not to expend too much breath on the initial 't' of 'Tosht'.

The light nature of this thoroughly enjoyable work makes it an ideal item with which to end a recital. It would be intriguing to compile a whole evening of works with a Scottish flavour, perhaps including Schumann's *Gedichte der Königin Maria Stuart* or his settings of Robert Burns. It would also be appropriate to perform Richard Rodney Bennett's *Garland for Marjory Fleming*, but it should not be sung in the same half of the concert as *A Suite o' Bairnsangs*.

# *Five Summer Songs*
## (1972)

### Ronald Perera (born 1941)
### Text by Emily Dickinson

T II; M II
Medium voice
Duration 12'

The songs show considerable delicacy and flair in the clear texture and skilful vocal writing. A flexible, light-toned mezzo-soprano or baritone would perhaps be best suited to them as too much heaviness might limit the range of dynamics. The songs form a nicely balanced group with good contrast and the accompaniments are varied and fluent. The musical idiom is straightforward, uncluttered and precise with great rhythmic vitality and a fine sensitivity to vocal sound. The style is reminiscent of Stravinsky's neo-classicism. The music is immaculately disciplined and its performance should be smooth to make a polished, elegant impression. The singer's refinement of tone will be displayed to great advantage and the charm of the texts comes across clearly. There should be no difficulty with pitch since the piano parts contain cues and doublings. The cycle is an ideal length for a concert and its appeal will be immediate. The composer's instructions in the score are lucid and helpful, making this an excellent choice for a young singer.

## 1. New Feet within my Garden Go

The singer should not find it difficult to convey the text clearly and the comfortable lie of the lines allows for full attention to dynamics. There is a hiatus in the last line just before the last note 'snow', but there is no need to breathe and, in fact, the sound is more likely to be well poised without a breath. A more rapt concentration for singer and listener always comes from using full lung capacity in this way. The audience should be drawn in by the performer's involvement in the physical process of singing long phrases.

## 2. South Winds Jostle Them

The composer's marking here is 'rippling'. The piano sets up a gently whirling figure of semiquavers grouped in tens within each 3/4 bar, while the voice projects a springing waltz tune which is imitated in canon two bars later in the piano. The song has a lovely swing and the singer must take care to preserve rhythmic security and yet keep a one-in-a-bar feeling to avoid hitting individual unstressed beats. The long notes at the ends of phrases will need firm, well-centred tone and consonants must be quickly and neatly articulated. The waltz rhythm suddenly dissolves into *alla breve* time and there are now whirls of 14 semiquavers to a bar, in the piano. The accompanist is responsible for setting up the new two-beat pulse, but the singer must remember that the crotchet speed remains constant. As before, the lilting feeling should be maintained with all its springing vitality, especially in the louder passage. The piano figure slows down for the apt setting of the words 'I, softly plucking' to a staccato phrase before the final very long notes and the return of the waltz at the end. There is a case for breathing before the last 'here' in that the 'h' will anyway provide a break, and it is often difficult to distinguish between an inhalation and an exhalation. A convenient *ritenuto* is provided in the preceding bar. As before, the word-setting is tailored to the singer's comfort. The lively rhythm is the outstanding feature of this song.

## 3. I Know a Place

Perera has written an especially impressive song for the centre of the cycle. An attractively lyrical, modal vocal line (marked 'gently rocking') is sufficiently low to be delivered with ease. The intensity and volume then rise to a peak in a recitative-like middle section. There is ample scope for dynamic contrast. The phrases are spaced out and thus set in relief. When the opening tempo returns the voice soars in radiant legato over pulsating syncopations which turn very suddenly into filigree flourishes similar to those in the second song. The voice is hushed to *pianissimo* but the singer must preserve rhythmic verve to the very end when the music dies away. The gradual fading of the voice will have to be carefully judged and consonants must still be clear and lively (Example 1). The tone should not become too quiet on the word

© E. C. Schirmer Music Company, Boston. Used with permission.

'quartz', which might be uncomfortable to place. Soft tones must always have presence and intensity. The line fortunately plunges down at the end, making it much easier to control the last tiny thread of sound. 'Shoe' is an ideal word here as it has no awkward consonant ending. Throughout the closing section the voice should keep an even, forward resonance, which can be felt at the bridge of the nose, so that the pitches are clear and accurate.

## 4. To Make a Prairie

An incisively clear, straight tone, together with rhythmic panache and verbal dexterity, is needed to perform this charming Scherzo with its appealing 5/8 time (Example 2). There is a central section for piano

alone after which the voice resumes, in a slightly calmer mood of warm resonance, with a lovely phrase which is supple and grateful to sing. The last few bars return to the brisk tempo. Precise intonation is crucial for a neat delivery as the notes tail off to delightful effect.

## 5. The One that could repeat the Summer Day

The composer's instructions again clearly indicate the interpretation he has in mind: 'floating, serene'. He suggests a freedom within the given tempo and the voice can weave its line flexibly within the natural span of the phrase. The singer should give full rein to a warm, rounded tone in the louder phrases, but vibrato must not obscure the words of this elusive, symbolic poem. The vocal line in the last two phrases, for instance, must be sung purely and clearly to offset the repeated *pianissimo* leaping 9ths. The composer's optional breathing marks suggest that he may not wish the wide descending leap to be interrupted, despite the sense of the words; here the musical considerations are paramount, and the two matching 't's of 'Orient' and 'Occident' can be neatly placed on the quarter-beat as the breath is taken, preserving the steady rhythmic pace. The last line must maintain tremendous force and momentum to the very end as no decrescendo is marked.

Perera's thoroughly pleasing and admirably written set of songs would grace any singer's repertory. The unadorned style and clarity of the musical language make the set an attractive proposition for a beginner to the field. The *Five Summer Songs* could be put with other Emily Dickinson settings. They would not seem out of place in a traditional recital programme because of their unpretentious and direct appeal. The set would form a good foil for late Romantic lieder with more exotic textures.

# *Dear Emily*
## (1973)

### Alison Bauld (born 1944)
### Text by William Blake and Alison Bauld

T II; M III
Soprano and piano/harp
Duration *c*.8′

Alison Bauld's tremendous flair and feeling for the theatre, based on professional experience as an actress, is evident in all her works. The musical idiom is extremely straightforward. Many modern conventions of notation are used. In the passages without time signatures time is indicated in seconds (which need not be timed with a stop-watch), giving the performer extra freedom. There are various styles of delivery, including pitched speech and half singing. A modicum of theatrical props is needed: a writing-table and a lamp (or candles, if fire regulations allow). The singer takes the role of Augusta, an Austen-like character who writes a diary entry to her imaginary friend Emily, complaining of a problem with an unwanted suitor. She breaks off from her writing to muse and sing her song, *Never seek to tell thy Love* by Blake, and ends by signing the letter in a resigned manner. This poignant and delicately gauged piece is sensitive in its understatement. Audiences are certain to find it refreshing and it would make a delightful surprise item in a programme. It is a perfect vehicle for a young singer who wishes to try some music theatre in an advanced idiom without being stretched vocally. A good sense of pitch and strong breath control are essential. Although the notation allows a degree of freedom, the vocal effects are precisely conceived and all nuances, dynamic markings and verbal inflections must be closely observed. A Regency style of dress would be appropriate for the singer.

Augusta stands at the writing-table and begins to read her letter haltingly in a natural speaking voice. The voice must trail away and dissolve almost imperceptibly into singing. The transition is difficult even within the low tessitura. The mood should be contemplative; the dynamics are almost uniformly gentle. Breathing has to be carefully planned as the composer likes to use a husky sound for expressive effect and this uses up air more quickly. The halting style continues in the main, sung part of the piece. Rests between words in the middle of sentences are common; they enhance the theatrical, otherworldly atmosphere, as well as holding the audience's attention. Diction is of the utmost importance. A bitter-sweet aura pervades the song in the crooning of the glissandos. An early example occurs on a hummed note (written with a cross for a note head). The use of the bocca chiusa makes for suitably smooth singing. The pace is slow and carefully measured within the 'free' notation. Pitched speech is used at the loudest point in the piece; it poses few problems as entries are short and clipped. (It is generally difficult to avoid singing if a note has to be sustained at some length.)

Changes of dynamics and metre are frequent but the dream-like quality must be preserved. The sudden *piano* in the middle of a long note is hard to accomplish smoothly without a sudden jerk. It must be stressed that the simple and sparse appearance of the score is deceptive; every detail is most carefully wrought, and meticulous adherence to instructions is essential. This is especially true of the closing section where tuning may present problems. The stuttering effect of repeated 's's before the long sigh which dissipates into a downward glissando curve is an excellent touch. The alternating pitched and unpitched words of the last line need to be practised to achieve perfect timing and poise, as the singer (metaphorically if not actually) dips her pen in the ink and signs off, a trifle wistfully.

Full of charm and originality, this piece would fit beautifully into a programme containing other period items, for example Schumann's *Gedichte der Königin Maria Stuart* or settings of Robert Burns. Any Romantic song cycle would be suitable, as would a major French cycle, such as Fauré's *Chanson d'Eve* and *La Bonne Chanson*, or the Baudelaire songs of Debussy. *Dear Emily* would be a perfect choice for a complete beginner with a fresh and appealingly unaffected stage manner. The piece must never be overacted; its simple and unusual musical language speaks for itself and the effect is genuinely touching.

# Five Lyrics of the T'ang Dynasty
## (1947)

## John Beckwith (born 1927)
## Translation by Witter Bynner

T II; M III
High voice
Duration c.8'

This brief cycle by John Beckwith is a gem. One rarely finds such assurance and panache combined with natural musicality and a perfect dovetailing of voice and piano. The music's appeal is immediate. A variety of contrasting moods is displayed during the cycle's short span. The singer should feel completely comfortable throughout. The economy of the writing is truly admirable and highly appropriate to the conciseness of the texts. A sparkling vitality is evident and it is no surprise to learn that this work brought the composer his first major success. It is difficult to imagine a better choice for someone seeking a short cycle with wide appeal; it ought to be recognised as a miniature classic. The vocal writing is expertly idiomatic, and there are some especially captivating and aptly pictorial figurations in the accompaniments. The songs would be equally well suited to a tenor or a soprano, preferably with a youthful and pliant voice, who is able to produce the purest tone and enunciate neatly. The rather conservative musical style sounds completely fresh and spontaneous.

### 1. The Staircase of Jade (Li Po, 699–762)

In Beckwith's delicious opening song a continuously shimmering texture in the piano supports a straightforward vocal line of great clarity. An airy lightness prevails and phrases soar naturally: there is a climax on a radiant high A on the word 'glow' closely followed by a long sustained F sharp on 'moon' which ends the song. Certain words lend themselves to special colours and timbres. The flow of the text seems so ideally conceived that it would be hard to envisage it set in any other way. A mysterious, slightly exotic atmosphere is magically captured in just one minute.

### 2. The limpid river (Wang Wei, 699–759)

The staccato figures on the piano set the scene delightfully. The vocal line is delicate and flexible, with graceful couplets to suggest the river's flow. Purity of tone is especially important, and once again words are set so perfectly that there should be no problems of articulation. It is a completely unpretentious and highly effective setting, devoid of vocal difficulty.

The final phrase is more sustained, over long chords in the piano, and the singer has complete freedom to place the notes comfortably without feeling hurried. The last phrase, 'and be at peace', falls naturally and allows the voice to settle easily on to the long middle G which is held *pianissimo*. The 'ee' vowel normally ensures a safe passage as it can be placed as if humming.

### 3. The Inlaid Harp (Li Shang-Yin, 813–858)

Beckwith displays much subtlety in this superb song. Sinewy chromatic semiquavers weave a fascinating web in the accompaniment as the voice comments in delicately shaped lilting phrases in 9/8. Suddenly spread chords begin in the piano in a most accurate imitation of the sound of a harp. The vocal lines trace a flexible path over the harp-like chords; the poetic effect of the lovely colours he creates demonstrates the composer's superb ear for sounds. The phrases become more ecstatic and the 'harp' expands into whirling cascades at a climax on 'sun'. The flexible triplets in the voice must seem unforced and natural. The contemplative ending shows a fine piece of musical judgment. The singer must exercise discretion and aim for a simple, burningly sincere approach, making the final diminuendo recede into inner thought and reflection.

### 4. On a Rainy Night (Li Shang-Yin)

The fourth song provides a welcome contrast at just the right moment. The deeply felt and lyrical vocal line should be a joy to sing. The simplicity of the language is an object lesson to those who feel that strong emotion can only be projected with dense textures. The delicate understatement of the poem is poignantly caught in the music. The piano's reiterated triplets underline the sudden anguished question 'Oh, when shall we be trimming wicks again?' The relationship between the voice and piano is well balanced and this contributes strongly to the enjoyment of performers and listeners. Beauty of tone will shine through most gratifyingly. The audience will feel closely involved with the underlying sense of despair in the words.

### 5. Parting at a Wine-shop (Li Po)

The final Scherzo scurries along with an infectious energy and the texture is light and sparkling. The singer must have a strong presence and display an extrovert personality. The words are set with exemplary crispness; this brisk, colourful narrative is a perfect way to end the work. Despite fast-changing syllables, the singer should project the text without too much effort. In the last paragraph the decision as to where to breathe is very important. It is best to wait until after 'farther' as the momentum will be sustained and the final expansion on to the high G will be easy (Example 1).

Ex.1.

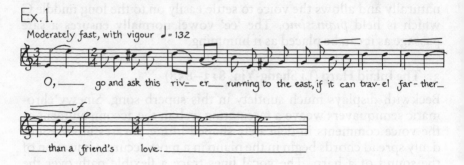

John Beckwith's cycle undeniably proves that the traditional art of songwriting is still cherished. Any recital will be enhanced by its inclusion in the programme and it will fit comfortably in the standard lieder repertory. Though brief, its impact is considerable and immediate; it would make an excellent start to a programme.

## *Three Poems of Robert Frost*
### (1942)

### Elliott Carter (born 1908)
**Text by Robert Frost**

T II; M III
Medium voice
Duration *c*.7′

This cycle is brief, colourful and highly accessible. Those familiar with Carter's later, extremely complex music need have no fears, because this earlier, neo-classical idiom is not exacting and will not tax the inexperienced singer. The songs make a bright, extrovert impression and abound in rhythmic verve. A high baritone with a youthful timbre would be the ideal voice to bring out the texts with freshness and clarity. As with much American song literature, the delivery should be frank and unaffected. Particular care must be taken to banish any trace of strongly English pronunciation of consonants which might result in a stylised preciousness that would be singularly inappropriate. Despite its straightforward musical idiom, the work contains many subtle details and an imaginative palette of colours. The underlying strength and vigour so typical of this major 20th-century composer are predominant features.

## 1. Dust of Snow

In the opening song the voice weaves in long lines over the nervous, jabbing piano part, creating a distinctive texture. Vocal phrases are steady, unadorned and relentlessly rhythmical. The second paragraph, by contrast, is slower and allows more freedom. The voice's role is declamatory and the accompanist provides the supportive continuity in its reiterated chords. The song is so undemanding for the singer that there may be a risk of too much dramatisation in the first section. At the end the deliberately calm mood should give way to a more warmly expressive characterisation.

## 2. The Rose Family

This piece is in 5/8 and a rhythmic pattern of two crotchets and a quaver in the vocal line continues more or less unabated through to the sustained D. The voice then delivers brief, energetic statements in varying colours and dynamics. The vocal demands are again modest, but rhythmic precision is crucial. The voice part is marked 'smoothly' to ensure that a natural, unforced flow continues through the irregular rhythms without any obtrusive pointing of beats. Breaths should be swift and shallow and taken strictly in time. A slight *accelerando* leads to a pause on 'plum'. It may be difficult to begin again *forte* and the singer must find a warm, easy resonance which does not need to be forced. The lilting uneven pulse encourages a light vocal touch, but short notes must be given their full value. A chanting, perhaps even crooning effect is appropriate but the words must still be enunciated properly. Singers who are not American should be aware that rolled 'r's may sound affected and are mainly unsuited to American poetry. Clipped word endings could become prissy if used, too much. An American style 'r' in the middle or at the end of a word is, however, extremely useful for extra clarity and should be encouraged here.

## 3. The Line-Gang

The third song is especially suited to a well-centred male voice as stamina is needed to punch out the strong accents in the middle of the voice. Cross-rhythms should feel quite natural and the rhythms must be precise. The loud, high notes may be strenuous for younger voices at first. All the composer's instructions as to dynamics, stresses and inflections must be carefully followed. The staccato phrase 'beaten out or spoken' is especially effective and the consonants are helpful. In the following phrase, which demands fine control of soft singing, the sibilance of 'hushed' can be used to good advantage, and the 'th' of 'thought' helps the singer to place the tone accurately. The *marcato* passage works up to a fierce climax. The comparatively low final section may be difficult since a *fortissimo* in middle or low register needs considerable supporting power and muscular co-ordination to avoid breathiness and unsteadiness. The physical effort of achieving this should have a beneficial effect on the sustained long notes at the ends of phrases once the singer's muscular apparatus is fully engaged. Rhythmic impact must be maintained by metronomically accurate timing, which must also be applied to the endings of each note. The full significance of the last line must be clear and the diminuendo carefully graded.

These songs will fit extremely well into a programme of works by a selection of American composers, including Ives, Copland or Barber. They make an ideally short group to be placed between larger, perhaps Romantic, cycles from the standard repertory. They stand in no danger of being overwhelmed and their quality will always shine through.

# The Exiled King
## (1984)

### Brian Dennis (born 1941)
### Text by Li Yin (937–978)
### Translated by Brian Dennis

T II; M III
Baritone
Duration *c*.14'

Brian Dennis, a singer—composer, has written a large body of highly original vocal music and it exhibits his special understanding of the medium. Progressing through several styles which reflect his constant awareness of the changing face of contemporary music, he has, over the past 10 years, forged an appealing and most accessible personal idiom, well suited to the economical but emotionally charged language of the ancient Chinese texts with which he first began working in the late 1960s. A fresh and direct approach is a strong feature of his music. He acknowledges many influences, from Ives and Boulez to the machine-like rhythms of recent fashion, from which he has evolved a fascinating and memorable musical style which is a curious hybrid of oriental and English cultures. It is a considerable departure from the more fragmentary settings of oriental texts more frequently found. Whole-tone scales are used; some of the melodies and harmonies are reminiscent of the late English Romantics, for example Delius and Vaughan Williams. The piano writing is extremely striking; it can almost be said to dominate and to dictate proceedings in the very best sense. Exciting, often.percussive ostinatos are a prominent feature. Changes of mood and colour are usually heralded by the piano, as it prepares the way for the voice to introduce a new thought and firmly underlines the emotional and dramatic implications.

The cycle contains several high Fs and G flats, so a warm-voiced tenor, as well as the high operatic baritone for which it was written should be able to sing it comfortably. The vocal lines are mellifluous and gratifying. The texts are set extremely well in a very straightforward manner, largely following the contours of each phrase and paced according to the patterns of heightened, declamatory speech. It should prove an enjoyable vehicle for both performers and audience. Its agreeably extrovert impression makes it a welcome item in a recital. Despite the antiquity of the texts, the words have a timeless relevance and a direct simplicity. There should be no difficulty in communicating their messages even to an unschooled or relatively unsophisticated audience.

## 1. The Past

The king speaks bitterly of his tragic plight in a series of impassioned outbursts. The piano establishes a *perpetuum mobile*, pausing briefly to allow the voice to enter. The right-hand part of the accompaniment is high, creating a brittle, glittering and quasi-percussive effect which appropriately evokes an oriental atmosphere. The vocal phrases are built out of note cells consisting of a limited number of pitches. From these the composer has drawn a wide variety of colours. Amongst several high notes in this song, the accented 'withered' on G flat works particularly well as the singer can use the 'w' to place the note carefully without being rushed. The lip action will be a great help. The vocal lines should be sung smoothly in a steadily graded tone, avoiding sudden changes of timbre, yet taking full advantage of emotional undercurrents. The repression and anguish should be expressed openly.

## 2. Love Sickness

This superb song, with its mercurial changes of mood, is led by a sparkling piano accompaniment of rhythmic vitality, which pinpoints the text and effects the many tempo changes. It is true lieder writing, perhaps reminiscent of Wolf in the attention to detail and the poignant brevity of the singer's utterance. The cadences into new sections are beautifully shaded and the pictorial imagery of the text is exceptionally well caught, especially in the staccato passage (Example 1). The singer will need to react quickly and deftly to the fleeting images. He must be able to place notes delicately and lightly in a disciplined rhythm but with flexibility.

Ex.1.

## 3. New Year

The central song is more ambitious in scope and warmly expressive, perfectly integrating the voice with the piano which again has a particularly dramatic and crucial role to play. The first unaccompanied vocal phrase is particularly striking after the listener has grown accustomed to the ostinato accompaniments of the previous songs. The texts are ideally set for comfort and audibility; it is a most romantic song in the best sense. The more obvious oriental features of the piano part (open 5ths and tritones) are blended into a richly expressive canvas, flexibly and sensuously shaped with smooth interplay between the two performers. The solo piano passage speaks volumes in its changes of mood, sometimes heavy, sometimes brisk and light. The ad lib vocal phrase which follows is probably the most difficult in the piece; since the piano holds one chord throughout, pitch problems may occur. The F flat in particular will need to be treated with special care, as will the interval after it (Example 2).

Ex. 2.

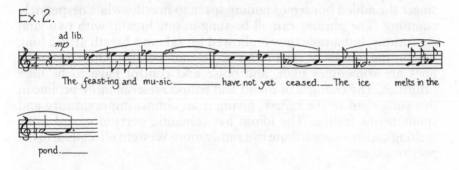

The legato final section is most beautiful. It must be sung *pianissimo* for the first two phrases, using sibilant and percussive syllables to enhance the poetic imagery without disturbing the tranquil, seamless effect. The singer's last phrase is heavy with understatement and must be delivered with absolute clarity and firmness of tone in an almost matter-of-fact manner. The music speaks for itself very clearly and the piano postlude makes a most moving conclusion which is guaranteed to hold attention.

## 4. Grief for a loved One

A reiterated G (marked 'bell-like') in the left-hand piano part and the icy, high treble part create a starkly miserable mood for the singer's bleak, *pianissimo* entry; the voice builds up to a passionate climax and then dies down again. The lack of vibrato can be used to good effect here, and the singer should allow the tone to become enriched a little only as the volume increases. A sense of unbearable grief is always present. The particularly telling piano solo which leads to the last verse is marked 'relentless'. As at the beginning, the singer has to control a cold, starved *pianissimo* line but at an even slower tempo. At the start of this final verse the dynamic markings are a little warmer, which is fortunate as it makes it easier for the singer to lift the voice to a high F while maintaining a smooth legato.

## 5. Spring Rain

The final song is the most elaborate and ambitious. It brings a few more musical problems, including irregular rhythms and unusual time signatures, for example 11/16 and 10/8. These are not as difficult as they look, as the piano's semiquaver groupings help to organise them into easily assimilated patterns which should soon grow familiar. A singer who is used to coping with Messiaen's additive rhythms will have few problems. The secret is not to be in too much of a hurry, but to maintain serene control, once basic security has been achieved through practising the song slowly. The composer has not given the singer the added burden of finding space to breathe while desperately counting. The phrases can all be sung in one breath, with two vital exceptions, but ample time is allowed for taking a breath after a long note in the middle of each (after 'exile' and 'petals'). Once again the lines are sometimes high, and poise and control have to be high priorities. The changes of mood and tempo are even more prolific in this song than in the others, giving it an almost improvisatory and spontaneous feeling. The idiom has romantic overtones, and some melting cadences contribute to a rather more Western effect than in the previous songs.

Dennis's cycle, with its intriguing blend of influences from East and West, should prove immensely popular with all kinds of audience. It would be fascinating to contrast it with other settings of ancient oriental verse, particularly if these are of the more usual miniaturist variety. Another good idea would be to place it amongst song cycles inspired by exotic subjects or translations in other languages from Eastern poets: the second of Webern's Four Songs, op. 12, or Schoenberg's *Das Buch der hängenden Gärten*, op. 15. Szymanowski's *Songs of the passionate Muezzin* could illustrate a different Eastern culture, as could some of the many settings of the Indian poet, Rabindranath Tagore (Frank Bridge's settings would be stylistically suitable). English songs by Delius or Ireland could be included. Wolf or Mahler lieder would also be compatible. The songs of 20th-century figures such as Weill or Eisler, with their close affinities with popular culture, share the accessibility of *The Exiled King*.

# Six de la Mare Songs
## (Nos. 1–4 and 6, 1966–71; no. 5, 1985)

### Elaine Hugh-Jones (born 1927)
#### Text by Walter de la Mare

T II; M III
Soprano/tenor
Duration 16′

It is a rare and special pleasure to discover a major songwriter, and I am much indebted to my colleague John Potter for introducing me to the work of Elaine Hugh-Jones. Her songs show complete mastery and understanding of voice and piano writing. Although they are firmly based on a traditional musical style – that of English post-Romantic – the songs are not in the least derivative. The composer shows a wonderful assurance and freshness of approach and an exceptionally sensitive response to words. It is extremely hard to choose from such a wealth of excellent material, all of it clearly and beautifully conceived, sensitive and full of character. Widely contrasting moods, pictures and situations are conjured up deftly and effortlessly. Elaine Hugh-Jones varies her material constantly yet always seems to preserve stylistic unity. Each song is a joy to sing and play. (The composer was herself for many years a staff accompanist for the BBC, which must have contributed to her unerring instinct for the medium.)

It is impossible to imagine an audience that would not be instantly attracted by this lovely music. The words should be easily followed, giving the listener immediate enjoyment. All singers will be grateful for the chance to be heard at their vocal best and to communicate directly to the audience, virtually unimpeded by technical problems. The music should be well within the grasp of a beginner; apart from some minor problems of rhythm and pitch, the writing is so fluent that the songs almost sing themselves.

## 1. Winter

The setting grips the listener's attention at once. It will be natural for even the most insensitive artist to keep the tone quality straight and starved as the accompanying figuration depicting an icy landscape is so apt. Individual words are heightened with precision and ease. The phrases are long and smooth but deliberately pallid; they are graceful and shape themselves so naturally that breathing places are obvious.

Much use is made of the middle of the voice until the lines move gradually upward. Ideally, the long paragraph beginning 'The rayless sun' should be as seamless as possible as the singer moves through the crescendo upwards and then down again (Example 1). The plangent

Ex.1.

qualities of certain vowel sounds (such as 'ur' and 'ay') are to be fully exploited in this song. They unerringly fall on pitches which make this easily practicable. The poem moves along at a perfect pace. The closing phrase is a delight: a *subito piano* on 'floats' on high G is vocally flattering and comfortable. The calm translucent texture of the piano writing creates a magical effect throughout.

## 2. Ghosts

Flowing arpeggios in the piano support and enhance a gentle yet intense legato vocal line which flows in perfectly timed paragraphs. The natural sweep of the music and relationship between voice and piano are reminiscent of Fauré's vocal writing. The high phrase 'Sweep softly thy strings' must be kept even in tone which is perhaps a little more difficult for a soprano. Dexterous timing of consonants is necessary to avoid pinching the tone. The natural rhythm of the words keeps a lively sense of pulse within the legato and there is ample time to point and colour special syllables. A sudden change to a slow tempo at the end makes way for a new atmosphere of contemplation and nostalgia. The 'subito piano' marking on 'Home', which follows a crescendo, is greatly helped by the aspirate 'h'. This would be a good case for covering the tone to make it sound more inward; the vowel sound helps to achieve this.

## 3. Echo

The sparkling lightness and bounce of this exquisite song is entrancing. Over a shimmering accompaniment with constant tremolando figures and rocking ostinatos, the melody alternates naturally from 6/8 to 9/8 time. A rising perfect 5th on 'who called' and later on 'who cares' is used as a recurring motto in a brilliant example of how a simple idea can be used with consummate skill and imagination to form a perfect whole. Through a delicious series of modulations the lilting song flows in one beautifully shaped long paragraph. At the final 'meno mosso' marking the opening F minor key returns. The last two lines are full of colour and dramatic contrast; the echo effect is used aptly incorporating some exciting dynamic changes. The duplets have to be carefully pointed in contrast to the basic triplet rhythms. The vocal lines are again joyously comfortable throughout and pacing is ideal for easy articulation.

## 4. The Hare

This delightful setting is full of vitality and yet delicate in the subtle and mercurial dynamic shadings. Repeated low staccato notes in the piano create a nervously tingling atmosphere and the vocal phrases are suitably intense. The music is marked 'misterioso' and the many sibilant sounds in the text help to create the right atmosphere. A hollow, rounded tone, is appropriate, especially for the low opening phrase, but the words must not lose their presence. This taut scena is full of fascinating musical twists and mercurial changes, as demonstrated in the central dramatic interjection. This is most aptly caught in the vocal line and the piano, too, makes a contribution of much character (Example 2). Then the music suddenly gallops off at a tremendous pace, stopping with equal suddenness for the last plain, bleakly simple phrase.

Ex. 2.

And I whispered 'Wh-sst Witch-hare,'

## 5. Silver

The composer has recently added this song to the cycle and its melting smoothness is the ideal contrast to the more intense songs on either side. The piano's gentle ostinato supports a dreamy, legato vocal line which must be sung with the silkiest tone possible. Extremes of range are wisely avoided so that the singer can gauge quality and evenness of the sound. The triplets fall naturally with the words of this exquisite text. The piano accompaniment gradually moves into more complex rhythms, including quintuplets, and the singer must be sure to maintain an even crotchet beat against them. The composer marks the phrase 'senza accelerando' to remind the singer and pianist not to hurry because of the slightly increased activity and the rise in volume to *forte*. The gentle motion of the *tranquillo* section continues undisturbed. It is essential to maintain a still and hypnotic atmosphere by not allowing any rubato as the sleeping creatures are described. The piano's figurations become more florid and there is a sudden flurry of activity as the harvest mouse appears. Light, scurrying figures on the piano depict this to perfection and the tempo quickens for a short while, only to slow down for the final phrase. The singer must exercise control to create as fine a legato line as possible, aided again by the composer's expert judgment of word-setting and pacing.

## 6. The Ride by Nights

This song is the most ambitious of the six, and it ends the cycle in tremendous style. The dashing piano part will suit a player skilled in fast fingerwork. After the gentle flurry of the high opening piano solo, the voice joins in the intense, though as yet suppressed excitement. Rhythmic sweep and dash are essential to this song. Dynamic markings, especially the short surging crescendos and corresponding diminuendos, must be strictly observed. The singer's middle range is used for most of the song. Rhythmic subtleties prevent the basic two-beat (6/8) pulse from becoming too square. The piano's filigree textures are spiked with staccato attacks, often accented on the beat. The vocal line has a decorative twirl on 'swing'. Great care must be taken in these dancing rhythms to account for consonants and give them an exact placing so that they all occur on a specific beat or half-beat. The word-painting is excellent: the swoop up a major 7th on 'whoop', for example, is a delight. A slight portamento may perhaps be allowed here and the singer should find it fun to do. The momentum and infectious liveliness of the music is captivating. A temporary gathering of strength for the final page is allowed by the 'poco allargando' marking. At this broadening of tempo there is a dramatic rise in tessitura and dynamics. By now the singer should be well into his or her stride and ready to enjoy the exhilaration of punching out the high repeated F sharps on 'huge Orion'. The brisk opening tempo then returns and plunges on into a heady *accelerando* to the final enormous glissando down on 'Home': a sure way to ensure a spectacular ending and a gift for the singer who must be very careful not to misfire and sink beyond the bottom note. Volume must not be allowed to subside during this last section. It may prove quite strenuous to sustain, but great physical excitement and involvement must be generated. The piano part is most helpful in providing clear cues in what would otherwise be a rather difficult passage to pitch.

Elaine Hugh-Jones's fine cycle ought to be a standard work; it is perfect for a recital programme catering for all tastes. It could be intriguing to pair it with the more avant-garde settings of de la Mare by Roger Smalley (included in this book). The stylistic assurance of the music makes it an ideal candidate to follow a powerful and substantial item from the classic repertory: perhaps a major song cycle by Schubert, Schumann or Fauré. Singer and pianist will find great satisfaction in performing the piece. Students and teachers should feel moved to seek out more of the fine work of this neglected songwriter. The songs will prove exceptionally suitable as examination pieces as they are so perfectly tailored to the needs of a young singer.

## *Letters found near a Suicide*
### (1954)

### Earl Kim (born 1920)
### Text by Frank Horne

### T II; M III
### High voice
### Duration *c.*5′

The wonderful directness of expression of this Korean (now US) composer is abundantly illustrated in this extended scena. Kim sets three poems in a continuous span, so the work is properly a song cycle (in the same sense as Beethoven's *An die ferne Geliebte*). Clearly the composer has an intimate understanding and a love of the voice, as is demonstrated by the comfortable lie of the lines throughout the tremendously wide range of dramatic colours. The extremely good vocal writing allows the text to be clearly heard and conveys the emotion concisely and poignantly. Key moments in the text tend to be set at a lowish tessitura so that the singer can subtly shade the voice without causing any stress in enunciating the extremely moving texts.

More extended vocal works from this most sensitive and assured composer, with his disciplined yet spontaneous musical style, would be welcome. Audiences cannot fail to find the piece deeply moving. The piano part is finely detailed. The many doublings of the voice mean that the singer need not fear pitching problems. The textures are expertly balanced and integrated with the voice part.

## 1. To All of You

The voice's delicate melody is heard first on the piano; its suppleness makes it graceful to sing. A reiterated B flat at the top of the piano part will secure the singer's pitch. Care must be taken to make the passage of triplets sound casual. The piano moves into semiquavers and the singer takes this rhythmic pulse into a soaring phrase, ending on an extended high F on 'kiss'. It may be easier for a tenor to make an open vowel here, but the preceding 've' of 'furtive' assures a comfortable start. A moving, one-line coda brings back the note cell of the opening bars with a gentle acciaccatura, adding an eastern flavour. Too much vibrato will spoil definition.

## 2. To Wanda

In the next poem the same economy of note patterns is found. The song starts very softly, set low in the voice. A pure tone is needed for clear intonation, especially as the intervals are quite close. The phrase lengths are flexible and varied and good breath control will be a prime requisite at such a steady tempo. The accents or dynamic gestures should stand out in the otherwise smoothly flowing vocal lines and the piano's accents help to point the words. The music builds up to a climax on 'black', only to calm down again for a particularly beautiful and rhythmically interesting melisma. The very steady tempo resumes in the coda, and the voice is now pitched at the higher octave. It is appropriate to keep the timbre thin and clear for these words. The sudden, delicate ripple, high in the piano, conveys the distant murmur of applause dying away.

## 3. To Telie

In his setting of the third poem the composer has again kept within a strictly limited range of pitch. The singer can orientate herself by the constant repetition of the same series of notes. Grace notes are used again, but this time they depict a catch in the voice, as if the singer were laughing. The device works easily since the tessitura is mainly in the middle of the range. The low Bs that occur in this section are set so well textually that they should give no problems, even to immature voices without much strength at the bottom of the range. The 'ng' sounds give the singer an opportunity to vocalise continuously with a loose throat.

The underlay of 'rippling laugh' seems incorrect (Example 1): the 'pling' should be directly under the note preceding the grace note, so that it lasts through the full quaver and grace note and not just the acciaccatura. The note groupings do seem to indicate this. It certainly makes it much easier to sing, and all the other grace notes are treated in such a way. The fascinating rhythmic melismas on 'crying' show how

Ex. 1.

Kim most effectively uses the instrumental capacity of the voice at a comfortably low range. All details of phrasing and accent are very important in this highly emotional yet controlled music. The high G on 'better' has a searing impact after so much low singing.

Scotch snaps and grace notes figure prominently in the closing pages. Much careful practice is needed to gain the requisite rhythmic precision. The almost unbearably sad final phrases demand intense control and dedication. The embellishments on 'fleeting kiss' must run naturally without disturbing the legato. Kim's use of the liquid 'l' and 'ng' consonants is skilful. The halting effect of the last few utterances is exquisitely caught by the composer as the voice sinks down to a gentle close.

This piece can be highly recommended for all singers as the tessitura is not beyond the reach of supple lower voices. It makes a happy choice for a recital which includes major items from the lieder repertory. Its effect is particularly good at the start of the second half of a programme when the audience is refreshed and ready to engage their emotions. It would be too great a shock to follow it immediately with something too lighthearted; tact and sensitivity of judgment in its placing are very important. Some English romantic music with nature imagery could be chosen to follow, or perhaps some late Fauré.

## *Five Songs*
### (1978)

### André Previn (born 1929)
### Text by Philip Larkin

T II; M III
Mezzo-soprano
Duration *c.* 12′

These fluent and pleasing songs, by a composer of wide-ranging musical tastes and experiences, show great flair and an innate feeling for vocal timbre. American composers seem to excel at setting texts in a relaxed way so that they are delivered without exaggerated accents. As in the simpler songs of Ives, the message is conveyed calmly and clearly with complete vocal comfort, and there is no danger of losing the words in the music. The accompaniments are delicately judged and the whole effect is unusually sensitive and simple. The songs would not tax the technique of a comparative beginner since they lie so smoothly in the voice and the timing of the phrases follows the natural flow of the text. The musical idiom is fresh, tuneful and instantly appealing, with gently shifting tonality.

### 1. Morning has spread again

The piano sets up easy lilting figures in 3/4 time. After the voice enters the beats are distributed more unevenly with changing time signatures; the resultant flexible lines ebb and flow naturally with the text, allowing the voice to produce a warm, glowing tone without stress. The effect of the words is all the more powerful because of the simple setting. The only possible vocal difficulty may be in creating a floating *pianissimo* sound on 'when' and 'hand'. Instead of the more usual device of melting into the sound by means of a liquid consonant, the composer here uses the opposite approach. Words with aspirate starts are chosen for the *pianissimo* because they do not inhibit the voice; the singer can set the note going without being too tentative. Obviously care should be taken not to let this jar the voice; it is best to sing the final phrase in one breath so that there is not too much air left to spoil the last note.

## 2. Home is so sad

This poignant song resembles a very slow recitative. It must be kept very steady and the rhythmic subtleties will then make their point clearly. The sudden expansion into a melisma on 'joyous' runs well in the voice at this tempo. The intonation must be carefully monitored. There is ample opportunity to colour the voice, individually painting such words as 'withers', 'theft' and 'shot'. Warmer tones can be contrasted with a bleak, starved sound without vibrato which is particularly suitable for the last few phrases which trail away wistfully into the distance. English pronunciation is easier for the final 'vase' because the continuous 'z' can be used for a humming effect. The word has to be controlled well, making full use of the opening 'v' and not allowing the vowel sound to slip back.

## 3. Friday Night in the Royal Station Hotel

This is a setting of great simplicity and therefore steadiness of tone is of prime importance. The effect of the acciaccaturas and metallic chords in the piano in 3/4 and 4/4 time is starkly disturbing and they emphasise the loneliness expressed in the text. At the end of the opening section in which a strict rhythmic pulse is maintained, a *colla voce* sentence gives the singer more freedom to speak the words naturally. The strict tempo then returns with more sustained support from the piano, so that the singer will need to use a fuller tone, singing firmly through every note. At the softer dynamic marking the texture becomes clearer again and the words are helpfully sibilant for added expression ('shoeless corridors'). This passage must be intense and quiet; its delivery requires more than a little concentration. The outburst on 'letters of exile' should have considerable dramatic impact. The enigmatic ending, with its legato couplets, must be clear and precise, almost bland; it is all the more effective if it is never overstated. The steady chiming motif, in slightly slower tempo, continues in the piano to the end.

## 4. Talking in Bed

Previn's response to the particularly touching text, which is full of suppressed emotion, is deeply felt and sensitive. Phrase lengths are varied; the vocal lines show great suppleness and a certain unpredictability which will keep the singer on her toes. This is probably the most difficult song of the set. Tuning may pose a few problems at first and it is essential to preserve a seemingly effortless delivery with no trace of hesitation. A legato style is appropriate for the most part, but sliding between notes is to be avoided. In the final paragraph a good breath must be taken so that the crescendo from 'find' to 'words' is not interrupted (Example 1). The best place to breathe is after 'isolation', but, if necessary, a quick breath could be snatched between the two 't's of 'difficult to' to ensure a smooth progress through the phrase. The last few notes must be well poised within the *ritenuto*, the singer making sure that every one is perfectly in tune and the somewhat equivocal, wryly resigned mood is not spoiled.

Ex. 1.

## 5. The Trees

This spontaneous song ends the cycle on a more affirmative note. Rustling triplet semiquavers in the piano provide a buoyant texture over which the voice dips and soars in the style of a true lied, building quickly to its first climax on a loud high G. The lyrical lines are a gift for the singer. The vitality of this song must never flag, even during the steadier and less active middle passage. The energy increases again in a flurry of semiquavers from the piano. The last phrase brings another long high note to end the piece in exuberant mood (Example 2). The repetitions of the word 'afresh' contribute to the excitement; rolled 'r's

Ex. 2.

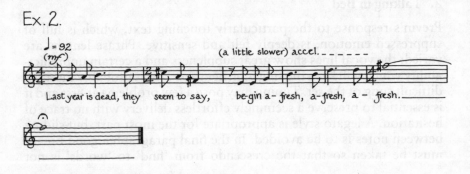

should add impetus. Intonation must be exact and the singer should be careful not to fall into the music's traps. The pieces are a perfect example of songwriting in traditional vein, which still exhibits a personality of its own.

It would be interesting to compare Previn's songs with the work of more established masters of the form, both of the 19th and 20th centuries. Fauré, Brahms and Warlock come to mind because they use the voice's and piano's inherent resources and colours to create textures which seem to spring naturally from their response to the words. Previn's cycle is well balanced and eminently practicable and it should make an excellent impression in the middle of a standard recital. A singer with a wide palette of colours will have ample scope to add subtle details of her own to those already implied. A beautiful tone quality will be well displayed at all times.

## *Bucolics*
### op. 28 (1968)

### James Wilson (born 1922)
#### Text by John Clare

### T II; M III
#### Soprano/tenor
#### Duration c.10′

These three songs have a wonderful freedom and naturalness, and the rhythm of the texts is most delicately and expertly handled. The words fit the music supremely well. As in all good vocal writing, there is physical enjoyment to be had in the action of enunciating and, in some cases, lingering over the expressive syllables of the resonant texts. The whole effect is fresh and exuberant. The drama flows with the music, as do the dynamics which are entirely appropriate at all times. The vocal range is comfortable for the singer, causing no strain or pinching on high-lying words. The musical idiom is straightforward and it has a strong individual character although the composer's touch is light. The piano figurations are attractively varied.

## 1. 'In the cowslip pips I lie'

The first song is marked 'Calmato'; its beautifully smooth lines are a pleasure to sing, allowing time to pinpoint particular words such as 'pips'. The singer should not breathe just because there is a rest mid-phrase: each 'p' should fall on the half-beat to keep the rhythm flowing. 'Clock-a-clay' gives the singer a perfect opportunity to emphasise the consonants and make a steady ticking effect. In the following low, gentle staccato phrase, the notes should not be too short. The piano texture is much busier and more impressionistic but still *pianissimo*. The sibilant sounds in the phrase about the winds and the forests can be used to colour the words. A dramatic glissando down the octave on the word 'fall' is simple to execute. The atmosphere is very tense (*ansioso*), with spiky staccatos for the repetition of 'pillar'. The rippling piano texture continues under fragmented lines set low in the voice.

The next verse returns to the simple, unforced gentleness of the opening and once again shimmering accompaniment figures charge the atmosphere, as the wind stirs the plants and flowers, and the music subsides in a coda. This perfectly constructed song is gratifyingly easy to sing.

## 2. 'When midnight comes'

The reiterated, muffled tread of staccato bass notes on the piano immediately grips the listener. As the voice enters, the sparse texture becomes still more ominous, with octaves in the right-hand and only an occasional decoration to illuminate the darkness. The whole opening paragraph sets an atmosphere of suspense as the hunters lie in wait for the badgers. The singer's *pianissimo*, legato narrative must be relentless and full of suppressed tension. A monotonous, steady thread of sound should be clear and always extremely soft. The sudden, furious outburst which follows at a brisk tempo should be a genuine shock. The piano repeats ostinato figures while the singer describes the fast-moving and lively action (Example 1).

Clarity of enunciation is essential as the excitement whips up to a frenzy and the dynamics rise accordingly. There is a possibility that the singer may be led into forcing the voice by over-zealous projection of the words. Ribs, diaphragm and stomach must be held very steady, and there should be no strain on the throat. Many percussive syllables help to illustrate the viciousness of the scene. The composer places accents in appropriate places so that the singer can use the labial attacks more effectively (for example the 'b' in 'bear' and 'bate').

This dramatic section is a real test of control and precision. It would be easy for the singer to become carried away and start making careless sounds. It is never necessary to push hard, for the text is set particularly

well. An impetus is provided for every loud note, as, for example, in the crescendo from *piano* to *fortissimo* from 'then' to 'everyone'. It is better to elide it without a glottal attack, as no accent is marked. The act of releasing the 'n' should suddenly impel the voice immediately to a strong, open sound. The sweeping arpeggio down this climactic phrase is enjoyable to perform. The music whirls along and paints the scene vividly with tremendous panache and infectious excitement. There are contrasting moments of repose as the chase progresses in fits and starts and the singer must be alive to every subtle change of mood. The song is filled with detail, right to the very last moments of the badger, whose brief death scene is devoid of sentimentality. The dramatic momentum of this song carries the listener along with such abandon that the suddenness of the ending should have a great impact. Tensions hover in the silence that follows, soon to be dispelled by the gentle relief of the last song.

### 3. 'The birds are gone to bed'

A gently pulsating piano texture high in the treble register, in which repeated bird calls are represented by grace notes, evokes the calm of the evening. The vocal line is plain and soft, remaining in the middle of the range throughout the opening paragraph. As in the second song, the piano heralds a change of tempo (though the bird-call rhythms persist) and the music gains speed. The voice rises higher, and longer, smoother lines which are delightful to sing float in a generally soft dynamic. Key words such as 'squat' and 'dance' are clipped off for an especially clear effect.

The closing section of the song allows the voice to float even higher, with the coming of morning (the silvery textures in the piano continue) and the stirring of human life again. Arpeggiated vocal twirls nicely illustrate the 'jingling yokes' and 'nimbling hare'. The final two phrases are crucial. 'Fear' may need special attention: if the 'f' is released quickly, the vowel sound should flow out without pushing. The delicacy and simplicity of this song makes an appealing effect.

*Bucolics* can take its rightful place in a standard recital as the perfect English song group, perhaps juxtaposed with German lieder or some songs by Fauré. Wilson's songs will suit a young voice extremely well, though the second song may seem strenuous at first.

# First Dream of Honeysuckle Petals Falling Alone
## (1978)

### Ronald Caltabiano (born 1959)
### Translated from the Japanese by Peter Beilenson (nos. 1, 3 and 4) and William Howard (no. 2)

T II; M IV
Mezzo-soprano
Duration *c.* 5'

The musical texture of this short cycle by a gifted young American composer is rather fuller than is often found in settings of Japanese poems. The vivid piano writing is most exciting and the abundant melismas in the voice part make it rewarding for the singer in exactly the same way as the bel canto writing of the past. Despite being brief, each song is eventful.

## 1. Spring (First Dream); Sho-u

After the piano's fast introduction the tempo slows down dramatically when the voice enters. The darker colours of the mezzo-soprano voice are immediately exploited: a low A sharp launches a complex melisma on the word 'dream'. Tuning will need careful attention to avoid smudging the sound. The tempo speeds up a little and, accompanied by running semiquavers in the piano, more fragmented vocal material with greatly contrasting dynamics is introduced. The enigmatic and simple ending of the song must be delivered with great poise and stillness.

## 2. Summer (of Honeysuckle Petals); Buson

The piano weaves an intricate web of triplet semiquavers in the right-hand part against duple rhythms in the left and the soft pedal is used. The constant quivering movement is most evocative of the hum of insects on a sultry summer day. The singer must make sure that she projects the smooth and rapt vocal line over the murmuring accompaniment. Her tone should be very pure and clear. The range is set in the middle of the voice and presents no problems, except perhaps for a sudden and sustained high G at the end of 'buzz' (Example 1). The 'zz'

Ex. 1.

Molto legato ♩ = 52

the mo-squi – toes _____ buzz.

can, of course, be vocalised, but clenching the teeth too much at such a high register may lead to a tightening of the throat. In this context the 'b' should not be too explosive. The final syllable of 'mosquitoes' (another 'z' which may be vocalised) can be used to continue the sound seamlessly through the *diminuendo* on to the G. It requires practice and skill to avoid an awkward bump on arrival or an unfortunate squeak at the end. It seems most appropriate, to finish with a very long 'zz' as a special effect; this is not clearly specified, but it would certainly be my own solution to the problem.

## 3. Fall (Falling); Gyodai

The vocal part is again mostly trouble free and undemanding. The rhythms are not difficult although quintuplets may take up some practice time. The melodies move smoothly, allowing the singer to check on purity of tone and finesse in the middle register. The two vocal paragraphs fall on either side of a brief and very expressive piano solo. In the final vocal entries the intervallic range is small; the singer often intones on one note and so the tuning must be faultless. The tone should be plain and uncluttered by too much vibrato, especially at the end when the voice is completely alone.

## 4. Winter (Alone); Chora

The strong, fast tempo, and largely violent character of this song suggests a vastly different kind of winter from the bleak, cold, shrivelled stillness often depicted in music. Vivaldi's 'Four Seasons' and Schubert's *Winterreise* are notable examples and there are many instances of individual words and notes being given a starved, pinched effect. Before the singer hurls herself into this with appropriate courage and abandon, the pitches must be sure. They should be practised softly in advance before attempting to sing the piece at full strength. Together with firmly emphasised accents, words such as 'Blows' and 'whirls' help the singer to convey the force of the blizzard. The lines range up and down but must remain incisive. A tranquil legato is more appropriate for 'drifts', but the rhythmic impetus and urgency must not be allowed to slacken. The piano retains its strict, spiky rhythms and jabbing chords. The singer must achieve a cool, relentlessly steady tone for the complete contrast of the final phrase. The last F must be controlled exactly so that the little staccato bounce for the 'n' of 'alone' can be brought off neatly. The new steady tempo is maintained without any hint of slowing down, so that the music cuts off suddenly with a feeling of chillness.

The cycle is beautifully concise and varied: the result of a young composer bringing an original mind and innate musicianship to the setting of oriental poetry. It makes an excellent item in a programme of longer song cycles. It would make a good, fresh start to a recital as it instantly attracts attention. Other songs which deal with the seasons could be included.

## *Anerca*
### (1966)

### Harry Freedman (born 1922)
### Translation by Knud Rasmussen

### T II; M IV
### Soprano
### Duration *c*.7′

These songs, by a senior Canadian composer, are fine examples of the best vocal writing of the 1960s. Although the lines are often more luxuriant than those in Webern's music they do show a similar delicacy of touch and a natural unforced shapeliness. The singer will find them delightfully easy and most flattering. Melismas are turned with subtle grace, the longer ones tending to close either on an open vowel or with a gentle downward curve. Even in the more dramatic moments there is plenty of time to poise the lines carefully without feeling rushed. The setting of the text is ideally smooth and there are no constricting consonants on high notes. The tone quality should be especially lovely as the writing ensures complete vocal comfort. Listeners as well as performers should relish the effortless flow of beautiful sounds. The piano gives discreet support and never over-powers the voice. It has a more dramatic role in the third song. The first song contains a number of spoken Eskimo words. There is no glossary, but pronunciation is straightforward; the only ambiguity is the 'ja' sound, which is presumably pronounced 'ya'. An explanation of the title's derivation is given. It is illuminating to know that in Eskimo the word for writing poetry is the same as the one for breathing: it is a poignant spiritual message.

## 1. 'Great sea'

The singer is immediately able to flex the voice in a series of rising 9ths. Large leaps are a fine training for a perfect legato technique. If the upper note is firmly anchored to the lower one, almost nothing can go wrong. The first small decorative feature, a quintuplet, can easily be joined up to the preceding long note and the notes should come out at their own natural speed. It is this that determines the exact tempo. The first expansive *forte* phrases should have loosened up the voice and made it ready for more subtle dynamic variations. The dip down to low B on 'me' should cause no trouble. There is an expert blend of phrases using recurring pitches within a close range with ones made up of wide intervals which suddenly broaden and stretch the voice in a spectacular way. The voice can be compared to a coiled spring, ready to leap out and unwind to its full length. The composer instructs that the Eskimo syllables are to be delivered in a ritualistic manner, 'like an incantation'. No note-heads are written but the appearance suggests a monotone. The singer should experiment with different pitches to test the balance with the piano. A low pitch always sounds dramatic, but it can be covered by the accompaniment. A slightly higher pitch, if notes are clipped, may be curiously effective here. The rhythms must be exactly co-ordinated with the piano's accented chords. The tempo becomes much faster without any preliminary warning, and the steady first tempo returns just as suddenly, with an expanded and embellished version of the opening music. The alternation between swift spoken passages and more easily paced arching paragraphs of vocal lyricism is repeated. The material is freely varied and enriched. The piano parts contribute to the well-tailored smoothness of the writing. Swirls of short notes before a long one, all on one syllable, are featured to particularly good effect.

## 2. Song of a Hostess

Although the tempo of this song is not a great deal faster than the main sections of the first one, the character must be quite different. It is a more intimate piece and lacks the first song's portentous declamatory feeling. It should be sung gently and sweetly without affectation. The vocal phrases are even more athletic, soaring and swooping up and down, always with perfect ease. The volume does not rise above *piano* until the end, when there is a swell to *mezzo-forte* on the last word, 'grand'. The composer marks 'no crescendo' in the middle of the piece to ensure that the performers do not forget themselves when the phrases rise ecstatically upwards. It will be an interesting interpretative task to convey this feeling without getting louder. The vocal writing is so skilled, however, that the performer will have no trouble in keeping the line smooth. It might be more effective to sing the repeat of 'All is more beautiful' slightly softer, as in rapt reflection. The disarming frankness of the last line must be conveyed with open and spontaneous pleasure and without a hint of artfulness.

## 3. 'I arise from rest'

The dramatic variety of the last song rounds off the cycle most impressively. The singer paints many vivid images and evokes old memories. She reflects on them with new-found wisdom and a broad perspective based on firm religious faith and optimism. The driving urgency of the opening lines is underlined by the piano's toccata-like fragments, which through an exciting *accelerando* depict the movement of the raven's wings. Quite suddenly, as if a plateau has been reached, with a view stretching all around, the music arrives at the steady tempo of the opening of the cycle. At this point the vocal lines become more stylised and confidently radiant, supported by stark chords in the piano which add to the atmosphere of spaciousness and ancient ritual. As the singer is moved to contemplate past events, a vivid, faster section begins and the piano's toccata is now fully developed, focusing on the frequent reiteration of single notes. Over this the singer has a series of strong, always shapely and rewarding phrases which describe a time of past danger. The portamento on 'shore' rises up and down again to illustrate the wind (Example 1). The word-painting is apt and the music brilliantly captures the flavour of each shade of meaning: it splinters into small fragments to convey nervousness and expands with exaggeration on 'big'. At the end of this paragraph the lines range more widely, particularly in the final cadence on 'reach', which stretches up a 9th.

The visionary confidence of the opening tempo returns in the final section in which the singer's lines cover a wide range even more swiftly and with affirmative abandon. A perfect legato throughout (also

Ex.1.

implied through short rests, where breaths must not be heard) should ensure comfortable placing of notes. The piano's ritualistic chords return and climb to a joyous and serene ending, which is only *mezzo-forte* and must not, in the elation of the moment, be allowed to grow louder. The warm joy of the last statement can be captured by the performer's own powers of concentration and inner integrity. An audience always responds to a feeling of deep involvement and the message of awed expectancy should be felt right up to the last chord.

No passage in this elegant piece ought to cause any vocal difficulty. A high standard of musicianship is required, together with a good sense of pitch, but these are separate problems. Any phrase taken out of context could form an exercise in how to set words comfortably for the singer and how to shape lines so that they are satisfying yet effortless.

*Anerca* will make a beautiful effect, and is best placed in a programme surrounded by Romantic music, especially the late Romantic music of Strauss or Rakhmaninov. The assurance and perfect proportions of the cycle mean that it would not be dwarfed by any major work from the standard repertory. Indeed, it would make a haunting and memorable complement.

# *Meditation*
## (1960)

### Gunther Schuller (born 1925)
### Text by Gertrude Stein

T II; M IV
High voice
Duration 2½'

This interesting sample of vocal writing from one of the leading composers in the United States is contained in *New Vistas in Song*, a splendid volume. Although the musical idiom is atonal, the extreme clarity of the writing should allow piano cues to be heard with ease, and the sinewy vocal lines give the singer much opportunity to aim and poise notes neatly. It is always pleasing to find such precision of language, and the work instantly appeals to the eye as well as to the ear. The tessitura will suit a light soprano or tenor voice with good control of vibrato. Much use is made of short, detached notes which have a fascinating, almost mechanical effect at times. Considerable subtlety of rhythm is shown and the technique of not breathing in successions of rests will be useful. The ironic humour of the text, with all its vagaries and stammerings, is perfectly caught in the music and the piano part is very rewarding. This delightfully concise and brilliantly written song makes a distinguished contribution to the repertory.

Opening on a low E, with a hesitancy appropriate to a setting of the words 'Why am I if I am uncertain' the voice moves through many changes of dynamics and rhythms, often sparingly set in tiny cells; the singer can enjoy precisely plotting the pitches and shading the smallest details. A segment of normal speech, which occurs near the beginning, is relaxing vocally. There is in fact nothing strenuous in the piece and the voice should feel very comfortable throughout. The first section of the song shows sensitivity to vocal sonority with great economy of means. The phrase 'let them be mine therefore' is marked 'espresso' and it lies beautifully for ease of tone gradation. Soon after this come the most remarkable and disjointed phrases; marked 'impersonal', they sound almost automatic. The singer must always treat such phrases as long spans, and stop and start the voice with strict rhythmic discipline so that the sound quality remains uniform and 'organised'. Singing in this way gives a very pleasant sensation of complete control and orderliness, and the purity of each sound can be carefully monitored. Scrupulous care must be taken to differentiate the various types of accent and attack, and no detail should be missed. The singer must decide where exactly to place final consonants. As with all composers who write well for the voice, Schuller's awareness of the vocal and sensual properties of syllables is acute. A suddenly loud phrase near the end is full of weighty accents which need solid support from stomach and diaphragm muscles. It is very important not to take a breath in the semiquavers immediately before sustaining 'come'. In this way the *fortepiano* will be much clearer and less difficult to sing. The bland, prosaic 'these stanzas are done' must be tossed off casually and with impeccable clarity, evoking comparison with the final phrase of Ravel's *Chansons madécasses* ('Allez, et préparez le repas'), or the last fragment of the David Bedford piece in this volume. The effect of this finely crafted song is all the more memorable for its subtle understatement.

*Meditation* would be well suited to a varied group of American songs, including some by Ives. It could also be performed with music of the Second Viennese School or, in lighter vein, songs by Satie and Poulenc. Baroque arias could be included to provide complete contrast. It is a sophisticated song in the best sense and should be much enjoyed by performers and audience.

# *Something Rich and Strange*
(1976)

## Trevor Hold (born 1939)
### Text by William Shakespeare

T III (soprano)/II (tenor); M II
Soprano/tenor
Duration *c*.6'

Any newcomer to contemporary music, however inexperienced, will find this delectable cycle an excellent introduction to the field. Most audiences will probably know the Shakespeare texts, and the economy and suitability of the settings inspire confidence from the outset. The moods of the texts are expertly caught in the music, and the simplest vocal devices are used with skill and unfailing accuracy. The strong resonances of the middle song are admirably framed by the two contrasting faster ones. Trevor Hold writes extremely well for the voice, as can be seen from his many other vocal works, all of which are worthy of much greater prominence in the repertory.

In the composer's programme note for this work he tells how some of the ideas, including the setting of such familiar texts, came to him in a dream. The opening melisma of the first song, and the unusual but appealing rhythmic setting of the last were thus inspired. The exceptional spontaneity of the songs may perhaps be explained by this. There can be no doubt that the composer has entirely succeeded in his attempt to capture the fantastical quality and atmosphere of Shakespeare's Ariel. The three songs are thematically linked, and well integrated, despite their continual contrasts.

## 1. Come unto these Yellow Sands

The *liberamente* flourish on the word 'come' (marked 'pp lontano') is most effective and gives a swing to the tempo. If the singer closes early on the 'm' it is easier to create the distant quality required. The long span of the first phrase provides a good 'singing-in' exercise for the performer. The song alternates between quick and even quicker passages. The rhythms are natural and pliant, and precisely tailored to fit the syllables. Syncopations may prove more difficult than they look; the rhythms on 'Hark, hark', for instance, can be quite troublesome at the extremely brisk pace (Example 1). These must be rehearsed rigorously until they become automatic as there is no time for any

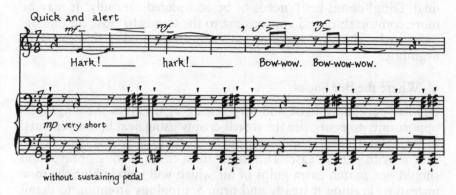

hesitation. The nuances are carefully chosen and graded, and the singer must adhere closely to staccato and tenuto markings. The lip-orientated alliterations in the text ('wild waves whist', 'foot it featly') are a boon to the singer; they aid clarity of enunciation as well as exact placing of the tone quality and attack.

When it comes to playing the dangerous game of onomatopoeias on 'Bow-wow-wow' and 'Cock-a-diddle-dow', this composer is as surefooted as ever. Using the lips on the 'w' gives it a more secure placing (Example 1 above). If breaths are taken in every rest, the sound will not remain clear. The 'k' of 'hark' should be placed on the next beat. The cockerel is especially well captured (Example 2) in the gradual fade on each of the three repeated glissandos, the last of which is suddenly cut off. In the slide, every semitone should seem like a large interval, and no microtone should be omitted.

## 2. Full Fathom Five

In the firmly dramatic opening statement of this beautifully constructed song, sonorous tenuto vocal phrases sound above changeringing patterns in the piano. To achieve bell-like sounds vocally, the singer must place the notes tellingly and accurately with a squeeze on each one falling away to suggest a diminuendo. A *semplice pianissimo* line, to be sung as ethereally as possible, introduces a suddenly fast tempo as the bells tinkle high up in the piano's right hand. The singer's final 'Ding! dong! bell!' needs to be considered carefully. It may be more comfortable, and appropriate to the words to close on the 'ng' quite early; the 'sfp' marking on each attack makes this easier to negotiate.

## 3. Where the Bee Sucks

Hold's sparklingly light and airy setting again gives the singer the opportunity to enunciate the words crisply using neat lip movements. It begins at a natural speaking pitch, so that the words trip off the tongue with perfect ease. The singer must think in long phrases and should not snatch extra gulps of air which will merely blur the tone instead of keeping it steady and firm. Scrupulous attention to detail will prove rewarding. The crescendo from the word 'fly' into the next phrase is especially grateful.

In the opening paragraph there are pauses at the end of the short phrases, as if Ariel were launching a fresh thought with each phrase. A vivacious performer should be able to capture this, as well as the gradual fading away into the distance, so that a light, mercurial ease of delivery prevails. The long *pianissimo* F sharp on 'I' at the very end is approached by a leap of a major 7th, thus giving it a natural spring, which propels the voice upwards from the 'ck' of 'suck'. A tiny glottal attack to separate the vowel from the preceding consonant is desirable and makes for extra clarity as well as a safe landing.

This extremely well-crafted cycle should slip easily into any programme, however diverse. Other settings of Shakespeare, for example those by Arne, Purcell and Tippett, could be chosen to make an interesting and well-integrated evening. Hold's cycle would make a delightful contrast to some more substantial and extended items from the established lieder repertory, particularly those of a totally different vocal idiom by Brahms, Mahler or Schoenberg. An interesting parallel could be struck with some Webern songs (opp. 12 or 25) whose brevity and crystalline precision would match Hold's succinct style.

# Twelve Moravian Songs
## (1957)

### Karel Husa (born 1921)
### Translation by Ruth Martin

T III; M II
Medium voice
Duration *c.*17′

Karel Husa, a Czechoslovakian composer now resident in the USA, has a most distinguished and varied output. These folksongs from his native land are a fine example of his sensitivity and expertise. The 12 brief items are properly balanced in mood and style to provide plenty of contrast, despite the overall simplicity of the vocal lines. The composer states that he has barely altered the original folk melodies, and in many cases especially idiomatic inflections are given added flexibility by means of grace notes. A full guide to pronunciation is provided for performance in the original language and it must be said that the English texts, though strong and evocative, inevitably lose something of the special character and unusual syllabic stresses so typical of Czech music. The composer's musical idiom successfully combines the appropriate national flavour with an up-to-date language. These folksongs deserve to be heard more widely alongside the well-known pieces in the genre by Bartók and Kodály.

Husa's songs are suitable for a beginner and make a charming and highly accessible concert item. With such simple lines, control and purity of tone must take priority so that the texts can come across clearly. To complement the plain melodies the composer has written the most imaginative and varied piano parts which immediately transform the pieces into art songs of a high quality and character; they are satisfying for performers and listeners alike. The final song has the highest tessitura and is best suited to a soprano or tenor, particularly the latter since the words change quickly in the upper register. A flexible mezzo-soprano or baritone should, however, experience little difficulty once the notes are thoroughly familiar and the text is fully assimilated.

## 1. Sunrise

Uninhibited piano arpeggios and trills introduce and punctuate the melody. The fast semiquaver triplet at the beginning each phrase requires careful practice to ensure that the tone does not fall away in the stress of negotiating the fast-moving syllables. It is important to give small notes their full value and not to gloss over them. The melodic line must always be heard clearly. The jubilant mood should be created without heaviness or gustiness. A wide dynamic range is covered, with a nice echo effect at the end of the first of the two strophic verses. In the second half of each verse the left-hand piano part treads out the beat while the right-hand chords convey excitement and tension by falling just after the beat. The final *fortissimo* on 'part' must be well prepared so that it is strong and firm; a slight crescendo towards the end of the note will help. A higher *ossia* octave is provided for the last phrase. The choice must depend on the penetration of the individual singer's voice at the given register. A raw, uninhibited chest voice rings out strongly on the lower pitch, but younger voices may prefer the upper alternative.

## 2. Who is that?

This deft and exquisitely simple song must be delivered with incisive clarity. The first verse is very delicate and precise while the second should perhaps be presented with a little more drama to reflect the words. Adroit tuning clears any vestige of doubt as to the exact pitches of the semiquavers. It is so easy to blur notes in the middle range, especially on unstressed syllables.

## 3. The Deserter

An extremely vigorous tempo characterises the soldier. The natural bounce of the melody is effectively enhanced by the *tenuto* marks which point certain crotchets for special emphasis. The *scherzando* second half of the verse flows in long phrases. The 'm' of 'come' can be used to swing naturally into the next word which is 'soldier'. The text of the second verse implies a fresh start. The singer should stop but should not take a breath as this is unnecessary at such a hectic pace and throws the whole line out of balance. Much greater precision is acquired if less air is used. A short coda prolongs the last word for two extra bars, but there is no repeat of the *scherzando* tune which occurred in verse one. The resultant elliptical effect adds distinction to the song.

## 4. Between Two Mountains

Husa's beautiful setting is a delight to sing with its sustained, cantabile vocal line and subtle atmosphere. Chromatic inflections in the melody and the Scotch snap rhythms make the music particularly arresting. The words in themselves have great impact. The ad lib instruction at the beginning of the song indicates a spontaneous, almost improvisatory style of delivery. The rhythms are prevented from becoming foursquare by the occasional garnishing of grace notes at appropriate cadences. It is important that the Scotch snaps should not be exaggerated but should seem to spring from the natural rhythm of the text. The fact that the song uses the most warmly expressive range of the voice is an advantage when the moods of the two lovers have to be portrayed. The drama of the scene is heightened by the woman's somewhat enigmatic final statement: the gentle tenderness is probably deceptive. This speech must be made to stand out, although the acting should not be exaggerated.

## 5. When I Sing

This two-verse song in perpetual motion has great rhythmic sweep. It may not be easy for a young voice to sound loud enough at such a low range. The turn (written out in full) in the first bar should run naturally; the notes should not be articulated separately as this will make it more difficult and spoil the swing of the two-beat rhythm. The piano texture is much more dense in this piece, which means that a strong, firm and relentlessly loud tone is absolutely vital.

## 6. What is wrong?

The characteristic rhythmic cell is used as an exercise in three-part counterpoint; the other two voices are in the piano part. The texture is light and transparent. The singer must aim for a simple style so that the musical structure can be clearly perceived. The dynamics are very soft, falling to *pianissimo* for the second half of the song. To sing a rising line gently, the placing must be perfect and there should be no vibrato. A singer should never be afraid to try a real *pianissimo*; it makes the people in the audience listen more keenly and increases their feeling of involvement as they cannot fail to be aware of the intense concentration of the performer.

## 7. Song for dancing

In this captivating song the dancing rhythm is provided on the piano by continuously repeated staccato chords. The mood is one of infectious gaiety and irrepressible verve. The delivery should be forthright and strong, with a well-focused, even tone. It may at first seem difficult to take swift breaths and to maintain rhythmic precision. It is inadvisable to cut the phrases up into small chunks as this proves unnecessarily exhausting. The crescendos to more enthusiastic outbursts are very important, and it would be a great pity to spoil their impact by breathing in places (such as after the first 'court her') where there is not enough time, even though they may be the most logical points in the text (Example 1). It is worth taking advantage of the chance to breathe at the natural interruption provided by the two percussive consonants between 'around' and 'to'. If this is negotiated absolutely in time, with the 'nd' on the half-beat, it would barely be noticeable; rhythmic sparkle would be added by separating the two words, and this is mirrored in the accompaniment. In the second verse, the 'h' of 'higher'

Ex.1.

gives a similar opportunity for cheating a little while enhancing the expressive effect. Taking a breath before 'higher' each time makes it much easier to sustain the last prolonged syllable 'er' and gives it the requisite staccato thrust. The whole song is more convincing if there are no uncomfortable moments at breathing places.

## 8. Echo in the Mountains

The setting of this short, atmospheric scene is highly dramatic and rhythmically varied, again featuring grace notes and Scotch snaps. The tessitura is rather high. Much of the opening section is loud. The melodic lines, though fleeting, are dense with detail. The 'ad lib' marking again suggests a free, declamatory style, unfettered by steady beats. The widely spaced piano accompaniment is sparse; it provides a sustaining texture and never moves while the voice is in full flight. This short passionate outburst gives the singer a fine opportunity to show imagination and presence, placing each phrase carefully and unhurriedly gauging the atmosphere. The soft ending is important. A break seems to be implied between the two syllables of 'tonight', perhaps to convey hesitancy. The rather unexpected quintuplet adds a special expressiveness. The cadence will need meticulous care, particularly for the diphthong on 'night'; the singer should not close it too soon as the sound needs to float into space over the vibrations in the piano.

## 9. The Snowball

This extremely short song is a perfect foil for the preceding piece, and will pose no problems at all. Its subdued statements and original phrase lengths are reminiscent of and equal to Charles Ives at his best.

## 10. Aspen Leaves

A strictly defined rhythmic pattern depicts the dry fallen leaves. The vocal line is extremely economic in its range of pitch and movement. Variety is provided by dynamic contrasts and, most importantly, in the only two legato phrases which must be sharply differentiated from the detached, staccato ones. When singing staccato, the singer must take care to place the consonants in rhythm: an excellent opportunity to practise singing with less air. Tempo must be strict throughout and breathiness avoided. The ending on a *fortissimo* E comes as a surprise. The passion must still be controlled, however, as this is not an extrovert song.

## 11. Lost Love

This song comprises just two repeated, smooth phrases, which rise and then fall. Rewarding and easy to sing, the piece clearly and effortlessly has a moving effect.

## 12. Homeland, Goodbye

The final song is the most problematic for the singer because of the high passages where diction must be clear. Words such as 'We heard him' are a little awkward in a high soprano tessitura, but in time and with well-spaced practice sessions, the lines lie more easily in the voice. The glowing E minor sonorities should ring out radiantly, and the *largamente* tempo allows a spacious unhurried effect. The crescendo on the high F sharp in the penultimate phrase of each of the two verses needs to be timed carefully. A comma is marked at the first occurrence so that the sudden *piano* immediately afterwards can be placed neatly. In the second verse it is better to continue without a break into the final rhetorical question. There is a clear opportunity for a quick, convenient breath after 'return', thus making the last phrase even more powerful and unrestricted by shortness of breath. The simplicity of the vocal lines is a trap for the unwary. Any lack of vocal control is painfully evident while command of technique will be rewarded.

This splendid collection of folksongs has great freshness and immediacy. It could be placed at the end of either half of a recital, perhaps after other Czech songs by Dvořák and Smetana or folksong settings in contrasting styles from different countries. The songs of Rakhmaninov also make excellent companion pieces.

# A Mini Song Cycle for Gina
## (1984)

### John Tavener (born 1944)
### Text by W. B. Yeats

T III; M II
Tenor/soprano
Duration *c.*6′

Tavener's highly individual cycle may appear simple at first sight, but a polished performance will require considerable artistry and concentration from the interpreter. The rapt atmosphere must be sustained through the almost continuous vocal line of this extended scena. The simple word-setting and natural rhythmic flow have a folk-like quality; the basically straightforward idiom is devoid of vocal gimmickry, but full of surprises. The piano part is extremely spare: chords only occasionally support the melody in the voice and the piano sometimes doubles the voice rather eerily at the octave. A shatteringly effective series of trills with a sudden violent crescendo occurs in the most overtly passionate section when the singer berates the curlew for evoking memories of the beloved. The work is in ABCA form and the close similarity of the opening and closing sections gives the piece a simple and satisfying symmetry. Apart from one impassioned outburst, the mood is contemplative and ripe with hidden overtones despite the generally steady pacing and unadorned lines.

The work is not so well suited to a soprano because of the higher passages in which a tenor will find it less problematic to achieve clear enunciation and undisturbed smoothness. However, a warm and well-controlled soprano voice could be appropriate, for the singer speaks as 'the poet' and more specific gender identification as 'the lover' seems unnecessary. The interpretation needs a good degree of refinement: the singer must adopt an almost impersonal yet deeply involved and committed manner without any feeling of constraint. Too much expressiveness could prove embarrassing and could easily seem insincere. The main outer sections require a hypnotic concentration as if chanting in a dream. The glowing quality of the words and images must be clearly conveyed with care and simplicity. The singer must not allow the line to become bumpy; some transitions may be awkward at first because the pitch rises and falls continually and there is very little respite from launching one long phrase after another. The folksong-like flow of the setting might prove tiring, especially as there are so few rests. At the end of the phrases, however, commas and carefully placed piano chords allow time for a poised restart. The dynamics are gentle and restrained and the quality of the voice is thus clearly exposed throughout. Chromatic intervals will need to be tuned meticulously without losing the supple naturalness of the line. Only very slight variations of tempo occur, but these must be strictly observed. The final 'stars' on high G at the end of the first A section should have an open, ringing resonance.

A very soft melody in triple time, doubled by the piano in octaves, is used for the setting of 'a cradle song' which is marked 'with extra tenderness'. The pauses between the lines avoid any rhythmic rigidity. This section has a lower tessitura. The text provides many sibilant and onomatopoeic consonants and the singer should use these to the full.

The highly dramatic recitative to the curlew follows. A sudden, fierce intensity is highlighted by the piano's trills which introduce each entry of the voice. This passage is marked 'liberamente' to give the singer full rein. An intense concentration in the voice part around the upper register (reminiscent of Stravinsky) gives a stressful, 'keening' edge to the vocal timbre, and this can be brought out most effectively (Example 1). The impact should be electrifying when, immediately

Ex. 1.

after this high point in the drama, the closing 'When you are old' section follows without a break and the passion is suddenly once more quenched. The whole opening song is repeated, presenting a challenge to the performer's expertise and control. This final section should, if anything, be delivered with even more simplicity and atmospheric understatement than it was at the opening so that the audience remains mesmerised. No artificial props are given to the singer in a work of this kind. It is an excellent test of straightforward 'artless' artistry, for though much vocal skill must be used to keep the tone clear and even, the effort involved must never be allowed to show.

A lovely piece, straight from the heart, it requires great delicacy and empathy from the singer. It would seem a good idea to consider placing it alongside other settings of Yeats: Frank Bridge's equally moving setting of *When you are old* is a clear candidate for selection and Peter Aston's unaccompanied *Seven Songs of Crazy Jane* would make an excellent contrast. The Tavener should come at the end of any such group of settings so that the singer is poised and well sung in.

## *Come in here child*
### (1968)
### David Bedford (born 1937)
### Text by Kenneth Patchen

T III; M III
Soprano and amplified piano
Duration 7½'

Bedford has an unusually fine ear for vocal sound. Though at first sight the music may appear dauntingly avant garde, it is simple and straightforward to perform. The lines flow smoothly and note patterns are constantly repeated, giving ample chance for secure pitch orientation. The space–time notation gives rhythmic flexibility in a direct and easily accessible form. Extra requirements include the suspension of a microphone over the piano strings to amplify the sound. The volume control of the connecting amplifier is operated by the pianist. (An extra stave, with graphic illustration of curves of volume, is provided in the score beneath the piano part.) In the course of the piece two milk bottles have to be pushed up and down the piano strings by the pianist; clear instructions are given as to how they should be used. Eventually, after a gentle push, they are left to oscillate on the strings like a spinning top. The resultant sound is rather beautiful and certainly arresting. The perfect voice for this song is a high, young-sounding lyric soprano with a steady and pure tone. It is an excellent introduction for a singer wanting to try a more adventurous idiom, for the vocal requirements are not at all taxing.

The chords in the accompaniment contain all the pitches of the singer's first phrase, and cues are given in the piano part at convenient points throughout the piece. This device allows the singer to feel relaxed and comfortable. The focusing on sensuous chromatic chords and their individual pitches evokes a comparison with Messiaen, whose music also has an immediate appeal to the listener. Bedford's simple and attractive writing is always lyrical and practical.

The performer should not be put off by having to open *piano* on a high B. For a perfect entry the 'th' of 'There's' should be gently pitched on the B before smoothly moving into the vowel. The performer should use only a little vibrato and aim the sound forward before opening the throat enough to warm the voice. A direct, clear sound is always easier to produce. If the singer is not afraid to feel immediate contact with the glottis, she is less likely to want to force the voice; increased awareness and precision of placing leads to greater care in the attack. This applies wonderfully well to similar high beginnings of phrases in Webern; it merely requires confidence to hit the centre of the note. Little pressure is required to make a clean sound and pushing too hard immediately impairs the quality. Once the ideal start has been achieved the phrase presents no further problems and should be sung as calmly and inscrutably as possible. It would be inappropriate to this music for the singer to use too much expression. The vocal lines are brief and pregnant with hidden meaning and forebodings. Enigmatic words drop one by one and the singer has ample opportunity to check the purity and steadiness of tone. Dynamics are extremely important for they add variety and contrast to the still, expressionless passages.

The white notes joined by ligatures are to be sung legato and the small black notes staccato (Example 1). As with other skilful compos-

Ex. 1.

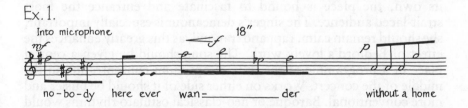

ers for the voice, Bedford knows that large intervals can be vocally flattering and exhilarating to execute, particularly within a legato. About a third of the way through the piece the singer walks to the piano and sings into the microphone, thus giving an effective extra resonance to one of the stronger, wide-ranging phrases.

The work's main difficulty occurs when a middle A flat, marked *ppp*, has to be sustained as long as possible on the word 'come'. A singer with a very good technique could be expected to hold the note for 20 seconds, but 12 seconds is probably a more practical length. The start of this note is crucial. A breathy 'k' will not land smoothly on the vowel and this in turn results in loss of poise and control, together with a wavering of pitch. It is ideal to place the sound well forward, with an almost metallic, instrumental tone and little vibrato, so that the sound penetrates further. This requires less effort and is easier to control through to the end. The 'm' of 'come' can be hummed early towards the end of the note. The low pitch presents the real problem, and it may be hard to stop the voice from trembling. The placing should be kept high and bright—soft singing does not have to be muffled artificially. Singers may feel inhibited when asked to sing very softly, and the sound can become tentative or tremulous. Solid muscular support is as important when singing softly as it is in loud passages. It helps to free the throat area and leaves the hard work to the lower part of the body. There is thus no strain in the sound which can then float effortlessly. The word 'moan' has to be sung without vibrato on a high A flat. It should be exaggerated a little to make an appropriately sinister, hollow sound and sharply differentiated from the other notes so that it cannot be mistaken for anything other than a special effect. Great economy is shown by the composer and so each small detail is of the utmost importance.

The last two extended phrases for the voice, one of which is again sung into the microphone, are particularly rewarding, as is the final lyrical shining legato line with its diminuendo on another high B. The milk bottles on the piano prolong the mysterious atmosphere and suspense before the voice intones (parlando) 'But I never heard of it' and the milk bottles' oscillations fade to nothing.

This is an example of 1960s avant-garde vocal music at its most simple. Easy to execute and possessing a natural, unaffected beauty of its own, the piece is bound to fascinate and entrance the most strait-laced audience. The singer's demeanour is especially important; she should remain calm, rapt and tranquil, as this greatly enhances the effect of Bedford's lovely work. The song should be given a central place in a programme at the time of optimum concentration in the middle of the concert. Works on either side of it should be busier and more conventional. Baroque or neo-classical ostinato rhythms would form a stark contrast. A group of songs by Ives would blend well with the freshness and originality of Bedford's concept. Pieces with a slightly exotic or eastern flavour (Szymanowski or late Debussy) would make good companions; Romantic music is not quite so appropriate.

# A Garland for Marjory Fleming
## (1969)

### Richard Rodney Bennett (born 1936)
### Text by Marjory Fleming

T III; M III
Soprano
Duration c.9'

Richard Rodney Bennett's cycle is an ideal and most tempting introduction to the repertory for a young singer. The unaffected, poignant charm and natural wit of the texts by Marjory Fleming (1803–11), a Scottish child, contribute to the piece's entertaining and enchanting effect. Misspellings in the text are left uncorrected except, as the composer says, when it would affect correct pronunciation. The remarkably direct stanzas with their uncanny wisdom find a warm response in the composer's characteristically mellifluous vocal style. The wit of the verses is aptly mirrored in music of striking versatility and delicate judgment. As the composer explains in the score, several of Marjory's poems are about her closest friend and cousin, Isabella Keith. The songs because of their freshness, are definitely suited to a young soprano voice. They sound even better when sung with a slight Scottish accent: the dedicatee and original performer is the Scottish soprano, Sasha Abrams. The five songs are perfectly balanced to provide interest in pace and mood. The vocal lines are supple and not quite as simple as they may seem at first and the rhythms are frequently surprising. Many subtle shadings underpin key moments in the texts. The central song, 'On Jessy Watsons Elopement', is the most difficult; it requires good rhythmic articulation and a wide variety of dynamics and melodic range. 'Sonnet on a Monkey', the last song, is a small masterpiece of artfulness and grace, sure to delight all listeners as it brings the cycle to an exuberant and tongue-in-cheek close.

## 1. In Isas Bed

In this *allegro giocoso* song a rocking 12/8 rhythm is established. Care must always to be taken to achieve the utmost precision in intonation. The delicate piano accompaniment will not cover the voice, even when it drops low; key phrases are virtually unaccompanied. A simple, almost bland style of delivery is appropriate throughout, without archness as the words and music speak so perfectly for themselves. The song swings naturally from beginning to end and poses few problems, except for intonation in more chromatic passages. Musical nuances and accents match the rhythm of the words. The song is followed by a priceless quotation from the authoress which should certainly be featured in a programme note or spoken introduction to the work.

## 2. A Melancholy Lay

The mock seriousness of this Allegretto con dolore makes it a perfect vehicle for the performer. The vocal line is plain and simple; glissandos are used carefully to emphasise special words (Example 1). An almost expressionless clarity and detachment should be retained while enunciating clearly and deliberately for maximum impact. Some particularly endearing quirks of vocabulary add to the especial charm and quaintness of this song.

Ex. 1.

Mourning for their offspring fair Whom they did nurse with tender care

## 3. On Jessy Watsons Elopement

A somewhat sanctimonious, even self-righteous, air pervades this song about a girl who has obviously gone astray. The dynamics are sharply contrasted. In the leaping vocal line accents and glissandos are again used to good effect. Rhythmic bite is essential to bring out the message which should be delivered with unconcealed relish.

## 4. Sweet Isabell

In this charmingly lilting *allegretto* song, the intricate figures of the accompaniment are used sparingly. Towards the middle there is a rather beautiful and unexpected shift from F major to E major; the first key returns later. The extreme simplicity of the tune is most appealing and care must be taken to avoid sentimentality. The song ends blandly with a slight *ritenuto*.

## 5. Sonnet on a Monkey

The finale is quite enchanting. The words are hilarious and include Marjory Fleming's unabashed admission of some problems with rhyming. The piano sets up a rumba-like rhythm, swinging easily between 7/8 and 2/4 time and the singer enunciates a syllable per note.

Each verse is more delightful and amusing than the last and the surprise ending, with its endearing frankness, caps them all.

*A Garland for Marjory Fleming* is a real treat for performer and audience and an ideal end to a recital. Stylistically the cycle would not clash with any item from the whole range of the standard repertory. It seems so complete in itself, and despite its brevity it is full of variety. The skill and experience of Richard Rodney Bennett are displayed in masterly fashion and the whole effect is captivating. The work represents the composer in his lighter vein; his other song cycles for soprano, such as *The little Ghost who Died for Love* and *Vocalese*, are warmly recommended for singers of more advanced abilities.


# *I Hate Music!*
## (1943)
## Leonard Bernstein (born 1918)
### Text by Leonard Bernstein


### T III; M III
### Soprano
### Duration *c*.10′


The dazzling gifts and versatility of Leonard Bernstein are demonstrated here in this captivating and lighthearted cycle of highly amusing and original songs. It is a perfect party piece for a young singer and her pianist, and great fun for the audience too. A youthful timbre is appropriate, but the composer states quite firmly in his introductory note that the temptation to adopt a falsely childlike manner, or to become arch is to be rigidly resisted. As he says, the music and the integrity of the individual performer should speak for themselves and no attempt should be made to impose artificial mannerisms. The title song, the third in the cycle, is fairly well known and can be used as an encore in a recital.

The whole piece has the musical flair and wit, and endless variety that might be expected from such an expert craftsman. Because the words and general impressions of all the songs have such immediate appeal, there is perhaps a danger that the performer might be tempted to cut corners and skim the surface of the music without rigorously attending to detail, merely relying on making a good effect rather than closely following the score. This is always a problem with entertainment pieces. It is sad when artists seek to convert pieces into personal vehicles and become less scrupulous about perfecting the music than they should be. The dynamic markings are usually the first to suffer; it is odd how often these come to be neglected at moments of high excitement. A more restrained and disciplined approach when learning such a work may pay larger dividends in the end. Spontaneity is, of course, the ultimate goal but this should come through confidence and secure knowledge of every detail of the score. The sparkling piano parts enhance the unqualified delight of these songs.

## 1. 'My name is Barbara'

The brief opening song is charmingly quaint. The delivery must be innocent and simple with very clear diction. Bernstein, as one might expect, is meticulous about interpretative instructions and his directions help to guide the performer: 'vehemently', 'almost resentfully'. The beginning is marked 'very legato, contemplative'. The subtly shifting chromatic line has to be tuned very accurately. A wide range of dynamics is covered within a short space of time and certain words have special accents. The final demure phrase, 'My name is Barbara' must be sung unaffectedly to avoid, at any cost, the prospect of eliciting a cheap laugh. Audiences will find the song funny and some gentle chuckling is likely, but the singer should be, or at least seem to be, totally unaware of this.

## 2. 'Jupiter has seven moons'

The quick alternation of 5/8 and 4/8 time makes an exuberantly extrovert opening for the recitation of information about the planets. As the child's imagination grows more fanciful the tempos fluctuate with the moods. The singer will need to cultivate an incisive tone to put across all the words at speed. In the exciting build-up to the central paragraph the accents and timing of consonants are crucial. The tessitura is rather low and the singer should avoid allowing too much breath to escape as the energy and excitement accumulates. The requisite hectic effect is inherent in the music. The words must be crisply enunciated in strict time. The more plaintive slower tempo returns for the closing lament in which notes are heavily emphasised by *tenuto* marks. The singer should not let the tone become too full or dramatic. The diminuendo on the final F has to be carefully graded and its nipped-off final quaver deftly placed.

### 3. 'I hate music!'

This song is splendidly apt for any musical occasion. The irony of its basic statement ('I hate music! But I like to sing') cannot fail to be keenly appreciated. The two contrastingly shaded phrases of this sentence, which occurs at the beginning and at the end of the song, must be clearly differentiated in style and timed perfectly (Example 1).

Ex. 1.

The singer's interpolations of 'la dee da' are marked 'freely, rather tonelessly and carelessly', which is easier to say than to perform. Too casual an approach could result in disaster, and deliberately out-of-tune singing can become embarrassing if the style is too much of a parody. Rhythmic freedom is an advantage in unaccompanied passages; a slightly breathy sound without vibrato would perhaps be effective here. The intervals are actually rather difficult, to add to the joke. They may need much practice. The important thing to remember is that there must be a complete contrast in tone and delivery to make these off-beat, seemingly effortless interpolations stand out from the more positive assertions of the main text. They are very apposite and must be given with a blithe unawareness of their overtones.

In the central paragraph which deprecates the singer's definition of music much attention must be given to breathing. The first breath can be taken after the reiteration of 'Music', but there are no rests before this. The decision as to when to breathe next is difficult. The best solution is probably to take two short breaths rather than one long one, as this may hold up the rhythm. I would suggest snatching quick breaths only after 'hall' and 'airs'.

The last batch of 'la dee da's' needs particular skill because the *subito forte* bravura phrase must come as a shock and the singer then immediately reverts to inward musing as if singing to herself. It is quite a demanding interpretative manoeuvre and it is essential to be wholly familiar with the pitches before daring to assume a casual air. The *subito forte* phrase could perhaps be performed in the manner of a child parodying an adult opera singer, with full vibrato; but this must not be overdone.

### 4. 'A big Indian and a little Indian'

This brief song is quite hilarious and has wonderful rhythmic verve. Unevenly grouped quavers are used to impel the music forward with irrepressible eagerness. The stresses in the text change constantly and accents are used to great effect. The singer suddenly breaks into speech at a brisk pace with much vivacity. The words are carefully underlined to aid natural delivery. The punch line, when it comes, must be devastating. A cheerful breeziness and enthusiasm is needed throughout the song.

### 5. 'I'm a person too'

The final song is the most ambitious and extended. It begins with a march-like theme of mock pomposity and then breaks off into a more conventional style based on speech patterns. The march keeps coming back, but the childish chatter always intervenes. The child's confidence begins to waver but it is regained with a splendidly impressive extension of the march in bold descending arpeggios. The steadier tempo means that the singer needs to control the tone carefully right up to the end. The cycle ends in the middle range with a crescendo on A; it is quite a difficult task for a young soprano whose middle notes may not yet be securely focused and may lack weight in this register. The pianist should take extra care to be tactful if necessary and not to drown out the singer, although the doubling of the voice above solid chords provides welcome support. The whole song lies in the middle part of the voice and it will be proof of the singer's high technical accomplishment if she is able to produce a straight, firm quality without becoming breathy or tired. A clear, penetrating sound, which has an almost instrumental cutting edge, will come over most successfully. All suspicions of woolliness from unsupported vibrato must be dispelled. The conversational sections should cause few problems, except for the danger of overacting. It is essential that the march tune be kept steady and cleanly produced each time and the singer must take care to maintain an even tone through the long lines.

*I Hate Music!* is to be recommended most warmly to all sopranos and their teachers. It is not as easy as it first appears but it presents a fine opportunity for a young performer to shine. There is no doubt that any audience will derive immense pleasure from it. It should be sung at the end of a standard recital, perhaps after a more serious and powerful lieder cycle or a florid Baroque cantata.

# The Pensive Traveller
## (1981)

## Donald Crockett (born 1951)
### Text by Henry David Thoreau

T III; M III
High voice
Duration *c*.14'

The outstandingly attractive, clear and simple appearance of this printed score gives it an immediate advantage. Other signs of enterprise and thoughtfulness are found in the excellent layout and the concise information given on the back page beside the full text. The publishers are to be congratulated, and it is to be hoped that singers will respond to their efforts.

*The Pensive Traveller* is an ideal work for a young or relatively inexperienced singer. It uses admirably simple means to convey a vast range of moods and emotions within a modest, yet fresh amalgam of chromatic and minimalist stylistic elements. The economy of the writing is quite remarkable: the vocal range is strictly limited and melodic figures and pitches are frequently repeated. The fourth and sixth songs allow the singer greater freedom, however, and employ avant-garde notational devices to create a dramatic effect. The musical demands made in these two songs and in the long fifth one are a little heavier than those of the first three, but the cycle in general should not tax the resources of the comparative newcomer. It is one of the most tempting pieces to come my way for some time. Technical hurdles, such as they are, are brief and straightforward. The piano writing is similarly practicable and appealing. It is most heartening to find a young composer who is so obviously aware of the practicalities of writing for voice and piano and who has the control and expertise to keep his music well within the scope of the average performer. The singer will be able to make a gratifyingly spectacular impression without being stretched.

### 1. I was born upon thy bank river

A bright bold start is always reassuring to the singer and it helps to clear away any areas of cloudiness and to dispel signs of nervousness such as tentative beginnings to notes. The singer opens *forte* in a series of wide intervals, which are imitated in octaves in the piano, first one step behind and then ahead. The 9th leap from low D to E flat is a feature of this opening phrase which continues to be prominent in the accompaniment. The simplicity of the phrases and the fact that many notes are repeated gives the singer an excellent opportunity to achieve secure pitch orientation, and tuning must be keen and precise. There is a Webernian meticulousness in details of articulation. The crescendo and diminuendo on 'thy stream' must be very carefully managed; the rolled 'r' on 'stream' should make it easy to reach the loud volume at this point. In music of such sparse texture, detail is especially significant. The *legatissimo* phrase on a repeated D, warming to a crescendo on 'ever', the last syllable of which floats off in a beautiful diminuendo, will sound lovely, particularly if the singer remembers to use the sound of the 'v' smoothly with the two vowels. The last line of repeated F sharps must be very evenly sung. No diminuendo is marked for the last, long note. Once again, the opening and closing consonants of this last word ('dream') could hardly be more perfect for controlling legato and maintaining steady tone. The next song follows *attacca*.

### 2. For though the caves were rabitted

The somewhat unfamiliar verb in the title, a carpentry term, is fully explained in a note in the score. In this song in particular, a tenor voice will sound better than a soprano, who may not be too happy intoning on a constantly repeated high F in the middle of the register break area. It is, however, an ideal way to practise overcoming any problems and to acquire the habit of relaxing throat and tongue muscles at will. Halfway through the piece the pitch drops to a more comfortable range and vocal and musical demands are otherwise extremely modest. The repeated 9ths in the accompaniment to the first song are used here to form rapidly oscillating patterns. The fact that the whole piano part is ingeniously constructed out of these repeated wide intervals should help the singer over any difficulties of pitch.

### 3. On the Sun coming out in the Afternoon

This song falls into the stylistic category of minimalism, but is also closely aligned to aspects of Baroque vocal music. Many ornamental vocal gestures require the technique used for Bach, and a clean pure line has to be maintained. In the piano's *perpetuum mobile* the two hands are out of step with each other. The irregular groups of notes in the right hand cross the bar-lines, but the left hand keeps a constant three-in-a-bar pulse which will be the singer's most useful anchor to keep the rhythm steady (Example 1). The effect should be marvellous.

Ex. 1.

The decorative figures in the vocal line must be sung legato and should not be overemphasised. Clean, effortless articulation of these may prove to be the song's only real technical test. The phrases are well judged, however, and fall naturally, with breathing places at just the right moments so that no hasty gasping is necessary. A poised and inscrutably controlled line can be spun out and delicately shaped with awareness and sensitivity to the subtle contours of the phrases. Dynamics are graded smoothly in long flowing paragraphs, rising to a *forte* near the end of the piece and then dying down for the gentle final verse.

This song should be a delight to work on. The syncopation and unusual distribution of syllables reminds one of some of Stravinsky's vocal writing (for example the *Cantata* and *Three Songs from William Shakespeare*), but Crockett's vocal lines are more supple and mellifluous. The singer should not panic at the complex appearance of the piano part. It only needs to be remembered to keep a steady inner beat going without being distracted, and to co-ordinate with the piano's left hand.

## 4. What's the railroad to me?

'Not without humour' is the composer's marking for this ironically dramatic scene, written alternately in 'space–time' and more conventional notation. *Accelerandos* and *rallentandos* are depicted in both the vocal and piano parts in the now familiar graphic way: ligatures thicken and divide up (getting faster) or converge gradually on one line from several (slowing down). The performer thus has the freedom to judge the progression and let the phrases emerge according to the natural rhythm of the words. It is a good idea to practise speaking the lines in order to become familiar with this device. Panache and energy are gained if trouble is taken to master these effects and to dispel any initial inhibitions. The strict tempo of the following phrases is all the more effective if the freer passages are delivered with an abandoned sweep so that the singer arrives on a splendid ringing note at the end, almost without being aware of how it happened. A flourish is often the best preparation for a strong sustained note.

The central part of the song is strictly notated with precise, fragmented vocal phrases. A brief passage of Baroque-like writing suddenly breaks into a sustained cadence of long notes, beneath which the piano has a dashing and intricate series of bravura passages which subside on to a soft tremolando. An extrovert performer should happily seize on the opportunities presented by such a bold piece of vocal writing; it is not at all difficult technically and is guaranteed to make a strong impression.

## 5. Sic Vita

A basic 4/4 time is split up into cells of teasingly unequal additive rhythms; it would be best if the singer were to forget the bar-lines and become used to the natural lilt of the rhythms which swing and sway with great spontaneity, helped by the neat staccatos of the piano part. It is important for the singer not to imitate the short attacks in the piano, but to keep an almost casual legato, flowing sound. Breaths at such a brisk speed (crotchet = 132) should only be taken at the ends of complete phrases; any snatched breaths will badly disturb the relentless pulse. Musically, and especially rhythmically, this is the most difficult and extended song of the cycle. Chromatic intervals have to be pitched very carefully, as it would be easy to slip down or up a semitone through inaccurate tuning. Many notes are grouped in couplets and these inner shapes within phrases should be sensitively pointed and turned to give a most elegant effect. Careful counting is the first priority and the singer can certainly never afford to lose concentration. Fortunately, though, the lines lie well and move around nimbly, avoiding the strain of lingering on register breaks.

More sustained legato passages occur in the middle of the song and the tone of the voice can become warmer and more expressive in contrast to the neat, cutting and precise sounds needed for the opening. As in the second song, the vocal line is concentrated on the top of the stave and a tenor will be more comfortable than a soprano. It is important not to get too loud too soon, as the song expands into a *poco maestoso* section and in order to make a stirring impact, the singer's strongest tone must be conserved for this moment. A short unaccompanied fragment has to be placed carefully (*subito mezzo-piano*) and if any forcing has taken place it will tend to show here. The lighter, springier lines of the opening are recalled briefly before the singer launches the last long note with a carefully gauged crescendo and diminuendo on 'here'; the piano builds up a frenzied series of repeated chords to create an exhilarating and extremely noisy climax.

### 6. I was born upon thy bank river (II)

This repeat of the opening text forms a magically atmospheric epilogue. The vocal line is marked 'Freely; with gravity' (Example 2). It is

Ex. 2.

mostly unaccompanied, apart from the occasional punctuation of a piano chord which helps to maintain security of pitch while the singer weaves a series of supple and improvisatory phrases which rises to a glowing high A. Careful attention to intonation will be needed, especially for smaller intervals. These phrases, which use elements from previous songs, lie comfortably in the voice. The final parlando is on low F sharp, as in the opening song, but instead of fading it makes a crescendo and rises to a sudden, short G sharp. The piano has the last word in a series of florid figures, typical of the cycle.

This beautifully planned cycle should fit easily into a recital of pieces from the standard repertory. Its variety is quite exceptional and its appeal immediate. It would be an excellent complement to a group of songs by Schumann, Liszt or Wolf; it would contrast well with English music of the early 20th century. Baroque music forms an obvious parallel, and the canzonets of Haydn or Mozart would also be a good choice. Despite using familiar vocal and compositional devices, the composer has achieved a work of delightful freshness.

## Voice from the Tomb
### op. 36A (nos. 1–6, 1980; no. 7, 1973)

### Gordon Crosse (born 1937)
#### Text by Stevie Smith

T III; M III
Medium voice
Duration *c*.15′

The sardonic but touching and unfailingly witty poems of this cycle are typical of their author; the composer has set them in such a way that the singer should not find it difficult to convey their meaning. When there is a profusion of words an almost parlando, recitative style is often adopted and there are very few melismas. Crosse creates a tremendous variety of mood and musical character. The balance between short, aphoristic and more extended songs is ideally judged, so that the whole cycle works perfectly within its time span and the interest never flags. The music of this superb piece of entertainment is never arch or predictable despite the traps offered by such texts.

A male or female voice is equally suited to the work. A performer of elegance and aplomb is given ample opportunity to display such talents. The manner of delivery is extremely important: there is absolutely no need to underline the humour in a heavy-handed way. Poised clarity will make the strongest effect. The piano part is relatively undemanding, yet full of personality. It is an ideal complement to the deceptively simple voice part which needs much subtlety and control.

### 1. (A soul earthbound by the grievance of never having been important)

The opening song consists of just one line which is unaccompanied until the last note. (The singer must be given the pitch very discreetly at the start, preferably backstage.) This tiny and extremely droll aphorism contains aptly pointed nuances and there is nothing to impede clear delivery.

## 2. The Blue from Heaven (A Legend of King Arthur of Britain)

The brief opening song is followed by the longest one. The composer might have been expected to set this poem as a strophic song because of the continuous narrative which includes dialogue between the characters. Instead, Crosse has evolved a scena which matches both the drama and sardonic understatement of the words. The singer has a real chance to exhibit a wide compass, even though all words are set syllable by syllable, and there are no spectacular vocal hurdles. The refrain 'Arthur, where are you, dear?' which punctuates the song throughout is so surprising and gently amusing that the singer must resist the temptation to overact. Continually reiterated single notes and simple repeated figures above sustained chords form the original and stark accompaniment, highly suggestive of a medieval setting. The singer should adopt a clear, firm and unaffected style to tell the story and to highlight the details. The lines are supple and flow comfortably. The notes are grouped in uneven rhythms to make a more natural effect at the passage which is marked 'more hesitant' (Example 1).

Ex.1.

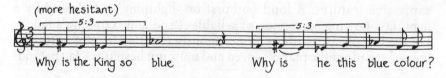

Appropriately, a blues feeling is immediately evident; the quintuplets should be sung very smoothly to enhance the effect.

A heavy voice may find the *mezza voce* phrase a little awkward, but an initial 'H' is helpful. The temporarily wistful mood is immediately dispelled by the resumption of forceful action. Guinevere should be characterised in her refrain, but not with exaggeration. The reference to 'blue' always provokes the sultry, jazzy mood, however fleetingly. The continual repetitions in the piano part provide a firm foundation which allows the singer to feel free and flexible so that his or her attention is not distracted from crucial descriptions and conversations. The timing of pauses as one character responds to another is very important and much concentration is necessary. As the dialogue between the king and queen becomes more heated, the accents and dynamics grow stronger and there are frequent contrasts. At the sudden diminuendo on 'After you' as Guinevere's resolve seems to die it requires expert control to keep the tone forward so that it does not disappear. The vocal lines plunge lower, and a more impersonal narrative takes over. The passage in which the tempo slackens and the tone becomes resigned and desolate is particularly effective. The low notes must not become unfocused; often they should be projected a little more strongly than the dynamic markings indicate or they may be lost in the piano texture which surrounds the voice part. Extra care will be needed for clear diction in this section.

An ominous feeling pervades the scene. The last 'verse', in contrast to the involved passion of the preceding music, should seem strangely detached and almost otherworldly. The final phrase is a master stroke: a long quintuplet and the delicate placing of 'cornflowers'. The high E flat could prove difficult; the preceding comma is necessary both to place the note and to point the word with suitable shading in such an understated ending. Nothing should disturb the sweet serenity of this last note.

### 3. Poor Soul, Poor Girl! (A debutante)

This is not, as one might expect, a frothy little piece, but a very black poem indeed, brief and chilling. A mechanical waltz figure on the piano underpins a recitative-like vocal line in which the tempo is left to the singer whose only instruction is to choose a speed slower than that of the piano, so that the two are not synchronised. This in itself is quite an exercise in concentration. Each phrase is full of highly characterised expressive features. A loud outburst on 'lightning' is followed by a light, fast-flowing succession of syllables ('suddenly crossing a field'). For the last phrase, with its monotonously repeated trios of notes, the voice does adopt the piano's speed and must not hesitate or lag behind.

### 4. 'I trod a foreign path'

This song is marked 'Numb' which, to any imaginative performer, exactly conveys the quality required. The voice, which is *pianissimo* throughout, chants the words, often set on a monotone, as if in a trance. It is no mean vocal feat to maintain a clear, precise and unchanging tone without any accents.

### 5. Avondall

This song has a lovely lilt and the 'one-in-a-bar' 3/8 feeling should always be sustained, even through cross-rhythms. Mellifluous vocal lines mirror the images of birds in the text and the piano part is delightfully exuberant with its abundant trills. There is, however, a sting in the tail. A slower ending brings the wan, impassive phrase 'All were inimical'. The pause in between the two entries must be well timed. The line is effective if sung without any expression.

## 6. 'I died for lack of company'

This pithy statement of great brevity and directness squeezes much emotion into a short space. After a somewhat languid beginning when the singer is directed to drag behind the pianist, the music becomes more strictly rhythmic with punched tenuto notes and then fades out in the very poignant last phrase.

## 7. The Frog Prince

The final song was written for the late Peter Pears and dates from seven years before the others. It makes a perfect and infectiously lively ending to the cycle. It is quite a substantial song in its own right, and could be performed separately. It is perhaps the only song in the work which requires considerable technical practice to acquire the agility necessary for the quick passage work with fast semiquaver triplets and extremely rapid enunciation. The composer's direction 'Nervous' gives the performer an opportunity for an imaginative interpretation (Example 2).

Ex.2.

The singer must occasionally deliver lengthy series of words conversationally and without regard to the piano's rhythms so that the words can flow naturally. There is a most effective swoop down on the word 'come', marked with a pause. It occurs in the middle of a sentence, which makes it rather a long breath, but the 'm' should help. The words 'frog's doom' at the end must be placed well and clearly separated. There is great charm in this song. The words come so fast that an appropriately nervous, out-of-breath quality will not be hard to achieve. More excitement is created towards the end of the song. The word 'heavenly' must be repeated with great fervour and the breathing must be well planned. It is best to make one breath last as long as possible; the rests in the part should suffice if the notes before rests are cut off smartly so that there is time to breathe without losing momentum. The longest melisma in the piece is a very soft and delicate septuplet on 'will'. It is worth spending some extra time on this moment so that it runs neatly and smoothly.

The last page of the cycle is a joy to sing. The loud beginning must be performed with gusto and bounce, while the answering phrase is plaintive and sweet. A final task is demanded of the singer in a most sensitive *pianissimo* staccato phrase which ends even more softly on 'heavenly'. It may take some careful practising to poise those last few moments, but the singer should not be satisfied until the tiniest thread of sound is found. Consonants must always be loud and this helps to keep the tone in line. The 'v' and 'nl' of 'heavenly' carry the voice through to the end.

*Voice from the Tomb* is beautifully constructed and sure to bring enjoyment to a wide audience. Crosse shows great sensitivity to the voice; indeed this is a fine vehicle for both performers. It is preferable to perform the cycle at the end of either half of the programme. It will go especially well with a traditional lieder cycle or a group of 19th- or 20th-century French songs, and would make a good contrast with more overtly romantic items.


# *Songs of Summer*
## (1954)

### Iain Hamilton (born 1922)


T III; M III
High voice
Duration 10'

The music of Iain Hamilton's charming song cycle is eminently practicable and direct in its appeal. Written in a neo-classical idiom, the lines ring out brightly and with exuberance. The large number of high passages would suggest that, at least initially, a tenor might sing the pieces with more ease than a soprano. The latter, however, simply needs to practise keeping her enunciation clear and separating the syllables so that they can be heard distinctly. A high and light soprano voice – perhaps an operatic soubrette – is better suited to the music than a singer with a heavier timbre. Flexibility is essential. The composer's high output of music, especially of opera, testifies to his appreciation of and identification with the sound of the human voice and its many colours. The singer must not be afraid to let the sound bloom naturally.

Rhythmic verve is a strong characteristic throughout the sparkling opening and closing songs; the mood of the central song is more contemplative, evoking as it does balmy warmth and quiet happiness. The piano accompaniments are most attractive.

## 1. Dawn (Anon.)

Although the mood of this song is irrepressibly jubilant, the music is not primarily loud and indeed covers an exceptionally wide range of dynamics. The beginning is lively yet gentle, and rhythmic discipline must be evident from the outset. The short rest after the word 'bank' does not indicate a breathing place but is instead a punctuation mark. The 'k' should be placed squarely on the half-beat. The staccato notes on 'musing myself' must not become breathy. The movement is marked 'Allegretto grazioso' and the graceful lilt of the music is best preserved with simplicity and clarity of style. The 'legato' marking on 'alone, hey ho' must be carefully observed. The singer can linger on the 'n' of 'lone' and thus span the interval seamlessly, perhaps with a hint of portamento to emphasise the point. 'Staccato' and 'legato' markings alternate rapidly and not a single one must be missed. The composer is meticulous in such details. The *tenuto* on 'Winter' is easier if the singer makes full and unhurried use of the 'w' to pitch the note securely. The crescendo down to the G on 'ho!' has a dashing effect and sustains the feeling of a celebratory dance. The repetition of 'dyry come dawn' high in the voice may prove awkward at first because of the hard consonants, especially the initial 'd'. The singer must remember to release each one immediately and keep neck and jaw muscles loose; the sound should not become 'throaty'. There is no need to breathe until just before the 'hey ho' at the end of the phrase.

The trumpet-like fanfare of the middle section allows perfect placing of the voice. Vibrato must not obscure such clean lines as these. In this passage in particular, breaths have to be taken strictly in tempo. The 'dyry come dawn' is now set to a crescendo on a fanfare. (As is carefully marked in the score the singer should not take a breath after the last 'dawn' but swing into the 'hey ho', ready for the recapitulation of the refrain which modulates freely and flexibly. The mood of extrovert joy grows right up to the scintillating climax on the *forte* high G.

## 2. The Rose (Thomas Howell)

The modal feeling of this lovely song is reminiscent of traditional British folksong. The music lies comfortably in the middle range of the voice, rising and falling naturally with the flow of the words. It is gratifyingly easy to vocalise. The singing must be as smooth as possible. Alliterative consonants in the text add presence to the undecorated lines. Each syllable is set to a note with no melismas, except for the gentle slow fading on to the long *pianissimo* on 'peer' (middle A). This gives the singer every chance to shine vocally and produce a warm, glowing resonance in an even and mellow tone, fully bringing out the shapeliness of the phrases.

## 3. Country Glee (Thomas Dekker)

This is by far the most difficult song because of its additive rhythms: the bars of 8/8 are divided into uneven groups of three notes and two notes and there is a great deal of syncopation. The piece should be practised assiduously at a slower tempo and the performer should speak the words at first until the rhythms feel natural. If the timing of breaths is not carefully planned the performance will collapse. The singer must achieve a good clear vocal attack in order to delineate the rhythmic and syllabic details and to convey the piece with the panache it deserves. A naturally swaying, almost jazzy feeling is to be encouraged so that the listener may not be able to tell where the bar-lines fall. Once mastered, such rhythms as those in the phrase 'Sing, dance and play' are a delight to perform and their effect is striking. The repeated chords and running semiquavers in the piano part are even more strongly neo-classical. At the passage beginning 'Each bonny lass' the singer must take care not to be disturbed by the piano's syncopated rhythms, which cross with those in the vocal part. The performers should be aware of the counterpoint between them.

In the more delicate section which dances along sure-footedly, the floating *pianissimo* on the word 'hollow' must be allowed to trail into space as a mere thread of sound. The images of 'skipping lambs' and 'bleating dams' are charmingly depicted in syncopations that will need good control, and in fleeting dashes of word-painting. The large crescendo at the end of this passage must be well judged. The verse about hunting starts quietly, punctuated by *secco* chords in the piano, and then lurches into rustic ebullience with figures which cascade down from F sharp on 'sport' and 'proud' in ever-increasing vitality and brilliance. The final declamatory paragraph is positively operatic, requiring a wide, expansive range and great conviction from the performer (Example 1). The sudden *pianissimo* should come as quite a shock. In the dazzling cadenza, rolling the 'r' of 'ring' (a potentially

Ex.1.

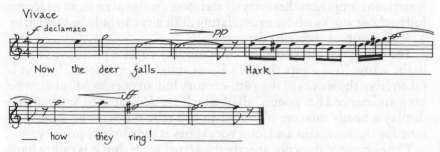

difficult last word) helps to launch the sound; the singer should not squeeze the 'ng'.

Hamilton's cycle will fit neatly into almost any space in a recital, preferably at the beginning or end of either half. It would go well with German lieder, especially those of Schubert, Schumann and Mendelssohn, and with other settings of old English texts.

## *Mirabai Songs*
### (1982)

### John Harbison (born 1938)
### Translation by Robert Bly

T III; M III
Female voice
Duration 17′

It is a real pleasure to find a substantial song cycle by one of the leading American composers of the middle generation; Harbison's music is heard less frequently in the United Kingdom than he deserves. This work has also been scored for instrumental ensemble because, as the composer states somewhat ruefully in the introduction, the voice and piano duo seems to be on the decline. It is to be hoped that the tide is already turning and that singers will eagerly take hold of the opportunities offered them by such powerful and highly accessible music, the latter quality being typical of a great deal of the music of young American composers these days. Harbison's songs are a most welcome foil to those works whose excruciating difficulty can only be tackled by a small group of specialist devotees.

The composer has provided an admirably concise programme note in the score. (It is a pity that this is not standard practice.) The text is taken from the works of the 16th-century Indian poetess Mirabai, who sang and danced her poems, all of which are dedicated to Krishna and display a heady mixture of eroticism and religious fervour. Beauty of tone for the luxuriant and long vocal lines is the obvious priority.

The composer does not specify the actual voice, but it is rather hard to imagine a man being suited to such overtly female statements. A sweet-toned, warmly lyrical soprano, with a hint of the darker *spinto* quality in the lower register, and a flexible operatic mezzo-soprano would both be perfect. Every chance is given to display the most ravishing quality of sound. Any lack of evenness will be clearly shown, making this an excellent opportunity to exhibit a healthy technique.

The six songs are well contrasted. The piano parts are fascinating, mostly based on continuous ostinato effects; they carry echoes of minimalism, but have greater flexibility and thematic interest. Rhythmic verve is a strong feature and the feeling of the pulse rarely slackens. Subtle dynamic markings will, if closely observed, make an important contribution to the overall effect, which must not be one of uniformity. Such seductive vocal lines are sometimes a trap, inviting a lazy singer to cruise through the music in a steady *mezzo-forte*. The softer dynamic shadings must be accurately gauged; a real *pianissimo* is essential. The work should not prove taxing as there are few intricate vocal passages and most of the fast-moving detail occurs in the piano accompaniments. The exotically Eastern origins of the words must always be borne in mind, especially with regard to the general tone quality. Each song is dedicated to a different singer who is associated with the composer's works.

## 1. It's true, I went to the Market

The continuous driving rhythms in the piano impel the singer excitingly along through leaping lines with many heavily accented notes. It is a splendidly extrovert way to begin and allows the voice to warm up without inhibition. The first section ends abruptly and the tempo slows a little. Tension is now present in a more suppressed form as the singer intones warmly passionate repeated As in mid-voice (a mezzo-soprano will have the advantage here), before the last, quiet descending phrase which is still well accented and must be crisply articulated. Clashing piano chords form a coda and maintain the intensity.

## 2. All I was Doing was Breathing

Once again the piano establishes a *perpetuum mobile*, but this time it is in quiet running quavers. The vocal lines are plain and undecorated at the beginning and must be sung very smoothly. A proliferation of detailed shadings within soft dynamic markings will need scrupulous attention. This highly sensuous and ecstatic movement must be spine-tingling and memorable; every thought, whether openly expressed or only implied, must be clearly projected. The pulse remains constant throughout, but rhythmic groupings are constantly varied to provide different emphases. A dancing passage of changing time signatures will fully engage the singer's concentration. Accents are used to point the text's natural rhythms. In the final, more emphatic section wide, spread chords support the voice as it rises to a sustained high G. Through the more active rhythmic passages in this song it is essential to obey the composer's dynamic markings as the longer, more sustained lines will then stand out in relief. The *sotto voce* phrase, in particular, makes a good effect if the consonants are heightened and the tone softened accordingly.

## 3. Why Mira Can't Go Back to her Old House

This song moves at a frenetic speed, making considerable work on fast articulation necessary. The piano's constant running quavers are again subject to varying pulses. The music has an irresistible vigour and sparkle. Some jazzy cross-rhythms add flavour, and evoke a richly exotic atmosphere of sunny warmth and vitality. Some pitch difficulties may well occur in the lines that move in alternating semitones at vulnerable points in the female voice. A great deal of care will be needed to achieve a clear, well-focused tone while maintaining rhythmic impetus, especially in the strenuous *fortissimo* passage (Example 1). The final wry comments can be delivered sardonically with dry humour and perfect control, never allowing rhythms to slacken.

Ex.1.

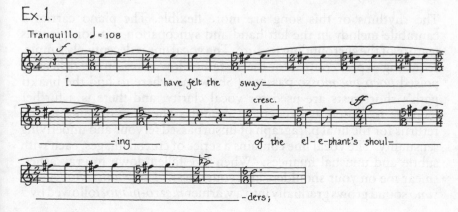

97

## 4. Where Did You Go?

The vocal lines are more sustained in a rhetorical, flexible recitative style, and there is more rubato than in the previous songs. The singer can display her vocal ability in the most flattering range, centred on the middle and upper registers and avoiding extremes. The voice can be allowed to glow beautifully; precision of placing and perfect control will be shown to fine effect. There is time to savour the quality of every note and gauge shadings and dynamics in the most refined detail. The graceful sextuplet melismas are especially rewarding. The piano part is contrastingly sparse. It provides rhythmic support, holding one chord in each bar; the first beat is divided for special emphasis, giving the effect of grace notes on the beat. The expressive quality of this song should be achieved with ease and comfort.

## 5. The Clouds

The piano resumes its continuous figures in a series of rocking semiquavers in uneven groupings in the right hand, while the left hand carries melodies in counterpoint to the voice. The vocal line moves flexibly above the colourful piano support. The accompanying figurations become busier, turning into triplet semiquavers, and the pace increases accordingly. The singer's stamina will be required to sustain the momentum and to project the strong lines in the heavily dramatic context with its colourful imagery. Firmness in the middle and lower registers is imperative in the last, more sustained section. The climactic outburst of the final few phrases fully exploits the singer's powers and she must take care to keep lower notes well in line with the more readily resonant high ones. Stark, dramatic tension must be sustained right up to the end; it is made more effective by the piano's shattering, gong-like chords.

## 6. Don't Go, Don't Go

The rhythms of this song are more flexible. The piano carries a cantabile melody in the left hand and syncopation is a conspicuous feature of the surrounding texture. The vocal line is deceptively simple, requiring expert control for the sustained low notes. In the delicately poised *poco più mosso* passage ('Show me where to find the bhakti path') short rests are used for vocal clarity, and there is a further increase in tempo as excitement mounts. The slow opening tempo returns for the final paragraph of unsurpassed fervour and underlying sensuality. The vocal line contains a series of crucial images, each with subtle and unusual nuances: 'When I've fallen down to gray ashes, smear me on your shoulders and your chest.' The *pianissimo legatissimo* sound grows gradually into a warmer *mezzo-piano*, followed by a fragment marked 'fragile'. The next, final phrase begins 'pieno' (full toned) but still within the *piano*; the difference can be highlighted by interpreting 'fragile' as a whispered tone with less vibrato. The last sentence warms to a *forte* on a low C sharp, which is then held through a steady diminuendo. This unkindly exposes any slight tiredness in the singer at the end of the cycle; she should be sure to keep the voice relaxed in moments of repose.

It is such a pleasure to find a large-scale work that achieves its dramatic effect through basically simple musical means. The piano supports and colours the vocal lines in a most positive way, and eases the singer's task. A clean technique is needed if suspect areas are not to be exposed.

The obvious comparison to draw, when considering such a potent blend of religion and eroticism, is with the vocal works of Messiaen. One of his large cycles would be an ideal companion. Other settings of Indian poetry or of Eastern texts (for instance, George Rochberg's *Songs in Praise of Krishna*, also treated in this book could make up a whole programme. The ecstatic, energised feeling of the songs will accord well with French music or with the music of that most cosmopolitan of English Romantics, Delius.

## *Wherever We May Be*
### op. 46 (1982)

### Robin Holloway (born 1943)
### Text by Robert Graves

### T III; M III
### Soprano
### Duration *c*.12′

The high opus number for a composer still in his early forties indicates a prolific output; much of it is vocal. The contrasts found in the five songs are most appealing. The vocal idiom is supply graceful and not too demanding of the singer's stamina. The delicately bubbling opening song has great freshness, vitality and natural impetus. The haunting legato of the next song makes a perfect foil for the first piece and for the third which is overtly dramatic and sometimes violent. The very brief fourth song makes way for the relentless gathering of intensity during the perpetual tread of the setting of the final poem from which the cycle takes it title. In fact, the balance of the five songs seems ideal; there is a fresh lilt and natural grace in the lines and rhythms throughout. This should prove a most enjoyable and tempting item for a comparative beginner as there is ample chance to show off a variety of vocal qualities within the fairly simple, tonal idiom. The piano writing is beautifully tailored to the vocal line in the best tradition of Romantic lieder.

## 1. Olive Tree

There is a lightness and bounce to this song which immediately attracts both the listener and the singer. The repeating bell-like and springy rhythms of the opening irresistibly recall the Flower Songs from Britten's *Gloriana*. The catchy and subtle patterns of notes are lovely to sing. At her entry the singer has to negotiate a subtle slackening of tempo (Example 1). It is not necessary, at a speed which is still brisk, to

Ex. 1.

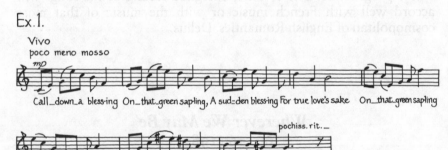

take a breath after two bars, at least in the first sentence; a four-bar phrase should be perfectly comfortable. A fresh start can be made on the high G of 'On that green sapling.' It should then be possible to go through to the end of the page without a break as it is much better not to disturb the flow and swing of the music.

In the second paragraph there should be time to snatch a quick breath after 'morning' which will allow the singer to enjoy projecting the alliteration of 'folded feathers'. The sibilant 'sh' of 'shake' at the end of the phrase should be used to full effect. In the high passage beginning 'Augury recorded' care must be taken to keep the sound open and free and to release all consonants once they are enunciated. Although the passage is loud, an unforced, floating and radiant quality is needed. The 'i' vowels will have to be modified to keep the tone round and even. There is an awkward moment during a crescendo when the vocal line swings off suddenly on 'flying', reaching a high G sharp. It is difficult to avoid feeling a little strangulated. Relaxing the throat quickly allows the larynx to drop once more for the new phrase but there is very little time in which to do this. The singer should make the most of the *sforzando* accent at the start of the word 'sting' and not close too soon on to the 'ng'. The radiantly serene motion then continues, rising in an exultant crescendo and quickening of pace to a full, glowing sound on 'heart'. The staccatos on 'in the' must be perfectly poised; there is another difficult 'ng' ending on 'morning'. After this the really fast opening speed returns fleetingly and the singer delivers the last words 'Re-echoing with quiet purity'.

Neat rhythm and an elegant style are essential for this song and it may take some time for the singer to avoid fumbling and to feel relaxed and natural. Consonants should be timed exactly to maintain the irrepressible momentum; the singer's enunciation must be extremely deft.

## 2. The Palm Tree

This song is marked 'smoothly flowing' and a seamless legato sound must be preserved throughout. Only a heavy accent on the final 'you' at the last cadence causes the slightest disturbance in the rapt, mysterious and refined line. Once again, notes are grouped in uneven rhythms which may take the performer by surprise. The *tenuto* marks emphasise key syllables, point and shape the phrases and colour the texts; lines steadily climb and fall with ease and sureness. The dynamics must be carefully controlled. The composer has marked phrasing meticulously, allowing extra breathing places only when one of the legato phrases needs punctuation. Since the text contains so many short and unvoiced consonants, such as 'p', 'f' and 't', much skill is required to keep the lines perfectly joined. The singer must watch for any tendency to prepare syllables too far in advance or to close on to consonants too soon. The phrase beginning 'Thorny branches' is a case in point: the diphthong endings on 'laced' and 'light' should not come until the very last moment and the vowels should be simple. The next phrase is all the more effective because of the *tenuto* markings which enhance the colouristic effect of 'wistful' and 'pasture-field' (Example 2).

The phrase which begins 'Never failing phoenix tree' should be sung in one breath so that the vowels of 'tree' and 'In' can elide smoothly. The cross-rhythms on 'From a desert of salt sand', again pointed by *tenuto* marks, must be precise yet flowing, perhaps even swinging. In the final phrase the arch up to a radiant high G, with a crescendo, is beautifully written; it undulates down again to the last, accented note, which must be held relentlessly at *forte* without a diminuendo.

Ex.2.

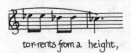

## 3. Robbers' Den

This is a marvellously extrovert display piece, full of a variety of expressive and vocal devices, which allow each statement to be vividly characterised. The vocal style is declamatory; the piece is marked 'Vivo: con vehemenza'. The softer passages, too, are full of suppressed intensity and passion. The syllables are spat out aggressively and the colourful nature of the text is fully exploited. The singer will need to support muscles tightly and not let out the air in a gasping and uncontrolled manner which would jar the larynx and tire the voice. The diaphragm must be as steady as a rock. Every opportunity should be taken to relax the throat, neck and face muscles after an explosive syllable. Each sound, however short, should have a full tone, so that the lines are heard clearly. So many percussive syllables tend to result in an unclear, gusty delivery. The pauses at the end of the terrifyingly vehement outbursts are especially effective because they are followed by calmer phrases. The dynamics are very important, as are the myriad staccatos, accents and phrasing marks. It is crucial that the singer avoids taking too much breath on fast staccato runs (Example 3).

Ex.3.

Similarly, if she does not breathe in the rest before the word 'Tilth', the sound will be better controlled.

Some notes are rather low: the *pianissimo* B should not cause problems, but middle notes need to be firm, especially in the phrase marked 'piangendo'. The approach to the soft, *dolcissimo* high G on 'Praise' is particularly well conceived with its ravishing diminuendo.

The singer should take plenty of time and enjoy singing through the 'th' of 'with' and rolling the 'r' in 'Praise'; a beautifully poised sound should then result without any trouble.

There is a fierce *molto animato* passage towards the end of the song. The lines are set in strict, spiky rhythms with heavily accented word endings. The violent *fortissimo* in the coda requires much control, but it is most effective. The slow diminuendo is followed by a very subtle *pianissimo* descent marked 'parlando, ma più cantabile' to a septuplet, ending on a firm middle C marked 'with contempt'. This phrase will probably need to be practised carefully to make the timing exact.

### 4. Fig Tree in Leaf

In this delightful, light song a natural spring and flow impels the performers forward. The lines move athletically up and down with ease. Intonation will need special attention: the performance must seem effortless with firmly centred notes. The words are set with the most meticulous care and attention to expressive details, so that each syllable can be relished.

### 5. Wherever we may be

The final, title song is marked 'stealthy' and the composer suggests a 'dark, full toned, intense' colouring. Such markings are of great help to the performer. The darker tone is well suited to the low phrases of this song. It begins softly and climbs to a series of loud, high climaxes on 'There is God'. The whole piece simmers with intensity and commitment. The tone must be sombre and full of foreboding even in louder passages. The steady, inexorable tread moves along to a final outburst at the top of the range on 'upon the stroke of midnight'. The music suddenly hurtles forward and it is a thrilling and unnerving moment. The coda is quiet and peaceful. The song's atmosphere should grip the listener.

Holloway's short song cycle is perfectly suited to the requirements of a standard recital and could easily stand beside major classics. The admirable balance of reflective and dramatic songs makes the cycle adaptable to all surroundings. The fresh immediacy of the opening song makes it a good beginning to one half of a programme. When the rhythmic details and vocal niceties are fully mastered the performance should not prove too taxing and will encourage young performers.

# *Beautiful Lie the Dead*
## (1954)
## Jeremy Dale Roberts (born 1934)

T III; M III
High voice
Duration *c.*6′

Each of these brief but finely wrought songs is dedicated to a distinguished figure from an older generation: the composers William Alwyn, Gerald Finzi and Howard Ferguson respectively. *Beautiful Lie the Dead* fits perfectly well into the English song tradition, and it has a fresh, distinctive appeal. The composer shows a good command of style, combined with an instinctive feeling for graceful vocal lines and the shaping of words. The piano writing, too, is beautifully idiomatic throughout. The high tessitura of many phrases perhaps suggests that a lightish tenor voice may be ideal, but a flexible soprano should have no real trouble in floating round the occasional awkward corner. Though an early work, it already shows the unpretentious craftsmanship and deep musicality that are the hallmarks of this unwarrantedly neglected composer.

### 1. Song (Thomas Lovell Beddoes)

A naturally mellifluous vocal line over a soft *tranquillo* accompaniment with repeated pedal notes in the left hand creates a gently shimmering texture. The opening section is easy and comfortable to sing and it is perfect for warming up the voice. The pace quickens as the piano figurations thicken and the vocal range increases dramatically, stretching in both directions in an atmosphere of growing excitement. The unexpected diminuendo on the highest note must be judged carefully; the *poco ritenuto* helps the singer to effect this. The end of the following phrase falls gently away to nothing on a *sotto voce* long note and again a slackening of speed gives the singer a chance to place the word 'happy' (without exaggerating the 'h') and then to slide easily into 'graves', making full use of the final 'v' and 'z' for smooth legato. This beautiful song flows effortlessly and lies well in the voice.

### 2. The Mourner (W. H. Davies)

The plaintively simple and touching melody is in traditional English vein but it has a very distinctive flavour. It begins in the middle of the voice and there is a most effective *subito piano* on 'lovely' (the 'v' helps to make a smooth transition). A slightly faster tempo brings a widely arching vocal line with some octave leaps. The singer will need a great deal of skill to attain the ethereal legato sound required though eliding consonants are sometimes helpful ('loveliness' and '<u>smile</u>'). The effect should be rapt and radiant. A sensitive singer will respond to the challenge of making the sound float out in the high register. The final statement is quiet and simple and must be kept clear and true with a minimum of vibrato.

### 3. Beautiful lie the dead (Steven Phillips)

The title song blends perfectly with the other two. The voice softly intones six phrases which are almost recitative-like in their pliability. The dynamics must be carefully controlled. The piano writing provides warmth and movement beneath the voice's starker lines. Tuning must be exact so that the finer shadings and colours of the voice can be shown clearly. The opening tempo is brisk, but the music quickly calms down to a considerably slower pace. If possible the long phrase beginning on 'satisfied' should not be interrupted by a breath.

This most refined piece of vocal writing deserves to be heard much more often. It makes a peaceful contrast if placed between more energetic, large-scale works from the 19th and 20th centuries. It is the ideal short cycle for the beginner who wishes to move into more adventurous vocal territory. It is unlikely to upset even the most conservative listener. Despite its brevity, the cycle exerts a quiet power which lingers in the memory.

# *Songs from the Thousand and One Nights*
## (1959, revised 1967)

### Richard Steinitz (born 1938)
### Translation by Powys Mathers

T III; M III
Tenor
Duration *c*.12′

This is a most striking and imaginative cycle of five songs, the third of which is especially arresting. A strong personality is evident in the voice part, to which the piano accompaniment is particularly suited. The music is flexible and there is a sense of constant flux in the changing tempos and moods which are occasionally mercurial and always colourful. The impression is of a vigorous and precise conception. The singer will enjoy launching into the long and subtly varied phrases with their original twists. The musical language is fairly straightforward, but there are many delightful details and flights of fancy to hold the interest of both singer and listener. The words are set with care and should pose few problems, even at the swiftest moments. The vocal writing is assured, giving the whole cycle great immediacy and presence.

## 1. 'She's here'

This is marked 'Allegro agitato' and the music conveys a tremendous sense of pace and excitement from the outset. The vocal melodies are quite simple and they undulate smoothly. The piano adds detail and creates an atmosphere of suppressed, nervous energy with its decorative and staccato lines. Tension increases with the volume in the *più agitato* section. Percussive beats sound in the piano, and on a long series of repeated Ds the singer is required to sustain and control a crescendo to *fortissimo*.

The dynamics are absolutely crucial and rhythms must be exactly defined in the fast flow of the music. Explosive consonants highlight the dissonance of the images of clashing stones; the sibilance of the word 'whisper' can be used to make the transition to a more mysterious mood. A dramatic climax comes; rather than being loud it is *pianissimo* and thus wonderfully effective. The singer repeats the words 'she's here' over and over to a crescendo, while the piano ostinatos continue independently. The voice is marked 'hushed but ecstatic with audible breaths' to heighten the intensity (Example 1). Although the sound of the breath is what is required the singer must not be tempted to gulp in more air than he needs. It is not really necessary to take a breath, since the phrases are so short, and the effect should be achieved by a short, sharp muscular movement each time. Gradually piano and voice come together again for the close on E flat with a diminuendo on the word 'here'. The unexpected disintegration of the regular pulse at the climax is a masterstroke which lifts the song out of the ordinary.

Ex. 1.

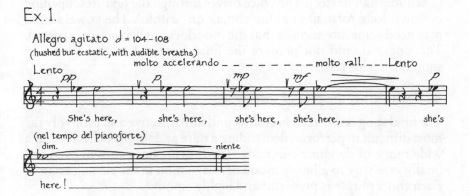

## 2. 'My joy'

This is a short *perpetuum mobile* with *alla breve* piano quavers in contrary motion throughout. The vocal line is made pliable by unusual phrase lengths and dynamics which follow its curvacious line. The music stands still for the interjections of 'Joy, my joy' which punctuate the steady flow of quavers. This delightfully infectious song makes the listener ready for something more complex.

## 3. 'The night is witchblown'

Despite its brevity, this is the big song of the cycle. The voice floats very softly above reiterated quiet pedalled octaves in the piano. At one point the vocal part is marked 'almost whispered', an effect which is difficult to achieve at the high range. It may be that the composer does intend a certain breathlessness to result, but it is safer to convey the hushed atmosphere by heightening the strong consonants. The dotted rhythms must be clearly defined.

The intensity of the evocative text rises rapidly to an almost unbearable level where the passion is scarcely controlled and the ecstasy verges on eroticism. The repeated notes at the top of the range may seem uncomfortable at first and the singer must find a true and steady tone. The expansive but rhythmically dynamic 'full tonight' makes a strong impact before a startling declaration ends the song quite abruptly and the piano fades away to a whisper.

## 4. 'The water-wheels'

The continuous ostinato rhythms strongly propel the music. The singer plunges in with an easy swing, helped by the frequent occurrence of 'w' in the text which smooths the line and controls it despite the pace. The churning of the wheels is heard throughout in the piano (a Schubertian device). The voice drives through the textures, opening out on a long *fortissimo* at the climax on 'within'. The vowel sound may need some attention so that the tone does not become constricted. The singer should not prepare the final, accented 'n' too soon and should keep his jaw loose.

## 5. 'I who grow the rose of sorrow'

The final song is the most brooding and introspective and probably the most difficult to perform, demanding a pure and simple delivery with a wide range of dynamic contrasts. The flowing lines vary in pace and finally give way to a heavy mood of resignation in the closing section. Each short phrase is powerful and highly emotive.

There is a most unusual flavour to these songs with their blend of Western and Eastern influences. Steinitz has avoided the obvious oriental exoticism that might have been expected, but the songs are rich in variety and true to the spirit of the texts. It would be interesting to compile a mixed programme of works either based on Eastern themes or influenced by them; Szymanowski's *Songs of the passionate Muezzin*, for example, or something in a lighter vein such as the well-known *Indian Love Lyrics*. Ideally suited to a young tenor, the cycle could be performed in a programme of Romantic songs, including an established cycle such as Schumann's *Dichterliebe*.

# *Five Songs*
## (1951)
### Virgil Thomson (born 1896)
### Text by William Blake

T III; M III
Baritone
Duration 18′

The wonderfully invigorating and original music of this senior composer is less often heard in the United Kingdom than it ought to be. His considerable output of songs belongs to the standard 20th-century repertory since it has the rare quality of being strikingly memorable through relatively simple musical means. Now that many younger composers are returning to a more accessible style, Thomson's work seems even more refreshing and up-to-the-minute. Whether in the serious vein of these Blake songs or in the more lighthearted mood of *The Courtship of the Yongly Bongly Bo*, Thomson never fails to engross the listener with beautifully turned phrasing and his highly individual way with words. The singer's needs are carefully taken into account so that an unaffected performing manner comes naturally.

A young baritone will find this substantial song cycle most satisfying. It is constructed so that each of the five songs is more extended and slightly more complex in texture than the last. In Thomson's setting of the poem we know as 'Jerusalem' the feeling of visionary exultation comes to a peak and then dies away as if dreaming. The whole performance should be straightforward, in a fearless and forthright style. All indications of expression and emphasis are given by the composer, and the singer must obey them exactly. Precious enunciation is to be avoided and a fresh, clear projection of the text is much more appropriate. Audiences will be delighted by the unconventional yet appealing language, and English listeners in particular will find it bracingly different from their expectations. The piano parts are most imaginative and varied.

## 1. The Divine Image

A gently rocking accompaniment figure over a slow bass tune in the left hand supports a graceful vocal melody of hymn-like simplicity. Despite the almost naive basic rhythmic structure and conventional cadences, the many individual rhythmic quirks and twists dispel any suspicions of predictability. The final verse brings a stirring tune built on arpeggios. The pause on low A flat is marked 'short' and *mezzo-piano* so that there is no fear of overemphasis or of a lighter baritone feeling constrained to plumb the depths for longer than is comfortable. The last few phrases cover quite a wide range, but there are no extremes.

A melting legato must be preserved throughout this song. The effect is most winning, with its straightforward sincerity and full range of dynamics which swell and subside with the natural curves of the lines. Musical demands are extremely modest and there should be no problems with diction.

## 2. Tiger! Tiger!

Short, clipped attacks on E in a brisk march-like tempo beneath long sustained notes make a steady, nervous accompaniment. The singer's phrases are brief and breathless, coming in sudden fitful bursts of varied lengths. Breathing must therefore be well organised. A bright edge to the voice is appropriate to project the strong high notes. Long pedal notes appear in the piano part and make the atmosphere darker and more mysterious for 'In what distant deeps'. Here the singer can cover and darken the voice a little more and keep the phrases as smooth as possible. The vocal phrases range more widely just before the highly dramatic fragmented outbursts. Some very fast articulation may cause problems; breath should be used economically (Example 1). The piano's steady march now appears in accented octaves sustained through the gaps in the vocal line. The singer must place consonants accurately on the beat and make sure that they can be heard clearly. The wild cries high in the voice must not be snatched but articulated cleanly, with a Scottish pronunciation of the 'wh' in 'what'.

Ex.1.

And what shoul=der, and what art,__ Could twist the sinews of thy heart?

And when the heart began to beat, What dread hand? and what dread feet?

There is a complete change of mood in a gentle, reflective passage, marked 'un poco meno mosso', of charming simplicity and sudden tenderness. The blazing intensity returns just as abruptly for the final tirade of tremendous ferocity and sustained aggression. The opening tune with its leaping lines returns and builds up to a searing high G on 'Dare'. The last few accented notes follow on directly and it is important to conserve breath. The composer is extremely wise not to allow the singer time to take too much breath as this would almost certainly result in the last few notes being forced if the alliterative 'f's in 'frame thy fearful' become too gusty. The very short rest just before the high G is a fine example of the useful device of impelling the singer on to a note at full stretch without giving enough time to get it wrong. Hesitation would prove inhibiting, but because of the setting the singer has no alternative but to hurl himself on to the note with only a moment to snatch breath after the preceding phrase. The piano's spiky staccatos make a strong contribution in this closing section.

## 3. The Land of Dreams

The singer can display a broad range of colours and dynamics in the shifting moods of this finely wrought piece. A reiterated triplet figure in the piano, like the fanfare of a trumpet, is used quite beautifully to evoke a mysterious and magical atmosphere. The boy replies to the urging voice in his dream in a very soft and smooth passage with silvery chords high in the piano. Perhaps the singer should cover the tone and use falsetto in this section to enhance the unearthly feeling. Sibilant consonants must be exaggerated and the singer must pay special attention to diction. An almost recitative-like passage follows in which the piano is instructed to follow the voice. As the intensity rises the dynamic markings change more frequently and the smaller details become important. The singer's interpretative gifts will be fully exploited to differentiate the voices in the dialogue. The warmly soothing voice of the father suddenly bursts into *fortissimo* on 'I could not get to the other side'. The child's voice becomes more agitated and the vocal line rises higher. The last section is quite demanding vocally. The awkward intervals must be pitched securely, and the crescendo and diminuendo in the rather high penultimate phrase firmly controlled. After the steep climb up the arpeggio, the high F sharp is held with a long fade from *mezzo-piano* to almost nothing. This considerable feat requires separate practice. The word is 'star' and it can thus be left to drift into falsetto without any final consonant.

## 4. The Little Black Boy

The opening tune evokes the attractive simplicity of 'The Divine Image' at a steadier speed. A folk-like melody lilts delicately above a swaying accompaniment similar to that of the first song. The opening section should be delivered in a matter-of-fact way to prepare for the complete contrast when a sudden change from F major to A flat major brings an exultant revivalist-style hymn tune. In the accompaniment running semiquaver broken chords in the right hand flow above a stirring counter-melody in the left. The singer conveys the message of hope in colourful images with affirmative fervour. Very clear enunciation is necessary and the rhythmic subtleties must be sharply defined. For example, the difference between triplets and dotted notes must be obvious. A quickening of speed leads to an *animando* section with a new time signature and a doubling of the tempo in an exuberant outburst. The wholesome directness of the singer's lines is created by the fact that they are largely constructed of broken chords. There is a considerable amount of upward and downward leaping in regular steps, as in a series of fanfares. The absence of close-set intervals is a most distinctive feature. This more florid section offers a momentary change of phrase lengths and the piano's sweeping arpeggios heighten the intensity. The tempo mark is halved (minim equals crotchet) with the time-signature reverting to 4/4 (although the beat actually remains the same). The tune is a varied and embellished version of the opening theme. Very carefully judged use of rubato points the interpretation of the unaffected optimism of the words whose artless innocence is most touchingly set. It may take a special effort for the singer to identify with the idea of expressing overt emotion of an extremely personal nature in a spiritual context. The simple trust of the final statement must be conveyed with the utmost dignity and restraint; the slackening of speed and *diminuendo* must be gauged with great care.

## 5. And did those feet

It is stimulating to find such a characteristically bold and original setting for these very familiar words. A long piano solo carries a high triplet tune in the right hand against cross-rhythms in the left-hand part, which is also set in the treble clef. This is evocative of the English folk dance idiom, presumably intended as a graphic illustration of the feet 'walking upon England's mountains green'. A highly decorative version of the triplet melody, now in semiquavers, follows and then the whole melody is repeated throughout the singer's first verse. As in the preceding song, vocal lines arch steeply in arpeggio-like figures and create a fresh and uninhibited impression. The left hand articulates sharp staccato chords, keeping strictly in time. At the words 'And was Jerusalem builded here' the vocal melody is imitated canonically in the piano. The singer should always be aware of such musical devices as the interplay of forces creates extra tension and authority. It may be a little hard to sound forceful at the word 'Mills' on a fortissimo low A. It is best not to take a breath in the preceding rest. The pause in which this note is placed gives a moment of repose before the pianist hurls himself into a veritable tornado of sound as a wildly exciting prelude to the second verse. A manic version of the semiquaver variation of the folk melody, set an octave higher, is hammered out, followed by the more simple version of the tune in *fortissimo* octaves and the dancing rhythm is also taken up by the left hand. The piano stops abruptly just before the singer enters.

The accompaniment is now very sparse and the singer can display his talents in the tremendously fiery series of exhortations which culminates in a high G, the work's most strenuous moment (Example 2). The rhythms need careful preparation, but there is time to gather

Ex. 2.

Bring me my bow___ of burn-ing gold ! Bring me my arrows of de-sire !___

Bring me my spear !___ O clouds___ un-fold ! Bring___ me my chariot of fire !

strength and breath between phrases. The last half of the verse consists of a loud and forthright repeat of the singer's opening material. The lines are now inverted and the piano's folkdance is an octave lower. In the last line the singer begins a *diminuendo* and the piano's semiquavers trip off into the distance as the music gradually dies away to nothing. This most piquant ending is an excellent illustration of Thomson's individuality and assurance.

It might be too much of a contrast to follow this major cycle with some of the lighter songs by this composer. There is a clear parallel with the works of Charles Ives which contain many examples of religous fervour alongside more lighthearted miniatures. It would be fascinating to compare the *Five Songs* with Britten's *Songs and Proverbs of William Blake* also for baritone. Each cycle could be used as the central item in each half of the recital, fringed by contrasting material – perhaps Britten's *Cabaret Songs* or some of the folksong settings. If another language is required, French is the obvious choice. Thomson's sophisticated taste and acute judgment, together with his penchant for avoiding excessive expressionism, have much in common with the music of early 20th-century French composers and thus make their songs particularly good companions. The *Five Songs* are ideal for a first recital as a fresh youthful approach is wholly appropriate.

# Extravaganzas
## (1963–9)

### Peter Dickinson (born 1934)
### Text by Gregory Corso

T III; M IV
Medium voice
Duration 6½'

This cycle of brief songs to evocative, disturbing and ironically humorous texts by the American Beat poet Gregory Corso makes a fine contribution to the recital repertory. Highly entertaining and full of variety, the songs are especially well tailored to the needs of the singer. The composer has special experience in this field through his many concerts with his sister Meriel, for whom these songs are written. The composer's interpretative as well as technical gifts are displayed fully, and the cycle is most enjoyable for all concerned. Wit and flexibility abound in the idiomatic writing for both voice and piano, and there is no chance of an audience's attention wandering. The moods change quickly; every detail counts in music of such conciseness; at times it is reminiscent of Webern's music in its precision and understatement. The singer is fully occupied with a constant parade of interesting vocal tasks and musical delights which are closely linked to the twists and sardonic flashes of dry humour in the text. The vocal part is wide ranging and well-placed clarity of intonation will be necessary. Immaculate diction (a strong feature of Meriel Dickinson's work) is a prime essential. The word-setting is splendidly judged and the whole effect is one of great sensitivity and natural flair. The composer's light touch and considerable expertise in many styles serve him well here in a basically atonal idiom. This cycle should be warmly welcomed as an antidote to heavier fare and a most pleasing showpiece for stylish performers with a disciplined technique.

## 1. Three

The first text consists of three contrasting and beautifully precise fragments. It requires concentration on perfect tuning and exact attention to details, especially the staccato and *tenuto* markings. The first is a slow-moving, simple and poignant portrait of a street singer, in which gentle melismas are used to highlight the more important words. The vocal line lies comfortably in the voice and tactfully allows the singer to warm up and feel the acoustic of the hall. This is particularly important for such brief fragments in which every word tells.

The second piece is even shorter and very fast. Perfect articulation is needed. In the *pianissimo* staccato passage the rhythm must be very strict and as light as possible. It is important to remember that the two longer but detached notes on 'man' and 'come' provide a useful springboard for the clipped notes if leaned upon a little.

The third fragment is in measured 3/4 time. The piano maintains a low tread of funeral march beats while the voice weaves high above with its bitter message. The vocal lines are smooth and angular by turn, but they all lie comfortably. The intonation of the last high *pianissimo* phrase will require close attention, especially for a female voice. Its shifting chromatic intervals will expose any insecurity in the area of the register break; each whole tone and semitone must be clearly defined.

## 2. On the Walls of a Dull Furnished Room

In this song the poet muses in brief nostalgia over his old girlfriends. Sinewy vocal phrases describe each girl's salient features, accompanied by piano flourishes; each phrase is followed by a reflective, unaccompanied and trance-like repetition of the name. The extreme brevity of the song is a challenge to the vocal interpreter. The upper octave is suggested as an *ossia* for singers who find a *forte* low A difficult. There is a lovely natural flexibility throughout which makes the piece especially rewarding to sing. The unaccompanied phrases, with their athletic leaping 7ths must be kept smooth and flowing and their dynamics softened to contrast with the loud phrases.

## 3. 2 Weird Happenings in Haarlem

These two highly colourful episodes are full of delightful details. The singer must exert scrupulous care over articulation and the wide range of dynamic markings. An incisive quality is useful in the *fortissimo* passages, especially for the first piece in which clipped, percussive consonants make a positive contribution. Scotch snap rhythms add character and bite to the attack; breaths must be short, swift and accurately timed.

The second song is much faster and full of sparkle. The 5/8 time signature creates a dancing effect of slightly exotic rhythms. The word 'weirdly' is split into three syllables, inviting an American pronunciation of the 'r' to keep the pulse constant and the syllables separate (Example 1). The impetus of this song is irresistible. The final staccato passage must be delivered delicately without using too much air.

Ex. 1.

## 4. Italian Extravaganza

A child's funeral is described in sardonic, grimly precise terms. The vocal line follows speech patterns and is kept carefully within restricted boundaries of range and volume, except for the sudden *fortissimo* exclamation, 'wow'. The last few lines drop low in the voice and seem to represent inward mutterings. A low *pianissimo* phrase must not invite slack enunciation; crystal clarity here will make a chilling effect. The whole song should be delivered in an expressionless manner with mechanically exact rhythms, so that the horrifying accuracy of the somewhat laconic comments comes out with full force.

## 5. Last night I drove a car

In complete contrast to the other songs, the last one features continuous running semiquavers in octaves in the piano. The vocal line lies in the middle range; it should be sung strongly and firmly so that it is clearly heard through the texture. Rhythms and note groupings fluctuate naturally with the swing of the words throughout the opening section. The motor rhythms halt temporarily for a simple recitative-like phrase of momentary tranquillity, and the pace then whips up again in relentless semiquavers. The final phrase should be punched out in an emphatic *fortissimo* of extreme callousness. The wayward and quirky reactions of the poet to his situation may prove difficult to convey, but a straightforward and clearly enunciated approach is best. The audience will be left with much food for thought.

The stylish economy and subtle humour of this cycle will find an apt parallel in the works of Erik Satie and Poulenc. French music in general goes well with Dickinson's work, as does much American music, especially Ives and Copland; many of the American cycles in this book would be appropriate companions. The cycle could be deliberately juxtaposed with a weighty classic from the lieder repertory. It would be wise to avoid placing it beside a piece which contains fast-changing words; a Baroque or early Italian aria in which words are repeated with melismata and fioritura would form a fine contrast. The economy of settings of Chinese or Japanese poems could also be used as a comparison. *Extravaganzas* would make a refreshing opening or an effective ending to a concert.

# The Hermit of Green Light
## (1979)

### Ross Edwards (born 1943)
### Text by Michael Dransfield

T III; M IV
Countertenor
Duration *c*.13′

There cannot be many finer examples of writing for the countertenor voice than this. Edwards, a leading Australian composer, is acutely aware of the special qualities of incisiveness and enviable evenness of timbre typical of this voice. The four songs are fluent, clearly conceived and well contrasted, and the style throughout is most elegant. The piano writing is invitingly idiomatic. The clear textures should allow the singer to pick out pitch cues. The whole-tone scales dominates both melody and harmony. The time signature fluctuates constantly and the rhythms are sometimes complex. The whole cycle is extremely practicable, however, and the composer's manuscript is a model of clarity. The vocal range is appropriately economical: there is much concentration on the most penetrating areas of the countertenor voice (the octave from middle C upwards). There are not many long notes, and those that do occur are so well placed that they avoid the need to sustain a note too long in the voice without vibrato. Dynamics are subtly moulded to the specific sound quality and musical gestures of the authentic style of Baroque music, which forms the corner-stone of the countertenor's repertory. The aptness of the setting is evident from the outset and finesse and clarity of judgment are sustained throughout the cycle in music of rare delicacy. All countertenors should welcome this addition to their rather limited repertory. It should also prove a satisfying vehicle for other voices, although it is important for them to adapt their tone qualities and dynamics accordingly. An alto or bass, for instance, will naturally command a fuller tone in the lower reaches, but might on the other hand lack the trumpet-like clarity for the middle or upper notes that is a countertenor's special attribute. The cycle requires skill and unusual sensitivity to timbre. It is important to avoid a rich tone which might blur the finely wrought lines.

## 1. The Hermit of Green Light

The gentle beginning in a low register allows the singer to ease himself comfortably into the piece and establish a discreet yet clearly articulated presence which instantly commands attention. It is always advantageous to start with phrases where there is no problem of balance. The listener's ears can then be quickly attuned so that they are alert to the finer details in the work. The rhythms follow the natural pace of the words and the tessitura remains low in a mood of restraint. Towards the end the voice is *sotto voce* as it drops to a low A flat. A slight huskiness would be permissible on the words 'the forest victims'. Every syllable is carefully placed for an unforced and precise delivery which is wholly audible. The vocal style should be plain and without mannerism or overt expressiveness; the extreme simplicity of the lines captures the atmosphere perfectly. The accompaniment is extremely sparse at the beginning and the end of the song, but there are arpeggiated flourishes in the middle when the piano provides a more continuous support and the singer will need to increase dynamics accordingly. In the unaccompanied passage beginning 'beside the moon' the singer must be accurate and sustain clearly defined pitches with no suggestion of imprecise scooping between notes.

## 2. Geography VI

The indication 'Andante, molto espressivo' which marks the piano's introduction to this song heralds a more varied and detailed programme of vocal shadings and nuances. At first the pace remains gentle. The ostinato semitones in the piano part form a useful basis for the singer's pitch orientation, except in the much more turbulent middle section when the tempo becomes more urgent and variable in the phrases describing the restless horses.

The central passage will need to be timed carefully to make the most dramatic effect possible in such a short time. After the piano surges to a climax there is a sudden relaxation of tension. A *molto ritenuto* phrase moves into the resumption of the semitone ostinato. The voice has to be poised on a *ppp* A and sustained through a finely graded crescendo into a line of steady, deliberate coolness. The singer must create an otherworldly atmosphere and maintain it with rapt concentration in an unwavering tone. The *sotto voce* ending must be well controlled and unhurried. Consonants, especially the sibilant ones, should be exaggerated slightly to heighten the intensity a little. The setting of the final word 'falling' is gratifying and flexible, allowing for a graceful, poised and comfortable ending. The changes of mood and subtle colourings suggested by the text of this song can be clearly projected without difficulty as phrases are of an ideal length and the tessitura is suitably undemanding. In the last section it would be wise not to breathe in the small rest preceding the perfect 5th which drops suddenly down to low A on 'mine'. The tone will then be firmer and easier to control and there is ample time to use the 'm' for a smooth transition.

## 3. Geography III

The singer must remain alert throughout this song to deal with the constant fluctuations of time signature and varied rhythmic groupings. The finished performance must seem entirely natural and effortless with no sign of careful counting, but this will only be achieved by slow practice. Pitches, too, are likely to give problems at first; there is a danger of glossing over unstressed notes if the piece is rehearsed up to speed too soon. The tempo is not fast, however, and a choice is given. The singer should definitely not feel constrained to adopt a speed which is not comfortable. The mood is dreamy and contemplative, and the music flows in lines that are supple and more wide ranging than hitherto. Expressive details are astutely judged with the utmost care for the vocal quality of each note. There are quite a number of low notes, but there should be no balance problems as the piano part is also low at the most crucial moments. A smooth timbre is essential. Meticulous attention to the exact duration of notes and rests will prove rewarding. The performer should take advantage of every opportunity to use colourfully sonorous syllables for full effect without disturbing the line. A low F sharp is reached on 'caring', helped by a slur from the previous note (A flat), allowing the singer to shape the phrase gracefully and securely even at this extreme. The higher passage which follows soon after makes an excellent contrast as the voice again rings out in its most incisive range.

The final melisma on 'spirit' must be sung carefully to prevent any loss of evenness which would mar the atmosphere. A truly seamless legato is essential for the leap up a minor 6th and if any break in register were perceptible here it would be most unfortunate. Very firm control of the support muscles solve the problem; the position of the throat and jaw must not be allowed to move with the notes. Physical strength and stamina, though unnoticeable to the listener, are needed for such passages. To allow any slackening is in fact more tiring in the long term.

## 4. And No Bird Sings

This brief song fulfils the role of a coda; it is simple and understated, with only occasional comment from the piano. The music evolves in a series of bland statements with sudden *sforzando* emphases on special words, superbly reflecting the text. The singer should hold something in reserve for this last test of control, and particularly for the last two phrases which hold the audience spellbound (Example 1). The boldly

Ex.1.

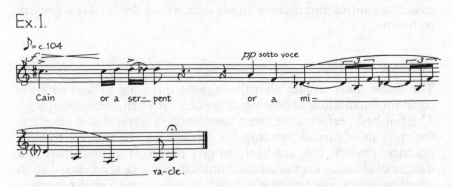

resonant *forte* at the incisive pitch of C sharp with a short diminuendo and immediate crescendo show the composer's understanding of the singer's need to banish any tentative waverings and clear the voice ready for the long *pianissimo* melisma. Full support is again essential and the singer must take care to sustain a legato sound through the wider intervals. A clear thread of sound is all that is required and there is no need to force syllables. The 'm' at the start and the 'le' at the finish help to make the sound continuous.

This is an impressive and expertly written cycle. The composer has obviously taken care to work closely with the work's original performer and to study the many facets of the countertenor voice in the utmost detail. Stylistically *The Hermit of Green Light* will make a perfect complement to early music and fit admirably into a programme which mixes Baroque or medieval music with contemporary songs. Its clarity and sense of proportion is sure to make a refined and pleasing effect and the performer should find it a joy to prepare.

# *Three Auden Songs*
## (1983)

## Hans Werner Henze (born 1926)
### Text by W. H. Auden

T III; M IV
Tenor
Duration *c.8'*

Today's major composers are now returning to the medium of voice and piano after a time of comparative neglect. Many have tended to regard the piano's resonances as unsuitable for a contemporary sound and too strongly evocative of the 19th century; they preferred to leave it in the hands of composers of a more determinedly conservative bias. Henze's present-day style is certainly accessible in every sense and it is a pleasure to find this recent set of tenor songs in the repertory. Its hallmarks are flair and innate musicality. The composer shows unerring sensitivity in his setting of the fast moving texts; the layers of subtleties are couched in beautifully concise language which rolls sensually off the tongue and is ideal for vocalising. The three poems are cumulative in their proportions and weight; a tiny, poignant tribute to a dead cat leads to a searing and intuitive portrait of Rimbaud in four pithy verses; this in turn is followed by the substantial love song, full of tenderness and passion which is sometimes overtly expressed but more often gently controlled in exquisitely wrought continuous phrases. The vocal writing is impeccable. For sheer enjoyment the set is to be warmly recommended to all tenors. It is not particularly difficult musically and gives the voice every chance to be heard to best advantage.

## 1. In Memoriam L. K. A. 1950–1952

Rising and falling minor 7ths give the voice a pleasing elasticity from the outset. This is a perfect way to begin a song, especially since the line is low at first. The encouraging effect of this flexing of the voice prepares the singer for the very soft high passage which is marked with the sign used for natural harmonics in string writing to indicate a falsetto or rather unearthly or 'white' sound. It is important to maintain a flowing tempo and not to slow up when approaching these specially marked notes. Several 'ee' vowels on high notes may need careful practice. Throughout this song it is probably a good idea to keep the voice fairly free of vibrato; a crooning sound, appropriate to the peaceful slumber of the cat, and a true legato is crucial. A seamless line will create a suitably hypnotic effect and no bumps must disturb its smooth flow, even when the singer takes a breath.

The vocal line stops suddenly with a comma just before the word 'weep' on a very soft, high F sharp. The consonant 'w' is in fact sung as 'oo'; the singer should fully exploit the alliteration. It is best not to take a breath at the comma but merely to suspend the sound to make the audience concentrate more acutely and to pin-point the word. The piano part here is soft and restrained, providing a simple texture of chords. The last note of the song – 'keep' on a harmonic on high F sharp – may be difficult at first. It is important not to overstress the 'k' as this may cause the sound to jump. A thin, pure strand of sound must be maintained with very clear intonation. The singer must concentrate on preserving a secure sense of pitch for the unaccompanied start of the next song; the C pedal note in the bass of the piano will provide the most reliable anchor.

## 2. Rimbaud

This much more extrovert song, marked 'harshly, rhapsodically', ranges over a whole spectrum of emotions amid fluctuating fast tempos. The vocal style is declamatory and sometimes parlando, as it is at the opening. Natural speech rhythms are adhered to and so diction should not be a problem. It would be a good idea, however, to practise declaiming the text in rhythm before actually singing. There should not be a breath between 'lie' and 'burst' since this may spoil the crescendo to the climax. As there is a convenient *rallentando*, it is practicable to place the 'st' of 'burst' exactly on the second part of the triplet (the rest) and immediately snatch a breath. The same applies to the subsequent 'p' of 'pipe'. These need only be small breaths and vocal impetus and position of supporting muscles should not alter. The vocal writing here is excellent. Henze clearly understands how to bring out the best in the performer and how to make constructive use of the voice's capacities. The quiet interlude which follows this dynamic passage must not be flaccid vocally, although the mood of the words should be conveyed until the volume rises once more (Example 1). Climactic, high phrases are potentially dangerous in that verbal clarity and control of vibrato may be lost. The dynamic markings must be carefully observed. The composer has tailored the lines to ensure vocal security and good pacing of breaths. The use of explosive consonants highlights and emphasises the lively rhythms. The 'f' of 'enough' should be synchronised with the piano chord on the third quaver and a breath taken immediately after to maintain a strict rhythm. The accents on 'That seemed the' are effective and easy to execute.

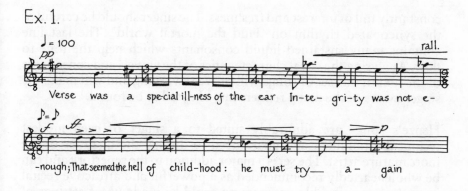

Ex. 1.

Verse was a spe-cial ill-ness of the ear In-te-gri-ty was not e-

-nough; That seemed the hell of child-hood: he must try— a- gain

It is not necessary to breathe in the rest between 'try' and 'again'.

In the last paragraph of this song there is a series of semiquavers high in the voice. The notes must not be swallowed and they must be even and secure, each one given its full value without rushing. The discipline of breathing at just the right moment from a physical point of view in a succession of phrases fortifies the singer for the tremendous high A sharp on 'truth', an ideal word to sing here because of the splendid impetus of 'tr' with a rolled 'r' and the following 'oo' vowel. The phrase then arches downwards and ends on a low B, which is eminently practicable in the circumstances. It is always a relief to swoop down deep from a strenuous high note and instantly loosen the voice again, thus removing any hint of fatigue.

### 3. Lay your Sleeping Head my Love

The marking 'utter simplicity' denotes the style required. The words speak for themselves and so the composer has set them to a smooth melody. Each verse starts with an upward whole-tone scale and the modal flavour is continued. The vocal lines are supple, with close-knit intervals, and although they are focused on the top of the stave they avoid extremes and never rise above G flat. The tessitura would be tiring for a soprano, but it is excellent writing for tenor. Good technical control is needed for the long phrases. Only in the centre of the song do loud notes have to be punched out in the contrasting *marcato* passage where percussive consonants (as in 'pedantic' and 'cost') again play their part in outlining the rhythms. In the phrase which begins with 'Every farthing', it is wise to breathe after 'cost' as this makes good sense verbally and enables the singer to go through to 'paid' where the line dips down. The sibilance of the text in the next section can be used to the full and consonants placed deliberately. The variety of rhythm in the opening whole-tone scale of each verse is a delight, and the last, hushed and halting one is especially apt. Subtlety and flexibility are to be found everywhere, making the vocal lines constantly full of interest and freshness. The singer should be careful of the syncopated rhythm on 'Find the mortal world'. The last line contains many sustained liquid consonants which help the tone to flow. Analysing the vocal characteristics of the vowels and consonants of the text in this set of songs will prove rewarding and will make the singer aware of the many refinements of detail to be found.

Henze's songs are admirably suited to a singer of even modest technical attainment and guaranteed to display the qualities of the more mature artist. The set is a major addition to the repertory and can be wholeheartedly recommended as a powerful and attractive recital item. A very enjoyable programme could be made up of settings of Auden's texts as there are so many fine examples; it would be wise to include something of a lighter nature, such as Britten's *Four Cabaret Songs*. Henze's songs would also go well with Austro-German Romantic lieder, especially those of Schumann, Liszt and Mahler.

## *Five Songs on English Poems*
### (1974)
### Daniël Manneke (born 1939)

### T III; M IV
Low voice and harpsichord/piano/organ
Duration 12′

In this welcome addition to the low-voice repertory, Manneke (a Dutch composer) employs space–time notation for the first three songs. Full explanatory notes are provided in the score. The fourth song uses conventional notation and, in the last song even greater freedom is employed in notating the voice part. The composer's first choice of instrument to accompany the voice is a harpsichord, but he states that the piano is also suitable. The pianist must then use his or her discretion in trying to mirror the timbre of the harpsichord by avoiding too much pedal and adopting appropriate dynamics and colours. Octave transpositions can be made if necessary.

Manneke gives a very clear index of vocal devices. A glissando is indicated by a wavy line between notes, rather than a straight one and small glissandos or portamentos have single curves. Heavy vibrato is marked by a wavy line over the note. Crosses through the stems of notes indicate Sprechgesang of the kind used in *Pierrot lunaire* and for parlando the note-heads are crosses. In the final song the two performers do not have to co-ordinate exactly (a reassuring thought); the parts should only come together at the points marked with an arrow.

Hopkins is by far the most recent of the poets set, and it is fascinating to observe how well the 20th-century treatment fits the older English texts.

### 1. Envoi (Walter Savage Landor, 1775–1864)

In this fine piece of loose-limbed and supple vocal writing, the voice moves easily and naturally through a series of smooth lines. Grace notes are used to stress special moments, a device which also serves to relax and flex the voice. The details listed in the glossary are used subtly and the singer must obey the instructions carefully, especially for the heavy vibrato notes which must be sharply differentiated from normal ones. The basic tone should therefore be straight, true and not too rich. The composer's Italian indications include some rather unusual ones, such as *sommesso*, meaning soft, subdued. It is worth taking extra care over these since the varieties of timbre stand out in an otherwise unruffled song. The semi-staccato on 'fire' is very effective. From Figure A onwards the phrases become more detailed and some are marked 'non-legato'. The *sforzandos* at the start of some of them help to relieve any hesitancy. (A bold start vocally is almost always a good idea.) There is a proliferation of grace notes in the last phrase; each note must be accurately poised and a plain timbre seems suitable. The composer has tactfully provided breathing places, not all of which should be necessary. It is particularly relaxing and comforting to skip across the large intervals on the grace notes.

### 2. Heaven-Haven (Gerard Manley Hopkins, 1844–89)

The stylistic and vocal characteristics of the first song pervade the second and third. They too are fleeting, with discreet and sparse accompaniments with chords lightly inserted between the statements of the voice. The lovely flexibility of the suave vocal lines is perfectly suited to Hopkins's poetry. The singer can enjoy the lack of strict rhythmic boundaries, but must meticulously observe all dynamic markings. The word 'dumb' is made to stand out by being written as Sprechstimme. The third song follows *attacca*.

### 3. The Author's Epitaph (Sir Walter Ralegh, 1552–1618)

This song is slightly more extended but similar in style to the first two. The composer helps to create the *inquieto* mood he requires by means of very varied dynamics. The grace notes can be sung with considerable force. Manneke again uses Sprechstimme, as well as *parlando* singing. The notes repeated within a melisma are particularly riveting. The song becomes very dramatic, with an *accelerando, sforzando* attacks, several heavy vibrato notes and Sprechstimme at wide-ranging volumes. In the final phrase, marked 'Feierlich, legato,' the singer must almost seem to be possessed or performing some ritual, helped by the very exciting series of small glissandos on all the rising intervals of the cadenza on 'up' (Example 1). Two Sprechstimme notes should then drift out as naturally as possible on the words 'I trust', with the singer using any spare breath to add an expressive hush to the voice. (This is permissible only in this kind of special instance.) The next song follows *attacca*.

Ex.1.

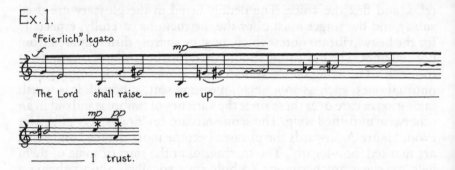

### 4. The world a hunting is (William Drummond of Hawthornden, 1585–1649)

The composer changes here to conventionally notated 2/4 time. The relationship of the accompaniment to the voice part alters with the piano now providing full support. The character of the vocal writing sharply contrasts that of the preceding songs: the singer should keep rhythmic pulses clear and disciplined to differentiate them fully from the free-flowing lines. Grace notes are still in evidence; some of them are written out exactly. Manneke strikingly uses the text to create drama. 'Inquieto' is again the instruction, and there is an urgent feeling throughout until the piece solemnly dies away. Considerable use is made of the singer's lowest register within fairly continuous, decorative phrases. Probably the most difficult task for the singer will be the long, *senza vibrato* low A which has to incorporate first a diminuendo and then a crescendo and decrescendo. This is very hard to control and requires a steady diaphragm. Since the vowel is 'ee' of 'breathe' the singer should keep the tone thin and straight, as if humming, and should not try to cover it. A sepulchral effect is highly appropriate to the text.

## 5. Silence (Thomas Hood, 1799–1845)

The last song makes a fascinating and comprehensive use of the speaking voice. The conventional stave is dispensed with and only the shape of the vocal line is shown within a blank space; a general guide to pitch is given by three markings: high, middle and low. The rhythms are notated normally, but there are no bar-lines (Example 2). The

Ex. 2.

accompaniment is full of character. Repeated staccato notes are a constant feature of the opening section; towards the end there is a much busier, five-against-four passage before the singer is left completely alone to speak the last few lines in quietness, obeying the composer's helpful instructions.

There are so many ways of performing this song that perhaps a few guidelines may help. It is really up to the individual performer to discover and exploit the many varied timbres of his or her voice which can be released when the rules of conventional singing may be broken. It is always wise to approach spoken lines as if they were to be sung, that is by supporting the phrases with the full apparatus provided by training. Neglect of this aspect tends to result in a coughing fit. It is only safe to make a special breathy sound when the dynamics are soft and hushed, for the action of pushing breath on to the voice box causes a dangerous, tickling sensation. The composer has made the contours of the lines clear; extremes of range are avoided and the phrases flow up and down quite easily. It is best to seize any opportunity to drop to the natural pitch of speech where there is no feeling of strain. Lower pitches are usually more comfortable, but attention must be paid to the balance with the accompaniment.

Consonants often suggest special colourings and inflections appropriate to the texts: all sibilants, for instance, create heightened mystery and can be exaggerated for clarity. Such words as 'clouds', 'shadows' and 'hush'd' are a gift for the speaker. Final consonants must be placed exactly in such a way that they keep rhythms steady and undisturbed. Long notes present the thorniest problems: as soon as a pitch is sustained, a singing tone results. (For the *quasi cantabile* passage at the very end when the lines have slowed down it is in fact appropriate to croon slightly, as in sustained Sprechstimme.) It is often a good idea to keep vowels a little shorter for parlando, but this, of course, must not interfere with the beat of the music. Liquid consonants, however, can be prolonged to help propel the performer through an awkward moment; the 'l' and 'n' of 'silence', which occurs so often in the poem, are useful in this way. Fortunately when the tone is at its loudest, the rhythms move faster and the long notes will not be strenuous to maintain.

Manneke's cycle has much to offer. Although it challenges the singer, it is not difficult vocally and it displays artistry without stress. It is tempting to place it in a programme with medieval, renaissance or Baroque music, especially if a harpsichord is available, or to include other settings of these poets.

# *Mutability*
## (1952)

### Irving Fine (1914–62)
### Text by Irene Orgel

### T III; M V
### Mezzo-soprano
### Duration *c.*15′

Irving Fine's music is typical of a whole generation of American composers writing in an accessible and tightly controlled idiom based strongly on European tradition. It is a wonderfully challenging cycle. Its powerful musical and verbal images make *Mutability* an outstanding vehicle for a well-schooled artist who is able to command a wide range of colours and dynamics and is adept at fast articulation. The variety and flexibility found within the fairly strict compositional procedure is truly admirable, and the whole work shows great confidence and integrity. The style could be described as neo-classical with serial elements. The singer thus has to deal with quite a few difficult intervals. An unprepared performance would produce blurred pitches and vague intonation. Careful practice will be needed to attain the precision demanded by this excellent piece and to perform it with the commitment and panache it deserves. As a recital item it will make a memorable effect. There are perhaps too many demands on skill and experienced imagination to make it suitable for the complete beginner unless the singer has the advantage of perfect pitch and an exceptional musicianship which would enable her to concentrate on tone quality, enunciation and aspects of interpretation.

A voice with a cutting edge is especially suitable for this work; the darker, fuller tones of a deep, almost contralto-like mezzo-soprano will sound well in the many low passages. Flexibility is the priority, however, and the voice must be able to move around easily and produce a clear tone at will without any delay. Heavier voices can sometimes be rather slow to speak. The piano parts are exciting and varied and make a strong contribution to the positive impression made by Fine's music.

## 1. I have heard the hoof beats of happiness

The opening Allegro needs tremendous rhythmic discipline and concentration. Breaths must be placed deftly in the short gaps provided and a relentless pulse maintained. Some of the words are not easy to enunciate at speed: 'hoof beats of happiness', for example. A straightforward and incisive placing of the sound is necessary to project the texts clearly without strain. A slackening of speed brings a more pliable, recitative-like line, and the piano's running semiquavers occasionally stop to allow more freedom of expression. The ending is particularly crucial: the singer reaches progressively lower, first to a B and then to the final sustained low A on the word 'eyes'. This is not easy to sing as the final part of the diphthong has to be elided smoothly with the 's' (pronounced 'z' and therefore singable) at the very end; if the vowel has been allowed to slip back and become too full and warm, this may prove difficult. A glottal attack is appropriate for 'eyes', but this must not be allowed to disturb the tone.

## 2. My father

The text and music of this poignant song are most arresting. It must be sung straightforwardly and clearly, paying great attention to intonation and exact tuning of intervals. The louder phrase in the middle is typical of the wide range; it is important not to neglect short notes when approaching a difficult interval. Although the word 'the' is set to a semiquaver, the note must be well centred and connected to those around it. There is an opportunity here to show natural warmth of tone and to keep the sound firm and even within the steadier *andante* pace.

## 3. The weed

The short Adagio is extremely well placed to provide balance and contrast. This highly concentrated song allows the singer considerable scope to show dramatic and interpretative prowess in the powerful diatribe. The repetition of the word 'weed', with the helpful 'w' to aid placing, makes a telling effect. Similar use of the lips' natural tendency to impel percussive attacks, if timed correctly, is appropriate for 'mine', which also recurs several times. The rhythms are particularly inventive, especially the triplet demisemiquavers, followed by quaver triplets which include a complex triplet within a triplet. The loaded statement of the text must be clearly emphasised and dynamic variations are especially important. The ending should be most moving and tinged with genuine regret after the forceful assertions of the opening.

## 4. Peregrine

The exhilarating sweep of the fourth song is a delight. The use of long notes sustained by the singer while the piano rushes along beneath is a recurrent feature. Strict rhythmic and musical discipline is needed to time the breathing perfectly and find a firmly centred sound for the often rather low beginnings of new phrases. There are many octave leaps, and pitch should cause little trouble except in the *poco meno mosso* passage in the middle and the last two phrases which must be delicately and accurately placed. There is no need to breathe in the expressive rest after 'no' in 'It was no canary'.

## 5. Jubilation

This is a most beautiful song, full of musical interest and variety. It is worth taking extra time to perfect the many subtle dynamic nuances in the wide-ranging lines of the opening section. Absolute clarity is essential, even though the composer marks the passage 'molto legato'. In the 'h' of 'hugged' and 'harp' the singer must not expend too much air or she will run out of breath. A sudden *allegro* passage, in which the voice is unaccompanied for a moment, brings a surge of passion and a stream of intricate coloratura and the close, chromatic cells are repeated relentlessly. It is best to join the notes smoothly together rather than trying to articulate each one separately. The speed of the passage can be determined by the pace at which the voice runs naturally. Good breath capacity will be needed. The singer then has to project accented attacks on each note of a *forte* phrase and, most difficult of all, to accomplish the *ffp* followed by a heavy crescendo through the long held B flat that ends the song on the word 'dismayed'. The final 'd' helps to make the ending emphatic and sharply etched.

## 6. Now God be thanked for Mutability

The final song follows *attacca* with a virtuosic piano introduction. The singer's deeply moving statements avoid extremes of range and volume, but they are ideally matched to words of great power and import. The piano's role is crucial here; the part is full of intense drama in the cantabile lines which move in counterpoint with the voice. Pitching may again cause the singer some problems, as any blurring of notes would ruin the atmosphere. A resigned and unaffected manner is a prime requisite to effect the final phrases with utter commitment and security and without faltering.

A great deal of emotion is contained in this concise and vivid cycle and any good singer should welcome the chance to rise to the challenge it offers. *Mutability* deserves a prime place in a recital programme. It would make an excellent companion piece to a major cycle by one of the leading Austro-German figures. One of Fauré's cycles, perhaps *Le jardin clos*, would also be highly suitable. It would be an especially good choice as the only 20th-century work in a recital, as it contrasts well with Baroque or early Classical arias. If another 20th-century work is to be included, something simple on a small scale in an avant-garde idiom (a piece by Cage, for example) would be appropriate.

## *Three Songs*
### (1961, revised 1970–71)

### Roger Smalley (born 1943)
### Text by Walter de la Mare

### T III; M V
### Mezzo-soprano or soprano
### Duration *c*.7'

Smalley's very brief and highly concentrated songs are almost Japanese in their economy of content and delicate fragmentary style. His piano writing is resourceful and varied, as might be expected from a fine pianist; some modernistic vocal devices, such as glissando and singing without vibrato, are used most effectively. In general the tessitura is suited to a mezzo-soprano. At the opening of the first song, however, the rapt *pianissimo* vocal line rises to a high F sharp with no vibrato and this might prove extremely hard for a heavy voice to control while it is relatively easy for a soprano. Likewise, the *pianissimo* fading on E at the end of this song and some rather long notes without vibrato, including one high G in the second song, suggest that a lighter voice may be more comfortable in this music. These are the only problems of this nature and elsewhere the voice moves easily over a medium range; the phrases lie well and are not at all taxing in either length or dynamics. Smalley's unusual rhythmic patterns set the text in a deft and original way. The vocal style is distinctly Webernian: the undulating lines flatter the voice and perhaps conceal any unevenness. The first two songs are mercurial in their changing moods and are seldom, except fleetingly, very loud. The third song, with its pattering figurations in the piano, is much more active and continuous, although the vocal line remains fragmented. Its range lies somewhat lower than the other songs. A different order of songs might be feasible; reversing the second and third might make a better vocal contrast.

## 1. Silver

This short and intricate song is packed with tiny details. As with Webern, the dynamic markings are extremely subtle and their strict observance is absolutely crucial. The opportunity of singing very smoothly must be firmly grasped to throw the wispy, more fragile phrases into relief. The wide-ranging intervals in the lovely smooth lines of the hushed opening are satisfying to sing. The F sharp mentioned above is made easier by being set to the word 'moon'. The position of the lips directs the aim of the thin, ghostly sound without strain. The sound should seem to float out through the top of the head. Thereafter the tempo quickens, and separately articulated fragments of text alternate with smooth ones. The singer may savour the particularly evocative sounds of the words: the sibilance of the recurring 'silver' is a case in point. The accompaniment is so sparse that it is not difficult to make the words clear. The appearance of the dog should form a marked contrast and that first *mezzo-forte* should seem very loud. It is worth learning to sing really softly for it has a magical effect and trains the listeners to tune their ears more finely. On the word 'silver' the glissando down a minor 7th from the loudest point leads to a steadier tempo to allow time to fit in the swift succession of syllables. The harvest mouse is introduced by way of neat staccatos while the fish appear in an appropriately still and rapt passage which ends in a difficult diminuendo to *ppp* on the final E. The 'm' of 'stream' should ideally be caught and held at the end. The singer should avoid cutting the sound off percussively and tightening the throat when the lips are closed. It is worth practising this because a bocca chiusa is quite commonly used by contemporary composers.

## 2. The Horseman

The more forthright text of this song makes a rather more extrovert impression. Care should be taken not to let vibrato obtrude. A pure, clear timbre is especially desirable in this more complex music; intonation must be exact with no groping or swooping even though the lines are invitingly flexible. The sudden *pianissimo* without vibrato on the high G on 'pale' is a fine example of word-painting. Fortunately the note does not have to be held too long and the singer can glide easily away from potential trouble before the sound becomes constricted. Eliding the 'l' and the 'w' of 'was' makes a smooth transition. As in the previous song, economy of means achieves maximum effect. The last phrase is strongly declamatory and it must come across clearly without a hint of gustiness. The singer should beware possible wastage of breath on 'h' sounds.

### 3. Rain

Meticulous precision with regard to details of shading and pitch is again needed. When singing these much deeper lines (incorporating several low A flats) care should be taken to keep the voice from speading into too rich a quality as vibrato might obscure the pitch. An almost reedy, instrumental sound seems appropriate and would cut through the texture well. Often singers are not aware that well-placed, straight sounds do not come out as harshly as they fear. A direct attack gives such a natural resonance (with all harmonics in line) that there is no need to round out the tone further to make it more expressive. The quintuplet groups, each marked 'tenuto', have to be carefully articulated. Short rests punctuate the lines but the singer must think through the silences to ensure that the feeling of long phrases continues. (This technique is nearly always a good idea in such passages.) The *sfp* on the word 'shrill' in the fourth bar can be made even more effective if the 'll' arrives early. The poised and delicate staccato syllables have to be picked out cleanly with perfect aim; they will be easier to control if only a small amount of air is used. The suppleness and grace of the lines should flatter the voice. The composer displays a natural feeling for the relaxing effect on the voice of lines which curve down at the ends of phrases, ready to spring up again quite suddenly.

If the singer has a fairly high degree of musicianship and is prepared to work hard to give an accurate performance of these songs, they should prove rewarding and relatively easy to vocalise. The delicate pointing of exquisite details is enjoyable for the performer. The fact that the poems will be familiar to many is an added boon. The general impression created should be one of translucent elegance.

This set would go well in a programme of works which encourage the audience to listen keenly to refined sounds: for example songs by Webern or French music, especially Debussy or Ravel. The brevity of the songs means that they can be used to break up a group of more substantial works. It is to be hoped that audiences, their appetites whetted by these delightful miniatures, will be tempted to sample more of such music in future. Imaginative programme planners could concoct a mélange of songs featuring themes and images from these poems: the moon, silver, horses, rain and so on. Pieces by Schubert, Schumann, Brahms, Debussy and Strauss leap to mind immediately. This thematic approach to the making of a programme often brings fresh audiences and can be most enticing to the fainthearted at a time when the traditional 'Liederabend' is going out of fashion and a younger audience needs to be attracted to the recital repertory.

# Scotch Minstrelsy
## (1982)

### Judith Weir (born 1954)
Text adapted from Scottish folk ballads

T III; M V
Tenor
Duration 12½'

The dashing wit, variety and characteristic brilliance of Scotch Minstrelsy makes it a most attractive addition to the tenor repertory. The clearly presented music (a model in this respect as all instructions are to the point and immensely helpful) even looks appetising on the page and instantly tempting to the performer. The vocal writing of this gifted composer is fresh and apt. The folk influences in the music are unmistakable, but they are given new perspectives. The composer has deftly captured a style that incorporates familiar idioms and sets them in a thoroughly original manner. Full of vigour and sardonic sly humour, the writing never falls into pastiche.

The word-setting is exemplary throughout. The phrasing and tessitura are so well designed that the piece is comfortable to sing, allowing maximum concentration on the abundant interpretative and dynamic subtleties. The piano accompaniment is most exciting and shows exceptional flair. An excellent player will be required for this rewarding part which greatly enhances the impact of the whole piece.

## 1. Bessie Bell and Mary Gray

The first song is preceded by a quotation telling the sad tale of the two ladies who in 1645 tried unsuccessfully to avoid becoming victims of the plague. This information is intended to be absorbed by the performers, but not read aloud.

The piano opens with a long, elaborate lament on one stave only, evocative of a Scottish fiddle. The voice enters very gently with a simple plaintive melody as the piano part moves on to two staves and continues to weave intricate rhythmic patterns. The one-stave figurations for piano solo resume, and the singer then repeats the second half of the verse simply and quietly at first, rising to a high G on 'plague'. The consonants make it easy to place the note; it begins *piano* and gets louder through the dotted minim. The effect should be clear and slightly eerie; vibrato must be kept to a minimum. An expression-

135

less delivery is appropriate. The spare simplicity of the vocal line directly conveys the chilling message of death by plague and contrasts with the extremely expressive piano part. Some difficulties may arise in co-ordinating some of the awkward rhythms in the voice and piano.

## 2. Bonnie James Campbell

The song is basically strophic, but each verse is heavily embellished and full of variety. The clear and bright traditional folk melody is in steady waltz rhythm with a few changes in tempo at the ends of phrases. The tune is subtly decorated in the second verse and there is an incisive galloping rhythm in the piano. The basic melody covers a wider range here as it whirls up and down. Slight shifts in rhythm add a freedom to the line. The words must be articulated bitingly with as little vibrato as possible so that rhythmic details are set in relief. At the end of the second verse the vocal line dips down and is *forte*. Younger voices may find this a little difficult. Exciting repeated chords underpin the vocal line in the third verse. More cross-rhythms are introduced and the more frenetic chord repetitions are notated in boxes; the resultant almost improvisatory feeling continues until the last two bars when the basic time resumes in its simpler form to round off the song. The singer should make the most of the opportunity to project the text strongly and to characterise it by pointing special words.

## 3. Lady Isobel and the Elf-Knight

A light timbre and precise attack and enunciation are essential in this song. The *perpetuum mobile* accompaniment in the treble clef in compound rhythm is set without accents. The tune is again traditional and extremely straightforward. The song's basic form is strophic. The first verse is fragile and delicate; tripping rhythms and fast-changing syllables move supply over a wide range. The high piano part should have a distinctive and magically sparkling colour with an even legato. Light pedalling is suggested to effect this. In the second verse the voice becomes higher and more declamatory (above an accompaniment of alternating bare 5ths) with greater contrast in the dynamics. The rhythm of the accompaniment in the second part of this verse becomes more complex; the four-against-three timing may need special work, and the rhythmic co-ordination of voice and piano is now undoubtedly harder. A particularly important phrase, 'till once my dear father and mother I see', is treated more flexibly to heighten the dramatic effect (Example 1). The dramatic dialogue between Lady Isobel and the Knight gives much scope to imaginative interpreters. It should not be difficult for a man to convey the idea of a woman speaking without exaggerating. Her lines could perhaps be sung extremely smoothly to

Ex. 1.

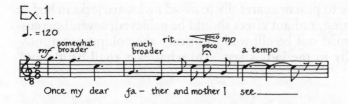

stand out against the bolder rhythms of the Elf-Knight. The passage beginning *piano* on 'O sit down a while' should be sung as sinuously as possible while maintaining the pulse. In the final verse the atmosphere should be sinister yet sweet, with evil fascination and chilling understatement. The setting of 'fast asleep' may cause problems in that 'fast a-' is *pianissimo* and there is a separate attack on '-sleep' which is marked *piano*. The singer should make full use of sibilant consonants and poise the sound close to the teeth; there must be no breath before '-sleep'. The words of the final bars should be crystal-clear to make their horrific yet seductive impact.

### 4. The Gypsy Laddie

The familiar tale (another version of the *Raggle-taggle Gypsies*) is given most arresting treatment in the form of a dramatic scena rather than a strophic song as might be expected. A restless, widely spaced piano figuration (marked 'pp: in the background') fluctuates between 3/8 and 2/4 to create a feeling of constant mystery and excitement. The dynamics in the vocal part are especially colourful and varied. It may initially prove difficult to fit together the uneven patterns of notes. The rhythm of the vocal line must be clearly defined against the subdivisions of the beat in the accompaniment which flows in contrary motion between the two hands. The narrative must be crisply delivered, not too loudly at first. The large number of 'ee' vowels on fairly high notes means that a soprano would be less comfortable in this song, but the composer has judged the tenor timbre perfectly. Potentially awkward moments are helped by well placed consonants which act as mellifluous bridges between the syllables, as in 'sweetly' and 'complete'.

The first verse sets the scene. The second verse must be seductive and smooth; it is marked 'very even'. The lowness of the line makes this easier, as do the sounds of the words describing the gypsies' aphrodisiac gifts. The vocal rhythms are straightforward, although they shift from duple to triple time. The piano weaves a complex web made up mainly of arpeggio-like patterns, except for a sudden, significant rhythmic unison of its *pianissimo* chords with the vocal line at the most spellbinding moment. The singer then personifies the lady and excitement mounts. The composer still asks for smooth singing; the singer may have to practise carefully to avoid awkward jerks in higher phrases. A shining, radiant effect should be achieved; several percussive syllables must not be allowed to disturb the voluptuous atmosphere, especially in the lady's last 'Ah! what ever shall betide me!' (Example 2).

Ex. 2.

The second part of the song is marked 'Epilogue'. A very fast piece of incidental music on the piano conveys the lady's departure with the gypsies and her husband's return. It leads directly to the forthright entry of the singer, now in the role of the avenging Lord. The fate of the gypsies is soon settled and without any slackening of the relentless, fast tempo of the music. The vocal lines lie low, straight and firm to allow for the greatest expression and subtle colouring of the words. The song should break off quite suddenly with no *rallentando* or warning that the end is imminent.

## 5. The Braes of Yarrow

The final, strophic song is very brief; marked 'distant and removed', it stands in sharp contrast to the dramatic fireworks of the preceding pages. The uneven rhythms of the voice in unison with the piano create a ghostly, withdrawn aura. The monodic tread continues within a simple series of intervals throughout the first two verses. Suddenly the singer resumes his centre-stage position and the last verse whips up momentum with busy whirls in the piano, still in octaves; meanwhile the same plain tune is sustained strongly and clearly by the singer right up to the sudden *pianissimo* piano octaves which conclude the work.

This brilliant and highly original piece will give the singer little technical trouble. The main problems are likely to lie in the music, and more particularly in the rhythms. These may inhibit vocal ease merely by providing many distractions at the initial stages. No singer should be deterred, however, from working carefully through the cycle, limiting the practice periods to short, intensive bursts with good rests in between. The end result will be truly satisfying. It would probably be wise to take the songs one by one without the piano so that the singer can master the vocal lines. It is pointless to run straight through the songs with piano, grappling with the problems of fitting the parts together before the lines feel natural and articulation is deft and smooth. This anyway would impede the singer's own ability to monitor the tone accurately and to avoid forcing, especially in the third and fourth songs. Only when the vocal line is absolutely secure should the singer attempt to sing all the songs with the piano. (Pitch and rhythm cues given in the accompaniment should all be noted carefully by the singer when practising alone.) Assiduous marking of the score before the full rehearsal will be a great advantage. The composer cannot then be held responsible for tiring the voice.

This superb concert piece is guaranteed to enthrall any audience. Its immediate appeal is supported by solid foundations of expertise and thorough, unerring instinct. It should form a centrepiece in a recital programme, perhaps followed by other Scottish settings influenced by folksong.

# *Mirages*
## (1970)
# William Alwyn (1905–85)
### Text by William Alwyn

### T IV; M III
### Baritone
### Duration *c.*22′

This fine and consistent composer, whose work is widely admired yet unwarrantedly neglected, will be greatly missed. *Mirages*, a substantial and passionate cycle, is a superb example of Alwyn's assurance, musical depth, refinement and warm conviction. Almost every song is a *tour de force* in itself: the baritone's resources will be fully stretched and the invigorating piano parts are similarly testing. The cycle is best suited to a singer and pianist who have often played together. A dramatic or operatic baritone with a command of vibrant vocal colours and an ability to control vibrato and dynamics to the finest degree will be ideal; a fiery and intensely committed stage presence will be a distinct advantage. Audiences will find the piece most stirring and powerful. The musical idiom could be classified as modern romantic, employing conventional notation. The cycle proves that there is still enormous scope within the well-tried paths for a composer of boldness and imagination to stamp his own personality on his music without sounding derivative. Alwyn's impressive work ought to become an established classic.

### 1. Undine

The opening song immediately attracts attention with its turbulent piano figures which begin gently and swell into small crescendos and diminuendos; the music eventually rises to a *mezzo-forte* and subsides slightly to provide a full texture for the first vocal entry. The singer's lines are warmly romantic, weaving lightly above the piano as the dynamics rise and fall according to the lie of the phrases and match the surging of the piano's arpeggiated figures. The forward propulsion of the music comes to a *forte* climax on 'Suddenly' on an E, the highest note so far. The impact is reinforced by a swirl of grace notes on the piano. There is no need for the singer to breathe after this one word as the dynamics quieten immediately to *piano*. The music proceeds with the same natural momentum. The voice soon soars to a more strenuous high *fortissimo* passage at the word 'gold' and a quick sweep of grace notes on the piano again precedes the voice's triumphal high E. The singer has a series of fanfare-like figures, which include a high F sharp (Example 1). An *ossia* is provided for those who find this note difficult. It would be a pity to lose impetus at this point and unless the higher version is completely secure in the voice it is much better to opt for the lower alternative, thereby making sure that the exultant ring of the whole passage is maintained.

Ex. 1.

With perfect judgment the composer immediately provides the singer with a more restful start to the next passage. The vocal line again builds up to a high loud note but stops to allow the piano to make the real climax in a wildly impassioned solo. The left-hand sextuplet figures slow down, the texture becomes thin and the music comes to rest on an exposed, *pianissimo* 7th. The voice has a telling recitative passage, marked 'sempre pianissimo'. Perfect timing is crucial for these small fragments, and the sibilant consonants will help the singer to attain clarity. The effect should be of an intense, almost whispered aside. The music of the opening returns in the piano, only to be interrupted suddenly by *martellato* octaves which herald the singer's trumpet-like calls. The piano part here is warmly impassioned; the right hand doubles the vocal melody while in the left hand triplet chords hammer out above a solid bass line, reminding one strongly of an aria from Romantic Italian opera.

The piano is left alone to make the transition to a sweeter mood, preserving the flowing romanticism and at the same time achieving a subtly mysterious quality for the soft and sensuous vocal phrases, with an almost Gallic use of whole-tones. The change of tempo to 'Andante sostenuto' consolidates the calmer mood. The singer must achieve the most beautiful legato for this central, high passage which is marked 'dolcissimo'. Excellent breath control is needed. The passion again increases and dynamics and tessitura rise accordingly. The high F sharp on 'all' should not cause problems, as the singer will by now be prepared for expansive phrases and should be supporting the sound securely enough for the leap of a 6th to seem natural and desirable. The preceding 'f' (which sounds 'v') of the word 'of' can be used to make a smooth elision; a glottal attack on the vowel of 'all' is probably best avoided here.

The singer should at this juncture feel confident enough to tackle the hurdle which soon follows: a diminuendo to a high and floating passage of sustained *pianissimo*. Again there is an *ossia* in case the prospect of holding the high E is too daunting. It is always my belief that performers should not punish themselves by choosing the more difficult course if it is at all unsafe and may endanger the tremendously potent atmosphere, especially near the end as it is in this case. The singer is more likely to achieve perfect control of tone quality and subtle dynamics on the most comfortable note and there is no reason to feel inferior if others seem to command a more spectacular range. The piano's opening arpeggio figures resume very softly for the singer's last phrase. Much attention must be paid to intonation as the notes are set very close together. The voice dies away as softly as possible on a monotone, without undue accentuation of words. This will require some skill and control, especially in preventing obtrusive vibrato.

## 2. Aquarium

After such a full-blooded opening, the brief second song could hardly be more contrasting in the spare, icy calm of its phrases and concisely described images, all to be articulated with cool purity and an unwavering line. A high degree of skill and technical control will be needed to maintain the volume at *pianissimo* throughout with suitably pure and unwavering articulation. A large amount of supporting energy is used up when sustaining such high, floating phrases in an undisturbed, steady stream of sound. The text is unusually rich in onomatopoeic and alliterative sounds which aid the interpretation of the images of nature, and this is especially true of the sibilant consonants. A very soft *tenuto* on high F will be safe when falsetto is used and the resultant pale tone quality is suitable to the text. The composer gives the singer ample time to poise the *marcato* notes, and the aspirate 'h's separate the sounds. It would be a mistake to allow the tone to slip back and become throaty as very fine tuning is needed throughout and a full vibrato must be avoided. Breaths should be kept to a minimum. An inscrutably calm demeanour is essential for the intense concentration of detail in this delicate haiku-like miniature.

### 3. The Honeysuckle

The highly erotic text, which compares the sleeping loved one to the honeysuckle, is enhanced by the constant presence of gently rocking semiquavers in the accompaniment. These create a sensuous, soporific texture full of rhythmic subtlety, over which the singer comments in smooth phrases. Each paragraph rises passionately to loud, high notes: an F sharp and then a G sharp. Every vocal phrase is fully integrated with the piano part in a way reminiscent of late Fauré. There is an irresistible flow and natural surge to the music despite the occasional changes from 4/4 to 5/8 time. The warmly lyrical lines should be comfortable to sing, even at the highest extreme which is ideally prepared. The 'l' of 'leave' gives the singer a perfect opportunity to slide smoothly on to the G sharp, keeping tongue and throat muscles supple and relaxed. The brief soft, recitative-like passage that follows this climax requires careful timing; precise adherence to dynamic markings is essential for the cadence into the recapitulation of the opening music. The repeat is not straightforward, however; the harmonies shift unexpectedly, introducing enharmonic relationships which end the song in somewhat equivocal mood.

### 4. Metronome

As might be expected from the title, a steady beat is present through most of this song in the slow tread of the left-hand piano part which is marked 'Tempo di marcia lento'. This is punctuated by dry, sharp staccato attacks in the right hand which create a bleak, unyielding atmosphere for the entry of the voice. In the singer's slow *pianissimo* chant the triplet figures must be meticulously differentiated from the regular beats. The lines rise inexorably and reach the upper octave in long sentences which require evenly graded timbres and good breath control. The singer must maintain the intensity at the *fortissimo* outburst on 'Measured against all these'. Immediately after this the voice resumes softly and is marked 'quasi parlando' in sharp contrast to the piano's 'legatissimo' line. The singer should not use vibrato. After the pause the song becomes much freer in a recitative style. The personality and presence of the interpreter come into the foreground, starkly exposed by the sparse accompaniment. Clear diction is crucial. Short bursts of the tread of the metronome recur in the piano, and seem to peter out in response to the singer's anxious self-questioning. This is an occasion when the singer, although not actually making a sound, is so closely involved in the music that his silence still speaks to the audience. His intense concentration must not waver and there must be no distraction. The silence is rudely shattered by the final anguished, *fortissimo* vocal phrase. Extra reserves of stamina must be saved for this searing moment. The singer requires considerable command of a wide range of dynamics to project the disturbingly poignant message of the text in this brilliant song.

## 5. Paradise

The superb versatility of the composer ensures a good contrast and balance of material. Exciting, rapidly pulsating triplet piano chords maintain the thrilling *Allegro strepitoso* pace while the rhythmic flexibility in the voice part adds spontaneity. The simple time of the vocal line prevails against compound time in the accompaniment, creating a feeling of restlessness. The seductive images of the opening verse are underlined by glittering high textures in the piano, but a rude awakening is imminent, heralded by a sudden upset of the triplet rhythm in the accompaniment at the cadence of the verse. The piano moves to a darker range of sounds with a low rumbling trill in the bass. The singer resumes in a vein of almost sneering pessimism, eventually rising to a snarling climax which reaches its height at the loudest reiteration of the words 'Fools' Paradise' when the piano triplets dissolve into sustained clashing chords, doubled in each hand an octave apart. In this shattering coda, the baritone has to reduce dynamics progressively so that the last repeated exclamation seems like an echo. Dramatic fervour and a compelling presence will be of great advantage to the performer.

## 6. Portrait in a Mirror

An almost unbearably touching and honest recognition of the effects of the ravages of old age brings the cycle to a close in deeply contemplative mood. The astonishing skill and seemingly limitless range of the composer's responses to different moods is demonstrated once again in his intricate piano part. The introduction is written in strict invertible counterpoint which continues for the first part of the song and resumes at the end. The baritone sings a series of recitative phrases in varied rhythms, tailored to the natural speed of delivery of the words. Images are once more strongly projected by way of especially suggestive syllables (Example 2). Good diction is of the utmost importance throughout the series of sometimes brutal descriptions of the aged face in the mirror. After a big crescendo to *fortissimo* the climax is unexpectedly *pianissimo*. Its subdued horror is chillingly effective. In the slow glissandos down a major 7th from E flat on the words 'Wrinkled' and 'neanderthal' the singer is given total freedom to make the most of the opportunity for drama. A pregnant silence follows. In the next *Andante sostenuto* passage the more flowing vocal line is supported by full but quiet chords on the piano. The dreadful dawning of realisation of the devastation of old age breaks out in surging despondency. The bleak recitative style returns for the last

Ex. 2.

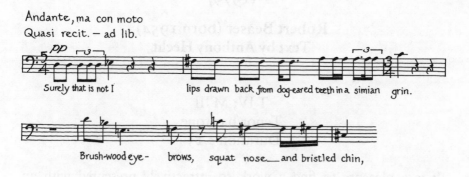

Andante, ma con moto
Quasi recit. — ad lib.

Surely that is not I    lips drawn back from dog-eared teeth in a simian grin.

Brush-wood eye-    brows,    squat nose___ and bristled chin,

paragraph. The singer is confronted with a particularly difficult task: the 'in' of 'innocent' is held *ppp* on a high E after a diminuendo. Again the singer should use falsetto to make a ghostly sound but he must be careful to avoid unevenness. A long piano postlude resumes the strict counterpoint of the opening, allowing singer and audience to contemplate the extreme poignancy of the final statement.

*Mirages* is a major work from a masterly craftsman. It is made all the more moving by the perfect marriage of words and music which results from the composer writing his own text. The piece demands a performer of the highest dedication; it is a superb vehicle for an established artist with an assured technique and compelling personality. It should also prove ideal material for a young singer wanting to expand his powers, as the vocal writing is so idiomatic and ultimately practical. It should have a central position in a recital and would balance excellently with a major classic from the lieder repertory, for example Schumann's *Dichterliebe*. Two such works of substance would form a satisfying and complete programme.

# The Seven Deadly Sins
## (1979)

### Robert Beaser (born 1954)
### Text by Anthony Hecht

T IV; M III
Tenor/baritone
Duration *c*.15′

It is a pleasure to find a work so attractively presented with an admirably clear and helpful set of performance notes in the score. The notes contain a succinct guide to the symbols used; the insight they give into this American composer's conception of the interpretation will greatly benefit both singer and pianist. Subtle vocal inflections and changes of timbre are suggested in readily understood terms. Both tenor and baritone versions of the vocal part are printed in the score. The methods of notation used vary according to the characteristics of each song, but all possible questions are answered in the introduction for the composer has considered all practicalities. In particular, the more avant-garde features, most of which are now standard practice, are lucidly explained. All the composer's markings in the text show meticulous forethought and are to be observed carefully.

The musical idiom is most appealing, containing elements both of neo-classicism and minimalism, and the songs should be extremely popular with audiences. Jazz style is needed for the third and fourth songs, but this will not prove difficult even for a singer with little experience in this field. The seven songs must be thought of in a continuous span, without long pauses between them. The vocal writing is straightforward and the line is set one note to a syllable for the most part. The strenuous Sprechstimme passages, some of which are almost shouted, will need special study and care. Range is agreeably wide and encourages a positive dramatic approach and vocal panache. The piano accompaniments are excitingly conceived, providing a gifted player with a satisfying variety of techniques and a chance to exhibit a strong personality of his own on equal terms with the singer. It is a fairly demanding work in terms of stamina, but not impracticable.

### 1. Pride

The opening to the cycle is brief and forthright. Accents punctuate the line to give added bite to individual syllables and indicate glottal attacks on vowels when appropriate. The short low B flat on 'is' near the end is Sprechstimme only if the performer is a tenor, a sign of the composer's good understanding of voices. Even a tenor may find it difficult to make a firmly centred sound, especially as the note has to be snatched so quickly. Lines are otherwise bold and starkly clear, with frequent 7th leaps.

## 2. Envy

The piano figurations in this song, based on modal note groups, make a most fascinating effect. The dynamic markings are soft but appropriately sinister overtones in the opening are underlined by the use of slurs between notes in the voice. These can be exaggerated to make a crooning sound and will prove helpful in smoothing the lines and making the approach to the high F comfortable. Uneven groups of notes which fall across beats enhance the sardonic wit of the text, delivered with deceptive sweetness in its Brechtian economy. The piano accompaniment alternates from conventional to free notation. The strictly rhythmic passage beginning 'Establishing in tissue' makes a violent contrast because of its more forceful projection of the text; the music rises to *fortissimo*, heralding a *senza misura* piano solo. The piano's repeated figurations create a texture that, as the composer says, can be deliberately blurred by the pedal and over which the voice has to be perfectly rhythmical. The interaction between voice and keyboard is especially subtle and flexible and a good rapport is essential. The piano's impressionistic textures continue and melt away into nothing at the end.

## 3. Wrath

This very fast movement requires much virtuosity and flair. It is marked 'con fuoco', and abounds in heavily accented syncopations and other jazz-oriented rhythmic gestures. Apart from a brief moment of respite at the start of the 'Dies Irae' section, the ferocity of the attack has to be maintained right up to the shouted ending (high A for tenor, F sharp for baritone), when the singer must exert great control to avoid damaging the vocal cords by too much air pressure. Percussive consonants are especially hazardous. The 'h' on 'hearts' must be supported by an iron grip on stomach, rib and diaphragm muscles to relieve the neck and throat and protect these more vulnerable areas from strain. A rasping quality would certainly be suitable for this song, but not at the expense of future vocal health.

The passage becomes less strenuous as the singer gains in capacity by means of cautiously regulated practice sessions; a short programme of warming-up exercises is an essential preparation. It is most unwise to rush impatiently at problems without first making sure that the voice is fully centred and that muscles are already in support. This is the cause of many unfounded accusations of harm resulting from new music. Breath should be conserved rigorously and rests used to place consonants dexterously in the spaces. The technique of using quick, shallow breaths and keeping the basic position of support muscles undisturbed will prove most valuable here. Once acquired, it ensures vocal safety for the future.

### 4. Sloth

In this much simpler song an aura of jazz is again evident. The tempo is now lazier and the singer can adopt a more casual style until this is suddenly interrupted by the forceful declaration 'The blind still lead'. The composer suggests using parlando if necessary during the first phrase in the tenor version, allowing for the fact that a lighter voice may lack firm articulation in the lower register and should therefore adopt an alternative which sounds more natural. It is important to avoid stylised operatic or formal concert manner of delivery. Vibrato should be kept to a minimum. The gentle last section has to be relaxed and precise at the same time. The soft low Bs help to loosen the voice in preparation for the octave leap up to a *subito pianissimo* C sharp. The dynamic markings and accents are crucial to the poise and effectiveness of the ending.

### 5. Avarice

This splendid song moves briskly and lightly. The tessitura is consistently high in the central section, although the baritone part is set a little lower when fast articulation of awkward syllables is required. The composer shows a strong sympathy with the different characteristics of the two voices and their individual assets. Flexibility must never be lost and the vocal quality must not be allowed to become too heavy as there is so much detail. The sardonic 'la la la' works extremely well and the text is most aptly set. There is a brief moment of coloratura in a *piano* passage when syllables must be neat and crisp in precisely timed rhythms. At other places there are slides marked between notes, as in the second song, and these are always easy to negotiate. It must be said, however, that a good degree of musicianship and sharpness of reaction will be needed from the singer to avoid being caught out by problems of rhythm. The expansive phrase on 'frankincense and myrrh' brings vocal relief from the constantly pounding rhythms. At the end the 'la la la' is marked 'seductively', and it dies *sotto voce*, trailing into nothing on a comfortable low note (E for tenor, B for baritone). The phrases are beautifully shaped to bring out the interpretative contrasts required and an enthusiastic performer should find them rewarding.

## 6. Gluttony

The clean-cut simplicity of the vocal lines is belied by the savagery of the text. The impact should be chilling. Phrases are supple and elegantly constructed with some gracefully dipping intervals in the opening paragraph, neatly pointed by accents. The almost continuous crotchet tread of the music is varied by changes of tempo and mood which are scrupulously annotated in the score and add a great deal to the effectiveness of the performance. It will be easier to create the desired *misterioso* atmosphere on 'the glutton worm' if consonants are given extra prominence, especially those which are accented, but the singer must be careful not to waste breath on the 'h' of 'head'. The subtle shading and diminuendos on the ·repeated 'parchment face' should provide a ghostly effect if placed clearly with hardly any vibrato. The baritone has a larger leap down than the tenor the first time, but both versions end the song on a sustained *pianissimo*.

## 7. Lust

The tempo marking of 'Molto presto' and the rapid ostinatos in the piano contribute to a thrilling climax to the cycle. The vocal writing is angular, with many octave leaps, but the lines are intentionally blurred by glissandos, into which the singer must fling himself with some abandon at such an impetuous speed. As the composer explains in the introduction, he underlines certain words to indicate that they are to be delivered in a 'menacing half-whisper'. It might perhaps have been safer for this instruction to appear on the relevant page as it is such an important feature. There is a possibility that it may be overlooked if a performer's initial perusal of the front pages of the score is cursory. It is difficult to manage the whisper when it occurs on the word 'blood' on high E with a glissando to F sharp and a sudden diminuendo from *forte* to *pianissimo*. It would be asking for trouble to use a breathy tone to convey the whispers at a forceful volume. This is probably why the composer says that 's' sounds in other similarly marked words should be exaggerated; they involve a safer, more muscular movement and produce a penetrating sound without effort. As there is no such helpful sibilant in 'blood' the tone should perhaps be allowed to drift back into a hollow quality, ending falsetto, to ensure that all consonants make the maximum impact: the 'ge' of 'vintage' can be used to provide impetus, and the final 'd' of 'blood' should be emphasised. There are several instances when a continuous sound on a 'hnn' or 'ah' is asked for to punctuate the lines between the specially emphasised words. The singer will inevitably lose volume on some of these. This final song, though short, may need considerable work if all the instructions are to be followed and the music is to be conveyed as the composer intends.

A singer's technique will definitely be improved by work on this piece. The performer is given ample chance to display his power, range and personality. Audiences should derive much pleasure from this exuberant *tour de force*, which never outstays its welcome. It would make a good contrast to romantic French or German music (Schumann, Brahms or Fauré). It would be appropriate to include some lighter items from the cabaret or show-song repertory. English 20th-century music of a traditional flavour is less suitable.

## Voices of the Prophets
### op. 41 (1952)
### Alan Bush (born 1900)

T IV; M III
Tenor
Duration 18½′

This inspired and substantial work from one of our senior composers deserves a prominent place in the repertory. It was commissioned by Peter Pears and first performed by him and Noel Mewton-Wood in 1953. The confident sweep and visionary intensity of the music is in close empathy with the texts and is sustained throughout in a most impressive manner. The composer's characteristically forthright, committed and authoritative approach is evident in all four movements. The work is truly on a grand scale. The composer's dash and virtuosity at the keyboard might be surmised from the exceptionally demanding piano parts which are full of colour and drama; they require a player of some stamina and considerable fire. A dramatic tenor voice with a good strong middle range is best suited to the piece. An operatic approach is in fact the most appropriate; the singer should use a rich palette of tone colours and an extrovert, often declamatory manner with excellent diction. A work of such boldness and fervour contains few reflective passages, giving a performer of the former qualities a wonderful chance to exhibit them without restraint. The work is also a good choice for an unassuming singer who wishes to develop and unleash his platform personality to the full. The vocal writing is guaranteed to involve the singer in hard work, but this is repaid by greater strength and security throughout the range. Conventional notation is used in a tonal idiom.

## 1. 'For behold' (*Isaiah* Chapter LXV)

The familiar resonances of the text conjure up vocal statements of equal grandeur, recitative-like in character, and wide ranging in both pitch and colour. The words are set spaciously so that clear diction is easily possible. Melismas are used as dramatic flourishes to extend key words and underline their meaning, as in 'rejoicing', 'joy', 'hundred' and 'long'. The piano part is characterised by stark intervals (4ths, 5ths and octaves) in austere and uncluttered textures, whose effect is ritualistic and noble. The first song does not present any vocal problems, but it does require energy and stamina in the projection of the text and a firm sound on lower notes. The positive start warms and exercises the voice in an ideal way; it is a lesson to composers who ask for delicate details early in a large work before the singer has settled down.

## 2. 'So at length the spirit of man' (John Milton)

A lengthy piano solo in two- and then three-part counterpoint opens the piece and is joined by the voice in a seamless flow of slower notes. The line only stops briefly and quick breaths must be taken strictly within the time allowed as the brisk tempo of this neo-classical movement must not slacken. As the song progresses the octaves in the left-hand part of the accompaniment carry the slower pulse of the vocal line; the texture becomes less intricate for a while, only to splinter into running semiquavers supported by octaves which grow increasingly slower. Both hands now play in the bass clef, giving a richer, darker underlay to the voice's largely unadorned lines in straightforward *alla breve* syncopated rhythmic patterns. A climax is reached on 'to him' when the tenor's sustained high notes must ring out firmly and breaths have to be timed exactly. The phrase lengths are very well judged; they allow the singer to use full lung capacity and to expand and develop his vocal resources.

The final paragraph brings a welcome tranquil mood and a quiet, steadily paced series of long lines. The huge range of the spectacularly arching last melisma has to be encompassed with especial skill and evenness of tone (Example 1). The inexorable pulse of this *perpetuum mobile* must be maintained, and although the music surges up and subsides in natural sweeps and curves, a disciplined rhythmic approach is the first essential. Dynamic variations must be created at an unflurried tempo with no hint of rushing or fumbling. Any lack of control would greatly spoil the visionary feeling engendered by such a positive setting of this inspiring text. The anti-climactic ending is all

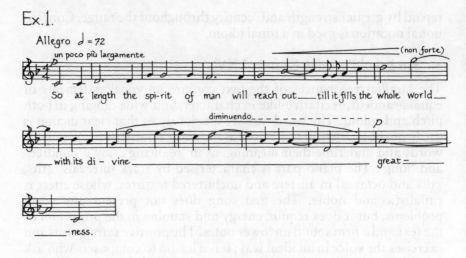

Ex.1.

Allegro ♩ = 72

un poco più largamente

(non forte)

So at length the spi-rit of man will reach out____till it fills the whole world____

diminuendo _ _ _ _ _ _ _ _ _ _ _ _ _ _     p

____with its di - vine____                                                              great =

- ness.

the more moving for its unexpected gentleness and air of quietly radiating confidence. The singer will need considerable insight and commitment to accomplish this convincingly.

### 3. 'Rouse up, O Young Men of the New Age!' (William Blake)

Jagged rhythms in the piano create a mood of nervous energy in the Allegro. An incisive vocal quality is necessary to delineate the urgent rhythms and the singer's enunciation must be crisp and accurate. The timing of consonants and breaths has to fit the relentless pulse of the music exactly, and added emphasis on sibilant and percussive consonants will be of considerable help. The singer must fearlessly approach the high G on 'destroying'; for the subsequent welcome leap down the octave he should articulate the 'y' fully to create impetus.

### 4. 'Over the years' (Peter Blackman)

The brisk Scherzo is followed by a movement of mammoth proportions. It is a vocal *scena* in its own right and could, I believe, be performed separately. The composer's passionate identification with this text and its personal social message is clearly apparent. The piano writing is virtuosic from the outset: thickly textured whirls and cadenzas surround the voice's first declamatory statement. It may prove difficult to enunciate the fast-changing words and this aspect might need to be practised with special care. There is a possibility that the voice could be submerged at times in the elaborate and rich piano scoring. A full heroic tone quality is especially suitable in this song and the singer's stamina will be tested to the full. Many of the lines are set low in the voice and powerful support will be needed to sustain them. Although it is necessary to emphasise the words, this may induce strain and the singer should take care not to jar the throat at moments of high excitement. It is wise to practise speaking the text in rhythm, especially the fast semiquaver triplet passages which are sure to trip up the singer at the first attempt (Example 2). When moving on to sing these

Ex. 2.

Allegro moderato, un poco largamente ♪ = 132

My heart sings in the lilt of the tear-twisted caress from the far lands of Chi-na

phrases it is imperative to keep tone quality firmly centred even for the briefest syllable when there may be risk of consonants obscuring vowel sounds completely. Even the most fleeting vowel must have a kernel of identifiable pitched tone. This section makes an exacting preparatory exercise but it must be practised separately so that no detail is glossed over. The piano part too is particularly elaborate here. It is a welcome relief when the line stretches out of trouble, although there are still strenuous moments to come and the rhythms have to be projected clearly. A calmer section with a very rich accompaniment brings more restful lines which are widely spaced and pliably contoured. The short, wide-ranging phrase on 'never may decay' must be encompassed within the whole, larger phrase so that it does not sound dislocated from its surroundings.

The pianist follows with even more dazzling display passages, similar to those of the opening. Vocal phrases are suddenly fragmented into sharp staccato bursts and it is useful to remember not to allow too much air to escape in all the enthusiasm. The exultant declamations resume; the music swings into compound time with irresistible vitality before winding down naturally and comfortably into a quiet section which must be sung simply in complete contrast to what has gone before. This passage is beautifully written for the voice. The few melismas melt easily into the gentle, smooth flow of the melody. The singer should take the time allowed to check the purity and focus of his tone in preparation for the final burst of wild excitement which follows immediately. The voice climbs high and the piano's figurations become correspondingly denser (semiquaver triplets within compound time), increasing tension and underpinning the singer's series of long notes which gradually grow calm. The vocal part descends to the middle range as the music dies down to a serene and warmly satisfying piano postlude, settling at last on an E major chord.

It would be extremely hard to overestimate the powerful impact of this major work, which represents the composer at the height of his powers and fully exhibits his qualities of fearlessness and missionary zeal. It thoroughly deserves to take a place as one of the finest tenor works in the repertory and should come to be regarded as a classic of the genre. When properly interpreted, it stretches the performer's resources in a positive sense, challenging both singer and listener to aspire towards new levels of insight. No one could fail to respond to a work of such inner conviction and intense utterance. It therefore needs to be placed centrally in a programme, perhaps at the end of the first half. Other items should be more modest in proportion and emotional range. French music might prove too violent a contrast, while Bartók's and Kodály's folksong settings, or perhaps some English folksong arrangements would be a very good choice indeed. The noble qualities of Beethoven's six Gellert songs, op. 48, would be particularly appropriate to begin the recital, and some of Schubert's Goethe settings could open the second half.

## *Escape at Bedtime*
### (1983)

### Corey Field (born 1956)
### Text by Robert Louis Stevenson

### T IV; M III
### High voice/unison chorus
### Duration 2′

This young American composer's exquisite setting of Stevenson's enchanting poem captures perfectly the glistening radiance of the night sky depicted in the text. It is especially well suited to a young and naturally high, bright-voiced singer using a light and well-open head voice. Considerable technical control and poise are needed to maintain the almost unbroken series of shimmering legato lines which cover a wide range and arch gently within the dynamics, which are never louder than *piano*. The pacing must be exact and breathing thus has to be extremely well planned. (The piece makes an excellent class exercise for young singers in small groups; breaths can be staggered to achieve legato.) Uneven rhythms feature throughout and voice and piano constantly move against each other's beats, with varied subdivisions. The rhythms constitute the song's only serious musical difficulty, and once they are mastered they add a pleasing suppleness. Accurate intonation for the many high notes is imperative. Too much vibrato will cloud the clean, pure lines. Notes are grouped in repetitive patterns with only slight variations. The singer can thus orientate pitches and become familiar with the feel of the notes in the voice. The mode of performance should not be too histrionic as that would spoil the entrancing atmosphere. Even though the unequal rhythms can be worked out mathematically and beats marked during the learning stages, there should be no awkward jerks of emphasis to disturb the luxurious seamless phrases. The sparse, simple accompaniment, like the vocal part, lies high in the instrument's range.

The voice opens in slow triplet minims which move against the regular minim beat of the piano. These first phrases are rather long. Ideally it should be possible, at such a low volume, to sing through to the word 'bars' without a break. It is important to mesmerise the audience from the very beginning, almost so that the listeners too hold their breath. The first melisma, on the word 'stars', is comfortable to sing. The minim triplets in the voice part quicken to sextuplet crotchets; the syllables have an evocative sibilance. The notes divide again into even quavers, and this time the minim triplets are in the right-hand piano part. Skill and dexterity are required to make the rhythms flow easily and naturally and to keep the words clear. The composer perceptively warns the singer not to succumb to tension or to rush ahead unnecessarily. The voice should float out gently without strain and without pushing on strong syllables. Quick short breaths must not hold up the flow of the rhythm and all melismas should be extremely smooth. The highest, most rapt point is reached when the voice returns to sextuplet crotchets for the final section. The fast regular quavers in the piano accompaniment create a delightful sparkling effect which highlights the text still further. The singer's high notes should have a natural sheen. An open throat prevents squeezing of syllables, particularly in a soprano voice. If the sound starts to become throaty, thick or constrained, the singing will be uncomfortable and tiring. The piece in fact gives very good training for even vocalising. In the last verse especially the singer must focus on the sinus areas for an added, bright resonance. Lip, tongue, palate and jaw movements made in enunciating the text must be as flexible and neat as possible to avoid changing the position of throat and jaw, thus disturbing the line. When the initial hard work is over, the song should become easier at each repetition. In the diminuendo on the last high G on the word 'head', the 'h' should not be overemphasised and neck and throat should not be prepared for the 'd' too early. The sound trails away until the swift but clear execution of the 'd' at the very end.

This song would make a charming interlude in any recital and is best set between two more richly textured pieces. If the singer is not fully sung in beforehand the resultant forcing might prove exhausting. The placing of the voice suggests the special silvered timbre also well suited to most French music. Other settings of Stevenson might be chosen to form an integrated group. The composer's *Yeats Songs* for high voice and piano are also warmly recommended.

# A Vision of Time and Eternity
## op. 61 (1972)

### William Mathias (born 1934)
### Text by Henry Vaughan

T IV; M III
Contralto
Duration *c*.10′

This skilful and attractive work is written in a continuous span but it contains many contrasting sections and can either be considered as a cycle or a short cantata. The voice is used in the most imaginative and colourful way and the singer's tone must be light and flexible enough to move speedily. The staccato passages must be articulated with aplomb. The notes at the higher part of the range (F, F sharp and one optional G sharp) need not cause trouble, for the dynamic markings are loud, and the voice is by then well sung-in. Much use is made of the contralto's strong and full chest register.

The piece requires quite a degree of stamina and experience to know when to conserve energy. It sustains interest most successfully through its constant varieties of musical figuration, vocal gesture and mood. The piano writing is also excellent and the work should have a very wide appeal for enterprising performers. The musical language could be described as 'advanced traditional', sharing some ground with Britten and Tippett, and employing harmonies redolent of Messiaen. It should not prove too difficult to a comparative newcomer to contemporary music. A good solid technique is a distinct advantage in order to give the work the authoritative interpretation it richly deserves. It should make a very strong and stimulating impression in a recital.

There seems to be a dearth of contemporary works for contralto, so it is an additional pleasure to recommend this one. The piece might also be suitable for a counter-tenor with a warm resonance and an ability to sing high without strain. The wonderful text is an added bonus to a work of distinction.

The chiming, bell-like effects in the piano form a clear, crystalline texture through which the singer has to intone, with utmost accuracy, a long series of repeated Ds with only slight ornamentation. Excellent focusing and control of vibrato are thus crucial from the outset. Extreme precision is desirable so that the staccato flourish on 'bright' can be carried off with expertise and élan. In the next phrase the singer again chants on D but at the lower, more sonorous octave. Rhythmic discipline is very important and if a steady pulse is kept, breaths need not disturb the beat. It is often a good idea to take advantage of emphasis marks by breathing just before them, thus using the added impetus of a new attack. For lower notes, the rule about not pushing too hard must be applied rigorously, particularly in the strenuously accented finish to the florid phrase on the word 'hurl'd' on a low B flat. It will be much clearer if no breath if allowed to cloud the sound, and also if there is no extra air to force the 'h' and risk jarring the throat. A good stentorian tone should easily be achieved by not trying too hard but instead using muscular resources wisely.

The rhythmic subtleties of the next passage, beginning with 'The doting Lover', are quite delightful. The many short rests are used for punctuation and to provide expressive clarity and attack; they are not an excuse for an out-of-breath hectic effect. Detail is all important here and the singer should enjoy perfecting the exact relationship between text and music (Example 1). The glissando on 'flower' heralds a most

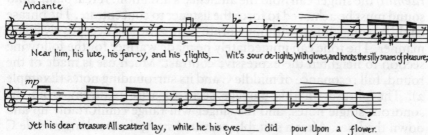

effective passage which features a series of slower glissandos over a minor 6th with a crescendo at the end of each phrase; the last one moves up and down and up again. It is always vocally beneficial to take the opportunity of exaggerating the slide and making sure that no microtone is omitted in its course. Much diaphragm control is needed to keep the sound firmly centred and unwavering in its intensity. Any lack of concentration may cause the note to leap out of control and produce a yodelling effect instead. It is an excellent exercise to maintain a perfect legato through register changes which should be so gradual that they are imperceptible. The result of holding on firmly to the strong resonance of the low B and sustaining the line relentlessly up to the G above is a new security and strength in the middle register. It is particularly good for all female voices (even soprano) to sing strongly below the stave, as long as they do not force the sound. The vocal cords become more pliable and the singer's range will widen as the voice swings flexibly up from a firm base.

The following section, marked 'Agitato', needs a biting attack with the words meticulously accented as marked. The piano launches into cascades of low descending arpeggios and the voice must aim at a knife-like penetration to cut through this thicker texture. The momentum is built up most skilfully, step by step, until the upper range is reached and the *fortissimo* Fs and G flats are uttered with great force and with tight control over rhythm and pulse. A toccata-like, softer piano figuration prepares for a vocal line of very short articulations and fragmented statements, beginning with 'The fearful Miser'. The lines become more flowing and gracefully fit the words in natural curves. The excitement builds up again, with frenetic staccatos, to a loud, high climax and the piano's figures become even more violent and insistent before they are suddenly cut off.

A serene series of smooth chords, strongly reminiscent of Messiaen, induces a rather liturgical atmosphere. The singer should match tone colour accordingly. The composer allows time to place each note cleanly with pure detachment so that the text speaks clearly for itself and no outside emotion obtrudes. The facts are stated with calm accuracy and every word tells. In the unaccompanied phrase with a *ritenuto* the singer can hold the audience's attention. A real *pianissimo* sound must be achieved to force the listener to concentrate. The phrase could be sung almost without vibrato in an eerie and deceptively bland manner. The tone can immediately be made warmer for the following section to heighten the expressive contrast. Much use is made of the round, full resonance of middle C and its surrounding notes (Example 2). The phrases in this passage seem to arise naturally from the sonorous single notes, and the singer will range comfortably up and down the lines. After a suitably accented start, the last long middle C should be left to resonate on its own, keeping the jaw relaxed on the 'ng' of 'wing'. The piano writing creates an easily flowing texture in this, the final, extended build-up of tension which blends together many previous elements and gestures. The song progresses in a natural process of musical growth through phrases which are ideally constructed and perfectly proportioned to expand and increase vocal

Ex. 2.

capacity. Grading dynamics is very important. It is particularly crucial not to grow too loud too soon and to remember to fall quickly away from accented notes so that the phrases maintain their liveliness and intensity and the tone does not spread to obscure the details.

A wonderful moment is reached when a drawn-out version of the first decorative staccato setting of 'bright' occurs on 'tread' (marked 'estatico'). Some care may be needed to accomplish this neatly and to avoid all suspicion of breathiness. For the work's highest note, a G sharp, an optional E is provided and it is best not to risk spoiling the climax if the high version is problematic. Singing a note just out of range at this point could be a distressing experience for listener and performer. The singer should not adopt a rigidly puritanical self-punishing approach and attempt a more difficult alternative if it induces real anxiety. It is true, however, that the extra adrenalin produced at a moment of high tension in a performance may suddenly release an unexpectedly ringing tone. Rolling the 'r' of 'bright' will be a great help. A singer will know his or her own potential in such enterprises. It should be a thrilling moment and timing must be carefully gauged.

The work then gradually calms down and the piano line thins into a fragmented version of the opening chimes while the singer chants the moving final statement. Although it is *pianissimo* it is marked 'espressivo', and it thus demands complete concentration and refinement of tone with words subtly emphasised. The tempo slows even more and the singer's last phrase requires very full control to the end in the long *calando* D on 'Bride'. A rolled 'r' will help to impel the sound forward so that the diphthong can be managed smoothly at the close. It will be marvellously effective if the singer, despite the strains of the climactic passage, has managed to conserve enough energy and poise to make this last note float out with utmost serenity and to hold it for as long as possible.

*A Vision of Time and Eternity* is a most admirable work for an accomplished singer and it will have a stirring effect on a wide audience. It should have a central placing in a concert and could also be performed in a church recital. It would contrast very well indeed with Medieval or Baroque music and it would be wise to include some items consisting of several short movements to create balance. Beethoven's Gellert songs, op. 48, or a selection of Schubert's settings of Goethe are also good possibilities. Mathias's piece would make a very powerful end to a concert. While to follow it with something in lighter vein may prove unsuitable, a group of Purcell arias might be an alternative ending. A singer with major technical problems would not be able to do justice to the fine details in this piece, but in many aspects it will prove a splendid vehicle for developing a young voice.

# Three Greek Epigrams
## (1937)

## Priaulx Rainier (born 1903)
### Translation by Richard Aldington from *Anyte of Tegea*

T IV; M III
Soprano
Duration 5′

These songs are typical of the originality and subtle craftsmanship of this most distinguished composer. Despite their brevity they are quite demanding technically, and the vocal lines need great control to sustain their intensity. Completely contrasting vocal styles are required for each song: the first flows smoothly with supple rhythms, the second involves florid coloratura and the last is an extrovert outburst of some strenuousness. So much detail and feeling are poured into each song that the cycle makes a substantial impression; in no sense could it be described as a set of miniatures.

The singer will have to make full use of her resources. The songs do not lie easily in the voice at first and they require and deserve a committed effort from the singer in order to attain security. The musical idiom is appropriately neo-classical; the piano accompaniments are clear and spare in texture, even stark at times. The powerful integrity which is generated throughout should have a lasting effect on the audience.

## 1. A Bird

In this swinging 6/4 Andante con moto the gentle arpeggio figures of the vocal line dip downwards in a steady legato. The vocal range stays mainly in the middle, and so verbal clarity should pose no difficulties. A loud, contrasting middle section brings a forceful climax on 'killed you' (Example 1). A short unaccompanied phrase is chilling in its

simplicity. The opening music is then repeated with a slightly different ending; a sustained D trails away in a diminuendo. It is quite difficult to accomplish this smoothly, but the 'ng' can arrive early and be carried through to the end. Lengths of notes must be scrupulously exact, especially the short quaver on 'throat' which ends the solo phrase. It is important to contrast the sostenuto smoothness of the main outer sections to the boldly etched phrases of the dramatic centre. A fascinating atmosphere is created by this short piece.

## 2. For a Fountain

The centrepiece of the cycle allows the singer to display her coloratura technique as she tosses off the running semiquaver rhythms which range up and down and are marked *dolce*. The long phrases must be uninterrupted. It would be a pity to snatch breaths and thus introduce a frantic, rushed quality to disturb the perpetual motion. It is in fact easier not to breathe in the middle of a paragraph. Each long phrase ends on a sustained note in the middle range, testing the singer's control to the full. At the fast tempo it should be quite practicable, however, and in any case it is a good exercise in discipline. Only two lines go up into the high soprano register and because the tessitura centres on the middle of the voice the singer may need to take particular care to keep the tone even. Emulating the sound of a woodwind instrument will help definition.

### 3. A Dolphin

The exhilarating octave swoops are a characteristic feature of this final, very exciting song. A sense of urgency and desperation is sustained until the very end, although the final, thrilling cadence is more expansive. Considerable stamina will be needed by the singer. Forcing must be avoided and the percussive syllables in the text can be used for extra impact without too much effort. Intensive practice of enunciation will be repaid by greater ease of delivery. It could be dangerous to sing this song at full volume without some advance preparation of this kind. The descending octaves provide a welcome chance to rest and elasticise the voice for the more rigorous phrases ahead (Example 2). The closing section starts softly but soon mounts

Ex. 2.

to a searing climax. The tension must be maintained to the very end of the last loud A, with no suspicion of a diminuendo. It is advisable to take a breath before the last three words so that the final crescendo is not at all inhibited.

These impressive songs make a stirring effect in performance. It would be interesting to include in the programme other songs with an archaic influence, for example Debussy's *Chansons de Bilitis*, and then to provide a contrast with some romantic English songs by Bridge, Ireland, Warlock or perhaps Delius.

# *Four Songs*
## (1970)

## Robert Heppener (born 1925)
### Text by Ezra Pound

T IV; M IV
High voice
Duration *c*.16′

This set of songs by the distinguished Dutch composer, Robert Heppener, allows a really accomplished singer to display virtuosity and a versatile technique. The vocal line is appealingly wide ranging, mellifluous and richly expressive; in some places it is quite physically demanding. Sprechstimme is used, together with other spoken devices, including whispering. The four songs are agreeably contrasted to each other. The piano accompaniments are characteristically full-blooded. They contribute strongly to the dramatic and powerful effect and extend the pieces far beyond the miniature style that such succinct texts sometimes inspire. A warm-toned, lyrical singer is best suited to the opportunities offered by Heppener's music.

## 1. N. Y.

Expansive and extrovert vocal phrases open the cycle in rhapsodic vein. The music moves towards a warm climax on 'soul', creating suspense by the imaginative repetition of the text (Example 1). The

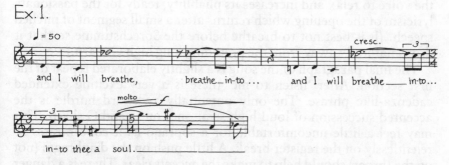

Ex. 1.

comma immediately after this is especially apt. The next passage is softer and more poised; it works particularly well because the singer has been at full stretch just before. (A sudden, gentle restart while support muscles are fully in action almost invariably comes out clearly without effort.) The following long 'reed' on E flat will therefore be much easier to control. The 'd' at the end of 'attend' can be nipped off neatly on the beat, and the lips can then mould the start of the lower note on 'me' without hurrying.

A violently active piano solo opens the faster section and makes a complete contrast. When the voice enters it is written out as pitched speech (with crosses instead of note heads), but the composer instructs that the pitches are only to be approximate. Since the piano part is so loud it is advisable to keep the voice free from breath, aiming for a direct and piercing sound. The singer should not be tempted to take extra breaths during the Sprechstimme, but should think in long well-supported phrases as if singing normally. It is particularly important to hold firm the rib cage, stomach muscles and diaphragm to prevent damage being caused by excess air grating against the voice-box, which often results when the singer is stretched. The line fortunately falls in a glissando on 'mad', which is ideal for resting the throat. The words must be projected with intensity, and the singer can thus never afford to stop thinking of protecting the larynx. The more energy that is used to hold support muscles, the easier it will feel. Muscular slackness and laziness at moments like this are most inadvisable. Extra practice of these passages will reap its rewards in the security gained, and help to build a good technique for the future. For each style of vocal delivery, whether it be whispering, shouting or conversational speech, there must be firm control and careful planning. If the singer learns good habits from the start, strenuous passages such as this one will cause few problems.

The transition from pitched speech into a sung tone ('No, No, No') is made extremely practical by the 'n' which can be used to place the sound safely at the start of each note. A declamatory passage, marked 'liberamente', gives the singer freedom. Its wide range of pitch helps the voice to relax and increases its pliability, ready for the passionate lyricism of the opening which returns after a small segment of pitched speech. (It is best not to breathe before the Sprechstimme so that it drops naturally away from the preceding long high G sharp.)

The final paragraph of the song is a slightly elaborated repeat of the first section. After 'listen to me' there is a very exciting extended cadenza-like phrase. The only potentially awkward hurdle is the accented succession of loud high semitones on G and G sharp. This may feel a little uncomfortable for a soprano as it concentrates so relentlessly on the register break. A little push on the diaphragm (not on the throat) should help to make the accents clear. There is a danger that the tone may spread and obscure the intonation at such moments, so extra care must be taken. The slow glissando from G sharp up to A must be enjoyed thoroughly, incorporating every microtone. The large intervals in this phrase are a joy to sing. The coda of the song involves continual repetitions of the text which fade and gradually wind down in slowing rhythms to sustained *pianissimo* murmurings. These will need scrupulous placing and well-controlled vibrato. The 'v' sound in 'ever' should be fully exploited. Simple intoning on a single note – 'C' in this case – always makes a beautiful effect. The singer must take the trouble to keep the tone pure. It helps to vocalise and pitch the 'v' before moving on to the vowel.

## 2. A Girl

This brief, memorable song is tremendously intense and the use of the voice is most original. Heavily accented rhythms provide a spring-board at the start of the long, hypnotic, sinewy phrases, which require great concentration in a strong, fully controlled tone. The word-setting is impeccable; there are some lovely extended passages on single vowels in a bel canto style. When dynamics become more varied and the piano textures thicken, care needs to be taken to keep the sound clear and penetrating. For the *pianissimo* on 'so high', a small bright sound is better than a veiled one. The repetitions of the word 'folly' at the end are set gracefully. The semiquavers must be neat and perfectly pitched in carefully graded crescendos and decrescendos. The number of breaths taken should be kept to a minimum. The groupings of the notes are also important for there are many subtleties and no detail should be overlooked. The unaccompanied last line has to be very well timed, with the notes poised unhurriedly. A clear-cut, though very soft tone is appropriate to the final C sharp. Accomplishing the diminuendo is made easier by using the 'l' of 'world' to keep the sound forward and to prevent it from slipping out of control.

## 3. Pan is dead

Full of rhythmic vitality, this piece fluctuates from 6/8 to 3/4 and to 2/4 time. The piano moves in fast semiquavers throughout the opening section of this song. By contrast, the vocal line is plain and it should be sung incisively, with fully exploited accents and no loss of momentum. The effect of the central section, without vibrato, is haunting; apart from two flourishes in the piano it is unaccompanied. Exact intonation is absolutely crucial as the notes are set very closely together. The lack of vibrato will aid clarity. The result is a cold, disembodied sound which is stark and chilling in its stillness. The motor rhythms start again and the voice has low, scooping glissandos, each of which is highly practical and easy to execute, including the one down to low G. If the 'd' of 'ladies' is projected too strongly it may impair smoothness.

The final paragraph, marked 'Meno mosso', is again highly concentrated in close intervals which require precise tuning. The singer must have good control of vibrato to sustain a gentle, somewhat plangent sound. It is essential that the middle notes are firm as they are exposed quite mercilessly and any unsteadiness would be obvious. The song ends with the slow, bell-like tolling of repeated low Bs, for which a hollow, rounded, covered tone is appropriate, making full use of the *tenuto* marks on each note. Much control will be needed for this song; it focuses on the centre of the voice and avoids any spectacular vocal tricks, relying instead on good, plain singing.

## 4. The Plunge

A wide variety of range and vocal attack is contained within the final song. It burns with fierce ardour and has some superb vocal effects and gestures. The voice drops quite low at times and a good legato technique is needed to keep the line flowing without awkward breaks. The pliability of the lines makes them an excellent exercise in improving technique as the singer must ensure that middle and low notes do not become unfocused or unsupported. The extra physical effort required to sing through every note to the last moment will be amply rewarded by the gain in capacity and control.

In the sudden *piano* on 'This that is all I wanted' the singer must retain the intensity of the louder parts as if the sound were being suppressed (Example 2). The following *andante* phrase, 'And you,

Ex.2.

Love', can be more warmly romantic in tone until the dynamics and words specifically dictate the moments of particular expressiveness: the unexpected *pianissimo* on 'loathe' should be aimed through the teeth so that the sound is clear and cutting. Consonants can be used bitingly to emphasise the mood. The word 'traffic' is set rather high and will not be easy for a soprano, but perhaps an uglier sound is not entirely unsuitable at this stressful moment. It is followed by an especially welcome melisma on 'You'. A more tender mood prevails and the music rises again to warmer passions. The lyricism of the closing passages is moving and vocally rewarding. As the work winds down, the vocal part is marked 'Bouche presque fermée'. (I interpret this as a comfortable, unemphasised vowel sound, somewhere between 'oo' and the German 'ö', but other singers may approach it differently.) The lips finally close at the end of the long descending phrase. The singer must take care to keep the sound in front of the teeth and open the throat so that the note does not cut itself off without warning. The words 'Out, and alone' are whispered like a sigh. The effect is lovely. At the end the vocal part is low and very soft. A crystal-clear and bleak sound seems appropriate, although it could also be effective with a hushed, almost breathy sound.

Heppener's extremely exciting cycle deserves a regular place in the repertory. It is deeply felt and highly imaginative; the composer responds to the words with characteristic fervour and commitment. A tenor or soprano would be equally well suited to the piece. The singer is given full rein to display his or her vocal and dramatic talents. The piece should be placed at a focal point in a recital. It would go well with any standard classics, perhaps Austro-German rather than French, if the programme is to be homogeneous. Russian songs might also be included or, as a complete contrast, Italian Baroque music. Other settings of Pound's poems that are more fragmentary in their musical language could be sung in the opposite half of the concert.

# *Care Charmer Sleepe*
## (1978)
### Peter Lawson (born 1951)

T IV; M IV
Soprano/tenor
Duration *c.*15′

This substantial and strikingly original song cycle by a young composer whose work deserves to be more widely known is not published, but has been broadcast and performed several times. Its appeal is immediate, and closer scrutiny reveals frequent use of subtle nuances, both verbal and musical. The singer is given considerable scope for variety of timbre and range, and should relish the dramatic potential of the highly resonant texts, the last of which was written some 200 years after the other three. The poems are set in a straightforward manner, mainly with one note per syllable and very few melismas. Their connecting theme is sleep in various guises: in the first song as the state preceding the discovery of love; in the second, which begins with the work's title, as a means of soothing troubles; in the third as a curtain shrouding life's light, and, in the final song, as a wasteful dissipation of energy, symbolic of profligate youth.

The piano accompaniment requires much virtuosity and flair. Full of ripe harmonies and distinctive leaping figurations, it is extremely satisfying to play. (The composer is a fine pianist and shows a thorough understanding of the instrument.) The musical idiom fluctuates between heavily romantic tonal and more mercurial atonal passages. Powerful and turbulent outbursts are often followed by moments of contemplative calm. Dynamics, tempo changes and smaller details are all carefully marked to give a clear guide to interpretation. The notation is conventional, apart from an absence of key signatures.

The singer will need especial security in the middle register and excellent breath control, and the cycle could serve as a good training to improve these particular areas. Skill in sustaining and controlling long notes will be fully tested. Several phrases end with the voice suspended on a note marked 'messa di voce'.

The tessitura is exceptionally wide ranging, but the supple vocal lines are rewarding to sing. There should be little difficulty in enunciating the words clearly, but considerable verbal crispness is needed for the quick passages, particularly those in the third song. It may take some time to master the difficult rhythms and rapid changes of time signature. A sensitive artist should respond naturally to the vocal shadings suggested by the piano sound, and to the positive imagery of the text. The general effect is rhetorical, yet warm and lyrical at times; the dramatic highpoints are carefully placed for maximum impact.

The first song could be performed separately and the third and fourth could be sung as a pair as they provide dramatic contrast. The composer gives a most helpful programme note in his immaculately presented manuscript.

### 1. The Good Morrow (John Donne, 1572–1631)

A note repeated in uneven rhythms on the piano, getting louder and then fading, creates a mood of muted tension. The voice then enters amid nervously disjointed figurations. The opening theme, which is repeated with slight rhythmic variations (as dictated by the flow of the words) at the start of each verse, is a simple declamation centred on A. The work's first technical hurdle occurs when the word 'loved' is held on the A with a crescendo to *forte* followed by a diminuendo.

Harp-like split chords add a warm, comforting tonal cushioning to the second half of the theme. The singer continues to make a series of firmly sustained recitative-like statements, relentlessly focused on the middle of the voice. After the opening tune is repeated at the start of the second verse, excitement builds up in an extended passage of steadily rising, long and sonorous phrases. The piano textures are full and florid and they should not mask the singer, even at the lowest point. Clarity of enunciation ought to be possible throughout the song. A telling climax is reached on the comfortable word 'world', which is sung *fortissimo* on G sharp; this coincides with a steadying of the tempo to *andante maestoso*. A gentle, fading passage with *sotto voce* triplet chords in the piano, forms a transition into the third verse. The mood becomes increasingly rapt and a ritualistic fervour pervades the song. The final *adagio*, one of the most beautiful moments in the entire work, flows naturally into the most sensuous harmonies of the piano's widely spaced chords, strongly redolent of Delius. The last note is perhaps the most difficult to sing: a magical *pianissimo* on the word 'die'. Some care is needed to make a perfect transition through the diphthong and to keep a pure thread of unwavering sound to the end. The piano finishes with resonant chords which slowly fade to nothing.

This first song already allows the singer to display and project a whole range of emotions within a tightly controlled legato line, whose flow is seldom interrupted.

## 2. Sonnet (Samuel Daniel, 1562–1601)

In this song the piano provides a continuous line: repeated minor 3rds pulsate hypnotically and continuously throughout the song. The voice part weaves sinuously above the piano with wide-ranging melodies which are agreeably relaxing to sing; the line swings easily over large intervals in a style reminiscent of Britten. The gentle tread of the accompaniment forms a secure foundation on which to place pitches, though the singer may need some extra practice to perfect this. The onomatopoeias in the text are fully exploited and liquid consonants help to keep a smooth line, as in 'Relieve my languish and restore the light'. Rolled 'r's may assist the approach to the wider leaps in an exceptionally adept piece of vocal writing (Example 1). Alternating time signatures (4/4 with 5/8) must not be allowed to disturb the atmosphere of calm introspection, and the transitions must sound natural. This is a most attractive song in which the mesmeric piano part exerts a delicately soothing influence over the athletic vocal lines. The word-setting is exemplary.

Ex. 1.

## 3. The Morning Watch (Henry Vaughan, 1621–95)

The freshness and joyful spontaneity of this, the cycle's Scherzo, make
a perfect contrast to the preceding song. Clear enunciation is important, for the music flows quickly, achieving its natural impetus from
some complex rhythms which will need careful study. The piano
writing is similar to that of Messiaen in its combination of rich, dense
chords with characteristic additive rhythms in irregular patterns of
twos and threes, which create unequal stresses. The mood is extrovert
and freely declamatory. A *meno mosso* section introduces strongly
dramatic material. The singer has to produce firmly centred low C
sharps over the deep sonorities of the piano chords. The vocal line rises
gradually and inexorably, with an exuberant piece of hocketing on the
word 'joyes'. Then follows an exhilarating paragraph in which expansive, arching vocal lines are supported by a regular 4/4 pulse of
repeated chromatic chords; the right-hand notes are so close together
that the singer may have trouble in placing the voice exactly in relation
to them. In a calmer mood the parts move smoothly on to a unison,
with plain octaves in the piano, for the words 'My lamp, and life' in the
course of a prolonged diminuendo. This beautifully worked preparation for the song's somewhat hazardous final notes culminates in a
long drawn-out *pianissimo* on C sharp, made more difficult by a
sudden *meno mosso* on the second syllable of 'abide'. This will have to
be placed well forward without forcing so that it floats easily, as if
humming.

## 4. Romance (Edgar Allan Poe, 1809–49)

The final song is the most vocally demanding. The singer is largely on
his or her own, and bears full responsibility for pointing the drama in a
series of rhetorical outbursts, sparsely accompanied by chords and
preparatory flourishes on the piano. The interpretation needs to be
carefully planned, using as wide a range of colourings and dynamics as
possible. Diction must be treated with especial care, since, for the only
time in the cycle, some lines lie uncomfortably high. The setting of the

words 'So shake the very Heaven on high', for example, makes it difficult to combine clear enunciation with a pleasantly open sound. Phrases are usually more gracefully arched, however, as in the second song, allowing the performer's full range to be shown to best advantage. The two verses are loosely strophic in form; at the end of each a climax is reached on a high G, approached by a sudden steep climb. (Example 2 shows the end of the first verse.) It is difficult for the singer

Ex. 2.

A child———— with a most know-ing eye.————

to sustain the intensity for such a long span at this extremely steady tempo, but if carried out successfully the effect is electrifying, especially when the last G is sung *fortissimo* on the word 'strings'. This is a singularly awkward word to sing at such a high pitch, and the singer may well have to put in some extra practice to find a comfortable and openly resonant sound, which should reverberate and mingle with the piano's final loud tremolando. The tension involved in overcoming this last hurdle ought to exert a powerful hold over the listener until the very last moment.

This weighty and memorable song cycle would be an excellent choice for a standard mixed recital programme, and is best placed at the end of one half of the concert. As it is strongly Romantic in nature and contains deep sonorities, the cycle could be suitably juxtaposed with a work of transparent, even austere texture, or alternatively something light and frivolous. It could follow a group of Classical songs, arias or canzonets or some early Italian arias by, for example, Pergolesi and Frescobaldi. A good balance would be achieved if the programme were to include another work of substance from the late Romantic or early 20th-century repertory, for example Rakhmaninov, Debussy or Strauss. It would be a good idea to place the Lawson centrally in a programme of British music, as a contrast to mixed groups of shorter songs by, say, Warlock, Bridge, Gurney or Finzi. The singer's most urgent requirement will be stamina, as the cycle fully engages the performer's physical and emotional resources and demands much concentration on detail. It would be impossible to envisage a light-weight treatment of such a deeply felt work. Audiences should be carried along by its dramatic sweep and intensity.

## *Evening Land*
### (1981)

### Anthony Payne (born 1936)
### Text by W. H. Auden

T IV; M IV
Soprano or mezzo-soprano
Duration 18'

This song cycle has an exceptionally strong and immediate appeal to the widest possible variety of listener. Despite its length, it never fails to hold the attention, largely because the words are set so that they can be heard with complete clarity and never fail to make their full impact. The audience can thus easily follow the poet's spiritual journey of discovery as it unfolds through a succession of nine songs which are joined together in a single span. A declamatory motto, 'May my heart's disquiet never vanish', appears twice in shortened form after its initial exposure as no. 4 and forms a balancing link between the sixth and seventh, and eight and ninth songs. The cycle begins gently and works up to a fierce climax in the central song of the spear caster. The poetic and musical images then pass through the changing seasons until a peaceful, whispered ending is reached.

Even a highly gifted pianist may blench at first sight of the score. The clear logic of the harmony and the rhythmic gestures that is characteristic of the composer means, however, that after the initial hard work, the piece falls quite quickly into place. Although it would be ideal to have a virtuoso pianist who can convey all the power and contrast while coping with the considerable rhythmic demands and intricacies of the part-writing, players with less natural ability can achieve a sound and musically satisfying interpretation.

The vocal writing is a model of smoothness, and the word-setting, as mentioned earlier, is exemplary. No distortion of the vowels is necessary. The lines are flexible, wide-ranging and of just the right length. The middle range of the voice is used a great deal and the singer can thus display a whole variety of colours and timbres. The dynamic shadings are extremely important. Apart from the spear-caster song, which does require stamina and relentless firmness for the loud sustained mid-range notes, the music sits well in the voice from the outset. Sprechstimme is used to great effect to highlight the important moments, sometimes pitched, sometimes unpitched, as naturally and easily as possible. There is exaggerated expressionism in only one place: 'but was only allowed to burn'. The rhythms preserve the natural flow of the text and encourage clarity of diction.

## 1. 'What did I experience that evening'

The opening phrase is spoken very quietly into the silence; it is unpitched and unaccompanied. In this first section the pianist plucks the strings inside the piano. (It may help to mark these with small stickers; this does no harm to the piano.) A fine, full-toned piano is essential. The singer proceeds in a gentle, almost casual, conversational style, until a sudden hushed moment leads into an upward *pianissimo* phrase on 'I saw the stars'. The pianist now moves to the keyboard. (He or she may need an assistant to replace the stand quietly without rustling at this crucial point.) The piano creates an impression of glittering stars and the feeling of repressed excitement mounts. The singer alternates between spoken and sung phrases, dipping low in the voice at one point. Suddenly there is a quickening of mood and tempo as childish things are set aside. The vocal lines are particularly gratifying and supple. The high A is the highest note in the piece; it is used to full effect on sustained notes so that it rings out naturally with full resonance. A quasi-conversational style is appropriate for the rest of this section. It must be remembered that a young boy is speaking; a simple, forthright and pure tone is appropriate in the free, recitative-like phrases. The first song draws to a close quietly, as it began, ending in an awestruck whisper. The piano writing is spare and will not spoil the piercing clarity of the vocal line. The audience should already be hanging on every word.

## 2. 'Into me he breathed his spirit'

The piano accelerates and asymmetric rhythms lead to the first of the loud, strong songs. The arching phrases are exhilarating to sing and must be firmly sustained, without allowing the tempo to sag. Correct pacing is extremely important. The singer must not be afraid of a wholly extrovert approach to this most significant section, in which the boy is almost intoxicated by his growing awareness of the universe and his relation to it. A crucial phrase, sung on a monotone and marked 'mp ma distinto' drops to a whisper before the biggest and most important phrase, which covers a wide tessitura in one large span of breath. It is absolutely imperative for there to be no loss of tension during the long crescendo (Example 1 overleaf).

## 3. 'The spear has been cast'

The music then plunges headlong into the most strenuous part of the cycle, a thrilling song with jabbing chords and intricate cantilenas in

Ex. 1.

To me this dread-ful thing hap-pened, namely, that he breathed ____ his

soul ____ in-to me

the piano. Above this the singer must sustain firm, emphatic and often very loud declamations, which are set in the middle register. It is a real test of technique and a good exercise for gaining strength and focus in this range. The song should move at an exhilarating pace, but not so fast as to obscure detail; the effect should be relentless rather than frantic. The flow of air must be well controlled to avoid breathiness and subsequent loss of tonal clarity. The song forms one long continuous paragraph, whirling along to a sustained D. It is a good idea to keep the crescendo going through this final note for the effect is electrifying. A short break allows a fleeting moment of respite before the piano leaps precipitately into an even faster passage, with jangling reiterated bell-like chords as the singer almost spits out the motto:–

#### 4. 'May my heart's disquiet never vanish'

No momentum must be lost and there should be a feeling of almost reckless abandon, right up to the next break. The calmer mood that follows should come as a physical and psychological relief to the performer and listener. The second part of the motto theme unwinds in a more comfortable dynamic range on 'unknowable goal'.

#### 5. 'I wanted to know'

The next song alternates between naturally poised Sprechstimme and sung phrases, including the wild outburst on 'but was only allowed to burn'. The composer likes the final word to curve slightly upwards and not downwards as might have been expected. The singer should not take a breath after the word 'light'; to do so would be less comfortable because of the temptation to overblow and jar the throat. The emotions change rapidly and the dynamic markings must be strictly obeyed. The final, unaccompanied spoken phrase 'but nobody understood' must be delivered blandly without emphasis.

### 6. 'I listen to the wind'

This song, evoking the sound of the wind, is light and flowing and must not be too slow. Spoken notes should be pitched low in the voice to sound entirely natural. Exaggerating the sibilance helps to enhance the poetry. The rhythms are rather subtle and worth the detailed practice necessary to perfect them. A gentle quarter-tone bends down on the word 'soft', followed by a more precisely pitched Sprechstimme for 'soft like oblivion'. The last section of this song is beautifully simple and without embellishment. The word-setting is well judged for unaffected clarity and the alliterative 'w's make an effective contribution. The *pianissimo* echo of 'my first steps' must be as clear as crystal without any vibrato. It is difficult to gauge the hushed Sprechstimme required at 'in the wonderfully untouched sand', and the singer will need some practice to gain confidence in projecting a sense of rapt wonder. A breathy tone is appropriate. The first half of the motto is then repeated as softly as possible without vibrato to make a magical effect.

### 7. 'Now it is summer morning'

This warmly lyrical song flows in graceful and athletic lines which are a pleasure to sing with their delicately controlled melismas and fluid rhythmic patterns. No extremes of dynamics or pitch disturb the mellifluousness of this extended passage. There is abundant word-painting. The contours of the lines curve naturally according to the words and images. It is important to keep this song moving. A slight quickening of pace leads into another crucial phrase: 'Far away are cold stars'. It is best to place the steely sound required well forward, making it bright with little vibrato. The sound should not waver at all as it climbs upwards and the volume increases. There should be no hurry after the word 'space'. The change of mood to *dolce* should be subtle yet unmistakable. The supple lines continue and the mood becomes languid and drowsy as the line sinks into the repeated 'summer time'.

### 8. 'Everything is so strangely removed today'

This song is fascinating and slightly eerie. The feeling of restlessness is emphasised by the piano's silvery, bell-like chords. Perfect clarity is all that is needed here. Consonants must be deftly enunciated and rhythms well defined. The speed should increase a little at 'Clear as a bell of silver and glass'. The syllables of this section are helpful for subtle vocal shadings to illustrate the text, depicting the sounds of wing-beats, bells and birdsong. Textures are clear and sparse to allow a crystalline purity of delivery and sibilants should be exploited to the full. The vocal line unwinds into a short-lived reverie, to be rudely interrupted by a repeat of the second half of the motto whose piercing *fortissimo* should have a shock effect.

### 9. 'Some day you will be one of those who lived long ago'

The final song is calm and resigned and must be sung gently, almost casually. The text is so economical and understates the ideas by means of implications. The listener has time between half-phrases to savour every statement. The Sprechstimme must be accurately pitched and carefully dovetailed into the sung lines to eliminate awkward breaks in tone (Example 2). The warm resonances of the piano chords support

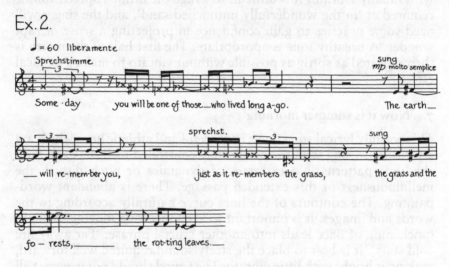

Ex. 2.

the vocal lines which are almost like folksongs in their simplicity. The legato in the last sung line must be as smooth as possible. After the piano has died gently away in a series of single notes in the left hand, it is best to place the final half-whispered phrase low in the voice to avoid any possibility of ruffling the calm atmosphere in which the work ends.

The impact made on an audience by this most substantial cycle is a tribute to its well-conceived structure and natural flow. People like to follow a text and a musical argument as clearly as this, and, if the dramatic pacing of the interpretation is correct, no singer need fear that interest will flag. It is best to perform *Evening Land* after the interval in a recital as people are once more ready to concentrate. English songs of the early 20th century and of the Second Viennese School make good companion pieces. Since the idiom is most original there is little danger of any stylistic clash. It is obviously not advisable to include another long work in the same half of the programme.

# On the Beach at Fontana
(1929)

## Roger Sessions (1896–1985)
### Text by James Joyce

T IV; M IV
High voice
Duration 1½'

This splendid song was originally part of the special collection written as a tribute to James Joyce, called *The Joyce Book*, which existed only in a limited edition. It is fortunate that the song is now available to a wider public. Sessions was one of the most cosmopolitan and influential of senior American composers, and he is sadly missed. It is perhaps surprising that this is his only song for solo voice and piano.

The lie of the lines suggests that the song is better suited to a tenor. There is a fairly consistent focusing on notes at the register break of the female voice; this could prove tiring and give intonation problems. It is not an easy piece to sing, but its originality and powerfully urgent atmosphere command attention and commitment, rewarding the rigorous practice necessary to make it flow smoothly and flexibly.

Subtlety of rhythm is the hallmark of the song. The interplay between simple and compound groupings of notes within a basic 6/8 creates a nervous energy with an ebb and flow appropriate to the text. It is essential to keep the tempo moving; only at the very end do the rippling semiquavers in the piano subside into calmer figures. The singer will have to work hard to attain total accuracy, and can then concentrate on adroitly dovetailing with the piano's rhythms. Words are quite often phrased across barlines, thus making fascinating cross-rhythms and creating a seamless stream of pulsations. The accents must not be exaggerated, however, but should seem natural, and breaths must be kept to a minimum. 'Slime-silvered stone' is particularly effective and comfortable to sing. The uneven groupings produce additive rhythms but in a very different way from those of Messiaen. The underlay of syllables is difficult, but it contributes to the feeling of a continuous flow. When the voice goes into 2/4 time over the piano's continuing 6/8 (which is slower, so the beat is the same as the singer's), a useful upbeat duplet makes the transition less awkward.

Joyce's texts are so resonant with vocal nuances that the singer should enjoy and exploit the sound of the syllables. The coloratura must be sung legato without separate articulation of each note. (The groupings of the notes in seemingly urgent pairs of semiquavers can be compared with the second song of Britten's *On this Island*.) The lilt of the rhythms must never be impeded.

The dramatic final section allows more scope for expansive tone colours. It is difficult to find a good breathing place in the last phrase. Snatched breaths in the middle of running passages can cause a collapse of rhythmic structure and create an air of desperation as the singer tries to catch up again. Since the line ends very low it ought to be possible to take one last breath after the word 'heart' and sing through to the close without another one (Example 1). But of course the *sempre*

Ex.1.

*forte* last note has to be powerfully sustained. It is feasible, if absolutely necessary, to separate the accented 'Ache' from its preceding note and to make a tiny break without spoiling the crescendo too much. If doing this it is best to make a feature of it rather than attempting to disguise it.

*On the Beach at Fontana*, a highly intricate song from one of the finest composers of his generation, casts a memorable spell. It will reward the accomplished artist of subtle, interpretative gifts. The obvious choice for a recital programme would include settings of James Joyce by other composers. One of the earlier Britten cycles would form a particularly interesting parallel.

# Graves Songs Set II
## op. 22 (1977–82)

### Hugh Wood (born 1932)
### Text by Robert Graves

T IV; M IV
High voice
Duration *c*.15′

Wood's five short songs make a stirring impact in their response to the passionate and extremely moving poems. The set seems to represent the composer in his most romantic vein. Always an excellent vocal stylist, here he finds an even more lyrical expression than in earlier works for voice and piano. The texts are comfortably set to enhance vocal tone and colour and to allow uninhibited interpretation. A warm and flexible tenor with more than a hint of the golden Heldentenor quality would be ideal for the glorious, expansive phrases and immaculately controlled nuances, aptly tailored to the words throughout. Such beautiful craftsmanship is extremely rare. Despite the fact that they were written in different years and the considerable time lapse between the earliest and the most recent, the songs make a cohesive and balanced set. (The printed order works very well, although it is not the order of composition: the earliest is sung later in the cycle while the most recent, according to the score, is placed first. The last song is not dated.) The effect on an audience of this fine example of modern lieder writing should be very strong indeed. The piano part is characteristically assured and colourful.

## 1. Symptoms of Love

Marked 'allegro nervoso', this song exploits most skilfully the use of staccato and tenuto speech rhythms, sharply pointing the words and helping the singer to project their import in a mood of bitterness that turns to poignant resignation and commitment. Rhythmic vitality is evident from the outset. An accented *pianissimo* on 'love' must be spun out until the moment when it splinters into short staccato notes. With small and precise lip and tongue movements it will work perfectly. On 'bright stain' the 't' of 'bright' can be placed neatly on the half-beat. No breath should be taken, and indeed the *fortepiano* on 'stain' will be all the better for lack of excess air. The liquid consonants of 'vision' ('v', 'zhi', 'n') make it easier to lean on the tenuto notes. The thread-like *pianissimo* on 'symptoms' can be achieved by using to the full the sibilance and percussive elements, and both the 'm's in the word aid the smooth crescendo through the phrase. The singer should not breathe in the quaver rest as it is there for clarity only. Such tiny gaps in the music ensure that ends of words are cleared and the start of a new word or phrase is then set in relief. The words 'leanness' and 'jealousy' can be well characterised. It is easier for a tenor than a soprano to avoid squeezing the tone on the 'e' and 'eh' vowels. Jabbing staccato chords in the piano keep the tension going and above this the voice sustains an incisive line up to a *fortissimo* climax on 'nightmares'.

The second half of the song brings a contrast in the softening of tone and a warmer mood. The staccato parlando phrases are effectively set to lie comfortably in the voice. The dynamics are meticulously marked. The beautiful cantabile phrases allow the singer to display a melting legato, swooping up and down. The final exhortation, 'Take courage, lover', must be very firmly sung; tenuto marks and consonants are helpful. The last sentence is quite unbearably moving. The singer must take special care over it so that the point is made clearly without over-indulgence. The *fortepiano* followed by a crescendo on 'grief' and the subsequent heavily accented notes must be controlled with a rock-like steadiness and an iron grip on support muscles.

## 2. The Visitation

The composer's instruction at the head of this song is 'Slow, tranced'; the gentle warmth of tone calls for strong control, especially when the lines move upwards. 'A trick of the night wind?' may need some practice before it sits comfortably in the voice without any pinching of the tone (Example 1). The throat should be kept open and left

Ex.1.

undisturbed through the changes of syllable. Often the lines dip down at the ends of phrases, making them easier to sing smoothly. The word-setting is impeccably judged. The staccatos on 'Do you cast no shadow?' should not be clipped too much. The word 'whisper' provides an opportunity for appropriate rustling sibilance to lighten the atmosphere. At this juncture the words are particularly enjoyable to enunciate and can easily be kept forward, close to lips and teeth. This is more important when the line becomes 'even softer' on those very words. The tone must be kept pure and sweet with the minimum of vibrato. When the volume increases suddenly in one of the lower-lying passages, more fullness of tone will be appropriate and it should become warm and securely placed. The *subito pianissimo* at 'single' on a high G, like certain other passages, will sound infinitely better when sung by a tenor voice. A soprano would have to cover and modify the vowel sound considerably and it is difficult to do so without obvious awkwardness. When the line returns to a lower, almost normal speech level, the voice can relax and prepare for the rapt ending. The whispered note requires just a breathy sound on the pitch, as if the singer were giving a little sigh. The 'w' and 'wh' sounds in the final few fragments help to poise the notes ready to radiate into glowing small crescendos (Example 2). These details will need a certain amount of practice, and breath control is vital.

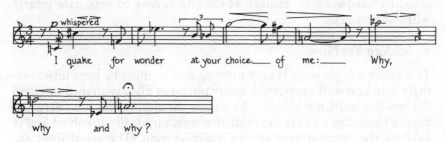

## 3. Fragment

The third song is marked 'Hushed, urgent', and the succinct indication of the composer's intentions is again immensely helpful to the interpreter. Feathery textures in the piano give a gossamer lightness to the music so that it makes a magical impression as it progresses inexorably through lengthening phrases and closes on shining notes. There are many lovely touches of word-painting and Wood exploits suggestive syllables for their full effect. Particularly rewarding are the arching phrases which provide an ideal launching pad for the long notes, together with increasing elasticity and vocal freedom.

The urgency of the opening phrases is perfectly captured in the gradual build-up of the succession of sibilant words, after which the smoother sounds of the remaining text draw out radiant legato lines that are extremely satisfying to sing.

## 4. Ouzo Unclouded

Wood's most sophisticated setting of this poem requires careful judgment and precision on the part of the singer. It takes the form of a reported speech containing mercurial changes of mood, unpredictable and hinting at coquettishness. As in the first song, staccato is used to heighten and accentuate the text. Tiny inflections and accents must be obeyed at all times. It is very important not to breathe after 'ice'; the crescendo to the staccato 'Not' works very well, and the 't' and the ensuing word endings can all be placed neatly on the half-beats to keep the rhythm lively. The 'oscuro' marking on 'Nor toped in secret' implies a darker, more covered tone set slightly further back with a very open throat. A sudden, loud command breaks the atmosphere of mystery; it is underlined by the piano's *vigoroso* which must be delivered with great purposefulness.

A glissando up to the word 'eyes' on high A is most practical vocally as the word before it is 'your'. In this particular instance, when a vowel follows, it is smoother to do the 'r' gently in an American style rather than rolling it, because the legato must be seamless. The delicate, staccato 'throw-away' remark at the end is easy to negotiate clearly without fussiness.

## 5. Seldom Yet Now

This short *adagio* song is very moving and so must be kept unwaveringly firm and well supported. Every phrase is filled with meaning and the tension must not relent. The singer should use the full energy of support muscles so that the audience feels physically involved and is held by the commitment of the interpretation. The vocal lines are uncluttered and contain very few extreme notes to distract attention. Subtle bass trills sound in the piano part at the reference to 'birds'; they are very soft and delicate and well below the voice range so that the text is clear. Individual words are given special accents and nuances where natural and appropriate, and not a single marking should be overlooked in this highly intense song.

The emotional power of Wood's cycle is sure to enthral all types of audience, and the singer must take care to surround it with suitably contrasting fare. A Classical group (Haydn, Mozart, Beethoven) would sound well before the Wood, while French music would be a good idea for the other half of the programme; some light-hearted songs should also be included. Wolf lieder would complement this music particularly well stylistically. It is best not to include early Schoenberg or Berg songs as they would not provide sufficient contrast.

## *Four Songs*
### (1958–60)

## David Del Tredici (born 1937)
### Text by James Joyce

T IV; M V
High voice
Duration *c*.14′

The composer says in a note in the score that the four songs were not
intended as a cycle, but that the printed order is his personal preference
if they are to be performed together. These extremely fine works
stretch the singer vocally, but in the most beneficial way. Del Tredici
understands the voice intimately and knows which devices are truly
effective. The wonderful variety of vocal figurations is most satisfying
for the performer who wants a challenge. Considerable musical ability
is needed, but confidence will gain as it quickly becomes clear that the
lines are rewarding and eminently singable once the difficulties (especially those in the rhythm) are overcome. An accomplished pianist
will be needed as the accompaniment is intricate. The fact that the
texts are familiar is an advantage. The four songs are all extremely
powerful and persuasive in appeal. The composer has a wonderful
flair. He has become more celebrated in recent years for his highly
diverting and enjoyable works based on *Alice's Adventures in
Wonderland* and *Through the Looking Glass*.

### 1. Dove Song

The first song is marked 'Andante frullante' (literally spinning or
fluttering). The expansive and softly floating vocal line is beautifully
paced for comfort. The composer's instructions and detailed requirements aid the interpretation greatly for he makes his intentions
completely clear. The two-against-three rhythms must seem easy and
natural. A lovely broad sweeping arpeggio line encourages the singer
to produce a ravishing legato sound over the whole span, joining the
notes so smoothly that a feeling of security is achieved. These phrases
actually extend the singer's technique, making it healthy and safe. A
gloriously satisfying glissando up a 10th is another example of this.
The voice should spring on to the high F which is ideally placed for the
sustained 'rise' of 'arise' and the gradual diminuendo. The vowel
should be kept forward so that the ending floats off into space.

In the much faster passage, marked 'Agitato sempre', it may be harder to bring out the shorter phrases clearly. The approach to the low B flat is sudden, but as the word is 'love' and there is a crescendo after it has begun, there is time to launch the note and monitor its progress. A more passionate phrase brings more glissandos. The singer should make the most of these as they give a wonderful feeling of relentless legato and sureness of tone. The singer's lower register must be secure and integrated with the rest of the voice. A quiet, low phrase dips down to A on the word 'head' and the note is sustained at some length. Full support and co-ordination is vital: a wobbly or slightly breathy start will make it impossible to achieve this. It is better to keep the sound as straight as possible and not too fruity. The tone should be covered as it diminishes. As at the beginning, the singer ends with gentle, resonating long sounds in the middle register. On the word 'Arise' there is ample time to gauge the quality and keep it warm and steady while the oscillating figures continue in the piano.

## 2. She Weeps Over Rahoon

The setting of this poem is masterly in its variety of textures. The opening is deceptively plain and simple: the rhythms are far from straightforward. The dynamic variation is extremely subtle. A most effective *subito pianissimo* on 'moon-rise' is made easier by the bocca chiusa. The change to 'agitato' is most apt. The composer allows the voice to change into a higher register ready for the *sforzando* landing on D sharp, which has to be held through a diminuendo, a big crescendo to *fortissimo* and another diminuendo. This is a good breathing exercise. It may require some practice to control the tone as the sound is the 'ing' of 'calling'. The section beginning 'Dark too our hearts' is marked 'sotto voce misterioso' and the music is low and fragmented. The singer should resist the temptation to take a breath in every rest; the naturally halting effect is most appropriate. There is time to inflect each syllable and place the pitch accurately. The gratifying glissando up a 10th on 'moon' flexes the voice beautifully. The singer should remember that the series of pauses means that the phrase will seem long and there is no way of cutting it up. The deep B flat on the final sustained 'rain' is made easier by rolling the 'r', and the diminuendo can be helped by lingering on the final 'n'.

## 3. A Flower given to my Daughter

The music of this brief and flexible *scherzando* song moves athletically across the full range of the voice. The notes are undeniably hard to pitch; vague groping for them would be horribly inappropriate and clarity of line is paramount. The song is beautiful and delicate with short radiant bursts of warm passion. The second phrase is not as difficult as it may seem if the singer observes the 'legato rubato' marking. It lies smoothly in the voice despite its angular appearance (Example 1). It is easier to make the desired suddenly quiet sound on

Ex.1.

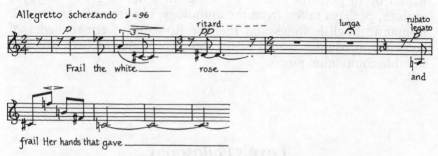

'soul' if the 's' is long, giving time to plot the note properly; the 'p' on 'paler' (also *subito pianissimo*) can be placed in the same way. The swiftly twisting legato line on 'Than time's wan wan wave' is made easier by the preponderance of long consonants, especially the 'w's. After a series of light, staccato fragments the voice swings up a 7th to a *sforzando* on 'wonder wild' and the singer should use the 'w' to control the attack. The short crescendo–diminuendo on 'gentle' works perfectly because of the slow consonants. Tuning is crucial in the *subito pianissimo* B flat on 'child' in the last line. The composer has carefully marked a linking dotted line towards the B natural in the piano part at the end of the bar.

### 4. Monotone

The final song is marked 'Adagio improvisando'. The composer stipulates that the initial 6/8 rhythm should be felt throughout in slow, flexible dotted crotchets rather than quavers. Many of the beats are divided into duplets (dotted quavers) giving a greater feeling of freedom so that the rhythms seem almost casual. Rhythmic complexities represent the most difficult aspect of this song. The vocal line largely avoids extremes of range, except for the sustained high note on 'cry' and a sudden build-up to a climax on 'blowing', which flows over into a descending accented arpeggio, again with consonants which help to launch the sound. The tone should be kept pure and not too full, especially in the passage marked 'sempre leggero'. The gentle rocking 6/8 motion returns for the final, low phrase, which fades to *ppp*.

It would be an excellent idea to feature these songs in a programme including other settings of Joyce's poems. The songs make a group of sufficient substance to be performed as the central item in a concert. There is much variety within their compact proportions. The last two songs together would make a balanced group. Another possibility would be to perform one of the songs in a mixed group of Joyce settings, perhaps taken from the anthology *The Joyce Book* (1933). Romantic English songs and the late Romantic German lieder of Strauss and Mahler would blend well. The songs of Berg are also suitable companion pieces.

## *Love's Philosophy*
### op. 19 (1968–73)

### Paavo Heininen (born 1938)

T IV; M V
High voice
Duration 8½'

*Love's Philosophy*, a short cycle of three extremely well-known poems, is a splendid example of this leading Finnish composer's work. His care for detail is always most conspicuous; the smooth and lyrical lines show his great sensitivity to the sound of the voice. The numerous phrases that focus on the top of the stave indicate that a tenor would be slightly more comfortable than a soprano. The musical idiom is well disciplined and highly chromatic; the intonation may require much attention. Rhythms are straightforward and there is scope for supple shaping of vocal phrases. The piano writing is full of character and exciting rhythmic details. The accompaniment is more intricate than the voice parts, allowing the singer to devote care to tone quality.

### 1. The Cloths of Heaven (W. B. Yeats)

Marked 'leggero ed espressivo', this short song must keep a springy quality and the tone must not become too full and heavy. It is worth special practice to achieve a thin, pliable web of sound, even for the high notes. This is helped by the melismas, roughly one to each line, which make it easier to glide smoothly from note to note with agility and grace. 'I would spread the cloths' is set high in the voice and may be a little constricting at first, but when phrases curve downwards at the end of high passages, vocal comfort is immediate. It is appropriate to emphasise the sibilant sounds of the text to bring out the rapt, ecstatically hushed quality and the volume must not get too loud. There are no dynamic markings and it is best to follow the natural flow of the phrase: the loudest part should be in the middle, ending on the high G on 'dreams'. It is not easy for sopranos to sing the word at such a high pitch; the vowel will have to be opened wide and support muscles engaged to avoid a tense tone. (The rolled 'r' will be useful here.) The next phrase, with its dip down to low B flat, is perfectly written. The gradually slowing pace of the ending has to be carefully controlled. The final 'ms' ('z') of 'dreams' can be placed high in the head; the singer should think of sinus cavities to keep it there!

## 2. Love's Philosophy (P. B. Shelley)

An infectious rhythmic impulse surges through this song, which again lies quite high in the voice with many 'ee' vowels on top notes. The word 'mingle' is set as only one syllable at a crucial point towards the middle of the song, but it is presumed that the second tied note takes the 'gle'. The elaborate piano part must generate plenty of energy as scurrying semiquavers alternate with punching chords. (The 'molto ritmico ed elastico' marking speaks for itself.) The voice must show flexibility and choose just the right tempo so that the notes fly along naturally as the weaving melodies flow with skill and suppleness. In the first verse the song builds up excitingly to an outburst on 'Why not I with thee'. The start of the second verse, like the first, is marked 'non f' to allow for the crescendo later. The excellent word-setting preserves rhythmic lilt and clarity, especially with the percussive sounds. The phrases soar luxuriantly and the singer must grade the increasing excitement carefully, holding full strength in reserve so that the voice peaks at the right moment. The climax on 'thou' is particularly flattering to the voice. There should be no need to breathe immediately after it, but merely to make a fresh start with the glottis on 'if'. An irrepressible jollity must be maintained for the last phrase; it is lighter in tone and must be sprightly and rhythmic. The final kick of the acciaccatura is an excellent touch, making the close suitably fresh and spontaneous.

## 3. True and False Compare (William Shakespeare)

The wonderful text is set with clarity and restraint so that the words make their own highly erotic, resonant effect without unnecessary distraction. High notes are carefully used at key moments when there is no danger of the tone obscuring the syllable. At the end, a truly lyrical outpouring on 'rare' (Example 1) allows the singer full rein in cadenzas of dazzling radiance and abandon (with a teasingly complex piece of coloratura), which flare naturally out of the highly romantic and sensual mood of the words. The composer's directions are very

Ex. 1.

helpful: 'affettuoso, legatissimo' is marked at the start of each thought, and the delightful, rhythmic ironic phrases are marked 'capriccioso, non legato'. A singer with good interpretative gifts will be able to display them fully in capturing the warmly affectionate yet humorously wise flavour of the lover's appraisal of his beloved. There is great expressiveness in the vocal phrases. The phrasing and breathing places are well judged throughout. (It is a subtle point, but the singer must consider how to convey the question marks in the text.) The luxuriance of the phrases gradually increases. The audience should respond warmly to the singer's physical involvement as it rises to a peak. The performance, however, must never become frenetic, and the tension eventually relaxes in the final *molto tranquillo* passage.

It is interesting to compare Heininen's highly original and warmhearted contribution to the English repertory with, for example, the well-known setting of the first poem by Thomas Dunhill or the familiar Delius and Quilter settings of the second. A programme made up of settings of English texts by foreign composers would be fascinating. Heininen has evolved a very different style of songwriting from that based on folksong elements; he shows a strongly romantic streak and great sympathy with the voice. A song cycle by Debussy would make an appropriate contrast, and there is no reason why Austro-German Romantic lieder could not also blend with this music.

# *Three Songs*
## (1955)

### Donald Martino (born 1931)
### Text by James Joyce

T IV; M V
Bass/high voice
Duration *c.6'*

These three brief songs are Webernian in the delicate conciseness and richness of expression that is concentrated within a modest framework. The composer is acutely sensitive to subtle sounds of syllables, and how they can be used as an aid to effective vocalising. The smallest sound is precisely gauged and placed well in the vocal range, which is comfortable and wide so that the singer can both relax and exercise the voice. The darker colours of the bass voice will sound particularly fine against the wide-ranging and angular piano part although there is also a version transposed by the composer for high voice. It is a good idea for a young singer to practise moving his voice about more than is sometimes required by slow-moving and ponderous bass parts. Each phrase is mellifluous; they are all of a comfortable length to be sung in one breath, and some are very short. Although the songs are somewhat difficult to pitch a skilful artist will find them a delight to sing. The wonderfully sensuous texts are beautifully captured in the music and should come across clearly without further emphasis. Each song has its own character: the first uses flowing melismas to highlight special words and in the second the melodic line is more fragmented; the last song is much more dramatic and intense. The singer is given the opportunity to show a full range of emotions and sensibilities within a very short span; it is a fascinating task.

## 1. Alone

The opening lines of the vocal part exploit the darker, lower tones of the voice, making full use of sibilant and murmured consonants. In the short glissando down to the word 'veil' the singer is able to maintain perfect poise and accuracy. The comma before the word 'trail' is comfortably timed for the launch into the first melisma (Example 1). The pace quickens a little and the dynamics become sharply varied before the warmer, slower legato phrases return and there is another gratifying downward glissando. The singer should keep the voice well

Ex.1.

The moon's grey-gold-en-mesh-es make____ All night a veil,____ The

shore-lamps_in the sleep-ing lake__ La-bur-num ten-drils trail.____

forward, straight and clear. If all the details in the score are followed closely the result should be magical. As with all good vocal writing, the singer will be able to respond naturally to the sounds of the consonants and relish the feeling of neat co-ordination between lips, tongue, teeth and palate. He should become especially sensitive to the quality of sound and the slightest changes of resonance engendered by the text. It is quite difficult to attack the last word ('shame') *pianissimo* on a high E flat. The singer should not hit the note too hard and should make full use of a long 'sh' to engage support muscles.

## 2. Tutto è sciolto

John Ireland has also set this beautiful poem magnificently. In Martino's setting the mood is almost unbearably rapt and tender at the beginning; the music rises to a passionate outburst which is suddenly suppressed and then it moves into a more reflective vein for the last verse. The treatment is wonderfully fresh and original and it highlights the text to perfection As in the first song, the tessitura is wide; nuances are finely drawn to accentuate important consonants. Rhythmic flexibility is needed. Rubato, together with the subsequent 'ansioso' marking, is used to highlight the imagery of the text towards the central point. Some of the more subtle effects may be difficult to bring off successfully. In the phrase beginning 'the candid brow', for example, the voice suddenly leaps to a high E flat, marked 'subito pianissimo teneramente', on the words 'the fragrant hair'. Falsetto is most appropriate here. It is worth taking a great deal of care over this spellbinding moment; the singer should resist the temptation to take in too much breath at the comma (Example 2). The vocal line becomes smoother and easier to sing thereafter. The *tenuto* low F sharps at the

Ex.2.

end must be resonated freely, like bells, using the mellow consonants 'w' and 'l' to the full.

## 3. A Memory of the Players in a Mirror at Midnight

The final song is quite dazzling. For the opening unpitched 'animated whisper' the singer should take great care to keep his ribs and diaphragm firm and to avoid catching the throat with an unguarded, forced sound. The throat, tongue and neck should feel loose and relaxed immediately after each percussive consonant has been enunciated. The sibilants must hiss as much as possible ('Gnash the thirteen teeth – your lean jaws'). The composer asks for a sudden crescendo through the end of 'jaws' to the word 'grin' with a heavily accented *forte*, almost as if shouting. It is extremely helpful to remember that the 's' of 'jaws' sounds 'z' and can therefore continue right through to the 'g' of 'grin'. The 'r' can be rolled to relieve the pressure and to effect the marked accent. This type of passage, which does not require normal singing as such, is inevitably strenuous and demands more physical strength and stamina than singers tend to imagine. Stomach and back muscles must also be used to give the vocal sound body and presence and, very importantly, to take the strain off the throat. The lower muscles may hurt a little at first but the throat should never feel roughened.

The real singing now begins, impelled by bold consonants; the singer should energetically use his jaws and lips to punch the notes out cleanly and securely without pushing too hard. In the middle of the song the sibilance is exploited in an overtly sensual way (Example 3). A

Ex.3.

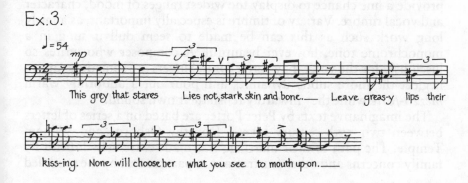

sudden *mezza voce* (a hollow, covered sound) contrasts with the last bright, ringing blaze of sound. A helpful 'v' launches the final vowel; the rhythmic impetus should not be allowed to flag. This is a most powerful song.

The brevity and economy of this delicious set of songs makes it an ideal surprise item for a traditional lieder recital. It would go especially well with Wolf, Schoenberg or Berg. It would also be appropriate to place it among other settings of Joyce's poems, especially those from *The Joyce Book* (1933), including the one by Ireland. Bax, Moeran, Howells and C. W. Orr have all written settings which would contrast well with Martino's style. The song would make a good prelude to a longer cycle in English: those of Britten or Finzi, amongst others.

# *The Voice of Love*
## (1966)

## Nicholas Maw (born 1935)
### Text by Peter Porter

### T IV; M V
Mezzo-soprano
Duration *c*.18'

This particularly satisfying and substantial song cycle rewards the careful study required to master its difficulties. It represents the composer at his most passionate and compelling, and the eight songs provide a fine chance to display the widest ranges of mood, character and vocal timbre. Variety of timbre is especially important, as a fairly long work such as this can be made to seem dull if sung in a monochrome tone, however beautiful. A composer who writes so lusciously for the voice may suffer for it. Singers are sometimes apt to neglect the more subtle dynamics and pour out a uniformly warm *mezzo-forte* while they inwardly relish their own sound.

The imaginative texts by Peter Porter are based on a series of letters between two 17th-century lovers, Dorothy Osborne and William Temple. The path to their marriage was made extremely difficult by family concerns and other frustrations in part created by the muddled political climate of the time: Cromwell had just come to power. The letters are from Dorothy to William (making this specifically a woman's cycle), but only the recurring, poignant phrase 'Shall we ever be so happy', which begins and ends the work, quotes her actual words. The vocal style is richly expressive; it is strongly influenced by the Second Viennese School, and more particularly by Schoenberg and Berg. Intervals need careful attention, but the lines are flatteringly mellifluous. Phrases are of a length to stretch and exercise the voice and to advance technique. (There are passages in Maw's *Scenes and Arias* which are also useful for training the student to negotiate long, sustained phrases at a high tessitura.) The ideal voice for this cycle is a light flexible mezzo-soprano with the clarity and range of colours to put the text across movingly and precisely. The voice must not become dark or unwieldy; rather it should have a springing, elastic quality and a light, fresh tone. The singer should portray and become wholly involved in the alternating moods of intimate reflection and passionate declaration which are punctuated by the heightening, by musical means, of important words or phrases.

## 1. Prologue

A series of improvisatory piano flourishes introduces the voice's first declamatory entry. The sweeping piano line continues beneath the voice, depicting the howling of the wind. In the second phrase it is easier to breathe after the word 'memory' at the beginning of the *rallentando*, rather than before 'cold'. It is then possible to sing through the 'z' of 'breeze' and place the *tenuto* on 'cold' more clearly and effectively.

When the singer recalls her memories (*semplice e con tenerezza*) a rapt and sweet *pianissimo* is required. A sudden burst of anguish instantly disturbs the serenity with *marcato* phrases which use the full vocal range. Considerable support is needed to sustain these impassioned lines with full intensity. The wry comment 'Time is a young enemy' should be intoned with almost no expression. The first occurrence of Dorothy's touching line 'Shall we ever be so happy' is unaccompanied; the words must be sung with simplicity and depth of feeling. The diminuendo on the C sharp is slightly awkward. It is worth giving this phrase particular attention as it is a recurring motif and the effect ought to be deeply poignant. The singer should not rush the line but take time to poise it properly in the (one hopes) rapt silence established.

## 2. 'We were two families upon the wharf'

The story itself now begins. The narrative style is flexible to suit the changing tempos and moods. For a fast and percussive succession of syllables it is less exhausting to take fewer breaths. Pliable rhythms are sometimes used to point natural speech patterns, as, for example, when a smooth melisma on the word 'slow' gently undulates downwards at one of the key moments. A seamless legato is essential here. Lilting, strict rhythms alternate with more flexible passages marked 'Recit.' and the music flows with a natural impulse. Words are strongly accentuated for the *maestoso* mock-heroic reference to 'the iron man' (Wellington). The subsequent *più tranquillo* phrase is sung entirely on B. A clear and direct tone must be sustained to contrast with the staccato ticking of the piano part. In the final phrase the singer jumps from the word 'born' on to a semiquaver rest and then immediately on to the last word, 'today'. There is only time for a very quick breath, as the natural impetus of this phrase may otherwise be lost. If this last note on E is launched properly, there should be no problems in sustaining its tone (Example 1). It is appropriate to make a crescendo here as the piano changes to a faster speed and maintains the tension.

Ex. 1.

Recit : sostenuto ♩ = 66                                    Molto moderato ♩ = 84–88

The world is old____ but love.____ was born__ to-day.____

## 3. 'Watching the doves in the drowned park'

The 'Lento e desolato' marking at the beginning of this song immediately suggests a plain and mournful interpretation. The singer should be open to the many possibilities of tone colour, each of which can be conjured up by a single phrase. Throughout the song it is useful to underline the liquid consonants in the text which contribute to the word-painting and help the sound to drift gently from syllable to syllable without disturbing the legato. The singer should relish the gentle vibrations of lips, tongue and teeth. The first line, for example, is improved by concentrating on this: 'W̲atching the doṿeṣ in̲ t̲he drowned'. The rolled 'r' of 'drowned' should be particularly emphasised. The tone is thus held securely in place without risk of unevenness. The sensuous feel of syllables, as in 'Ev'ry leaf dripping its colourless wax', can be savoured to the full and sibilants exaggerated.

The audience should be made to hang on every word. The delightful parlando passage about 'high ladies and their little dogs' must be adroit and natural. The words of this song give special opportunities for vocal and interpretative flair. The melisma on 'changing' must be extremely smooth and it should swing naturally out of the text. The galloping rhythms of the piano, marked 'poco allegretto', are heightened by careful placing of consonants in strict tempo. The bleaker mood of the opening returns for the final section. The dynamic markings are subtle and must be scrupulously followed. The suppressed emotion of the text is so strongly projected by the music itself that it is unnecessary to use too full a vibrato; indeed, a slightly starved sound is more suitable for the last phrase.

### 4. 'Your love for me is my ruin'

Rhythmic bite, perfect pacing and clear consonants are essential for this angry and extrovert outburst. The song hurtles along to a wild climax on the cadence on the word 'Bedlam' (Example 2). The singer

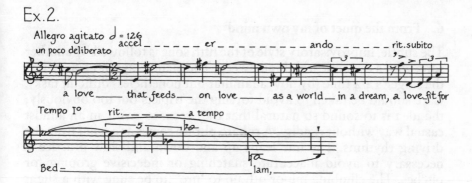

Ex.2.

should hurl herself into this, throwing caution to the winds. The 'f' of 'fit' provides a chance to engage support muscles to control the air as it comes out. The explosive lip movement on the 'b' of 'Bedlam' should have a trumpet-like attack. Once launched the vowel must not be allowed to tighten during the melisma but must be left open and the 'd' should not be prepared too soon. The special accent on the final 'm' means that there is an unusually percussive bounce on this consonant, rather than the usual sustained resonance. The grace notes which are used to emphasise key words produce a hocketing effect at high speed. The song closes with a solemn, low section; it flicks back for an instant to the very fast *agitato* of the main section before quickly subsiding. It may be difficult for a young voice to get a firm attack on the word 'quarrel' on low B flat with a big crescendo. The sound should be intense and kept well forward. At the quiet sustained ending of the song the voice leaps up a minor 10th to a most effective placing of the word 'world' on an accented D flat. The final two words, 'is silence', could be sung without vibrato to achieve a clear *pianissimo* sound and to separate the syllables as marked. As ever, nuances are of the utmost importance.

## 5. 'After darkness, how welcome the sky'

This is perhaps the most difficult song to capture with its subtle rhythmic and dynamic features and elusively mercurial mood. The music is complex and requires detailed study to ensure a comfortable and secure projection of the text. The little roulade on 'pleasure' is particularly original and deft. The *dolce cantabile* vocalise on 'Ah' must flow evenly but be well articulated. It is much harder to achieve this when there are no consonants to provide a springboard over intervals. The atmosphere is highly sensual. The decorative style of both vocal line and accompaniment suggests a light and spring-like feeling. The song has freshness, spontaneity and openness, as well as a gentle ironic humour.

## 6. 'From the quiet of my own mind'

The subtle, improvisatory style of the fifth song is followed by another song with a dynamic, rhythmic sweep. The piano plays in 12/8 against the singer's 4/4 time (by now a familiar but nonetheless difficult task). Care should be taken to avoid forcing the triplets out too obviously; the idea is to sound so natural that they seem to swing in an almost casual way without rigidity. A rubato phrase comes as a relief from the driving rhythms. The line leaps up and down and slow practice is necessary to avoid inaccurate snatching or indecisive groping for pitches. The climbing minor 9th up to 'fire' (to be sung with a slight glissando) is comfortable and gratifyingly spectacular. This makes an ideal preparation for the *fortissimo* climax on 'There is my heart', the effect of which should be impassioned and almost searing. It is hard to avoid too shrill a sound on 'effigy'; the 'fi' should be joined as smoothly as possible to the last note and the 'g' must be dispatched very swiftly with as little jaw movement as possible to avoid an awkward bump in the sound.

## 7. 'Long faces and stiff looks attend a marriage'

The mood becomes much heavier in this song with its references to such events as a wedding, widowhood, loss of children and its reflections on lost happiness. As in the fifth song, much thought, dedication and attention to detail are needed, as well as an empathy with the shifting moods. It is very rewarding to sing because of the richness of expression, and it must be carefully paced. The first phrase is rather long, but the singer should try to sustain it in one breath. A relentless weightiness enhances the effect of the text. The phrase 'brother's curse' is particularly telling; the hushed *sotto voce* must maintain the intensity and involvement. A poignant return of the 'Shall we ever be so happy' motif is beautifully placed, again unaccompanied, and it should perhaps be sung with a touch of irony. A pulsating figure in the piano accompanies the dense narrative which, touching briefly on the events, leads to the agonised cry of loss and culminates in a series of melismas on the word 'siege' (Example 3). It is difficult to pitch these melismas and the passage requires much practice. The voice can relax on the low B flat which is repeated with a diminuendo. The singer must be careful not to force the highest and loudest part of these final outbursts, as it will then be difficult to hold steady the last hushed tones. The final *ppp* can be allowed to fade into the distance; a covered sound is appropriate here, and the 'n' of 'night' helps to place each note securely.

Ex.3.

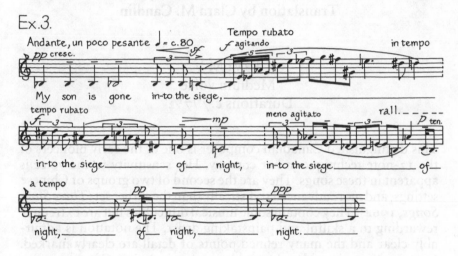

## 8. Epilogue

In an almost conversational style the singer comments on fate; she resigns herself to it in a clever telescoping of all that has gone before, each phrase with its appropriate piano figurations. The sensual awareness of nature found in the fifth song is recaptured. The tone is set for a peaceful ending of serene acceptance. The poignant *dolcissimo* line on the words 'love, come now to me' is followed by the last, bitter-sweet 'Shall we ever be so happy'. The final C sharp must again be held purely and calmly.

Maw's powerful cycle should be placed at the beginning of the second half of a recital when the audience is relaxed, refreshed and ready for sustained concentration. Nothing of similar length should be placed beside it; it could be followed by folksongs by Britten, or perhaps by Stravinsky's *The Owl and the Pussy-cat*. Schumann's *Frauenliebe und -leben* is an apt parallel with which to end the first half of the programme. The work would make a good contrast to music of a sparse texture in a more strongly avant-garde idiom, for example the Cage and Bedford songs treated in this book.

## Sung Songs nos. 4 and 5
### (1971)

### Barbara Pentland (born 1912)
### Translation by Clara M. Candlin

T IV; M V
Medium voice
Durations $c.7'/7\frac{1}{2}'$

This distinguished Canadian composer is one of the early pioneers of the 12-note technique in her country. Her sensitivity to the voice is apparent in these songs. They are the second of two groups of Chinese settings, and more advanced stylistically than the earlier set (*Three Sung Songs*, 1964). They contain some musical difficulties but are extremely rewarding to a skilful and painstaking artist. The notation is admirably clear and the many refined points of detail are clearly marked. Great attention is paid to the problems of articulation. Grace notes are often found, together with other small decorative devices which highlight special moments. It is interesting to compare Pentland's work with that of Elisabeth Lutyens in this respect. They both show a rare delicacy in their vocal and verbal shadings.

The Chinese poems provide inspiration for songs of graceful fluency, using the voice's full range and enabling every sound quality to be minutely examined. An accomplished singer with excellent technical control will certainly be needed. Soprano, mezzo-soprano, tenor or high baritone will all be suitable, as long as they have the necessary suppleness. The quarter-tones are the real test for the performer; vibrato has to be well harnessed to clarify these. However, the composer's vocal language is so assured that real pitfalls are avoided, and a magical effect should be achieved. The piano parts are delicately moulded to balance with the voice and not obtrude. It is a great pity that these splendid songs are not heard more often in Europe. Each song is quite substantial and will provide a gifted performer with an excellent opportunity to make a lasting impression on the audience.

#### 4. Midnight among the Hills (H'sin Ch'i-Chi)

The atmosphere of stillness and inscrutable resignation of this song may be difficult to capture. Intense concentration and a steady tone are needed, particularly for the quarter-tones. These occur during the slightly more restless middle section and are marvellously appropriate. They give an even more distinctly Eastern flavour to the music and pin-point the plaintive shadings of the words.

The real musical problem of this song, however, is caused by the fact that the piano and voice move at different speeds. Arrows are provided to mark the instances when they coincide. The seemingly simple outer sections of the song, with their smoothly arching lines, therefore need a confident singer who can take advantage of the rubato recommended by the composer and proceed at a slightly faster tempo than the pianist while keeping an eye on the piano's steadier progress to make sure the parts converge at the signposts. Fortunately, the score is very clearly written to show the alignment of beats. After some practice so that the singer is well past the sight-reading stage, the performers should be able to solve any problems. The effect of the uneven beats contributes greatly to the fascination of the song.

#### 5. The Tune of the Stream (H'sin Ch'i-Chi)

In this song the singer has a more virtuosic role with a considerable sprinkling of coloratura passage-work and arresting details of rhythm and accent. Quarter-tones are again used; one in particular will need careful practice, especially for a female voice, as it occurs during accelerating semiquavers in an already complex passage. Tuning will need to be worked out with great care if the effect is to be achieved clearly (Example 1). The composer asks the singer to gaze skyward at

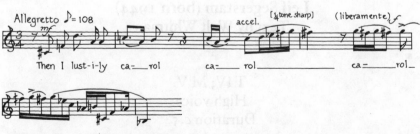

one moment for added dramatic effect during the *liberamente* passage that also includes two exceptionally well-placed quarter-tones. The singer has thus quite a number of tasks to consider at the same time. Early preparation is a wise precaution against tiredness. The piece requires a dedicated approach and deserves the best that the performer can give.

Another delightful detail is the 'mocking tone' asked for near the end. This can be enhanced further by facial expression but the singer should also evolve his or her own personal way of conveying this feeling by means of tone colour. Since the words by their piercing nature seem to invite it, a bitingly direct tone can be used, perhaps clipping the words smartly almost in the manner of speech. (The composer herself suggests that the phrase may be half-sung.) A chanting delivery often works very well when putting across a cynical or ironic message. The singer should not be afraid to experiment with the individual shadings found in his or her voice.

Such exquisite examples of 'the acceptable face of serialism' are a good weapon against the ill-informed. The sensitivity of this composer's vocal writing is a treat to hear, and an imaginative singer will find these songs highly rewarding. Stylistically, Barbara Pentland has a tremendous rapport with the later songs of the Second Viennese School composers, but the best idea would be to contrast her work with classics of the French repertory or songs of Copland, Britten or Barber. The pure-voiced singer that is ideal for these songs is also likely to feel comfortable in earlier music, especially of the early Baroque. Such strongly atmospheric and finely wrought songs will cast their spell in any context.

## *Three Leaves of Grass*
### (1967)

### Leif Segerstam (born 1944)
### Text by Walt Whitman

T IV; M V
High voice
Duration *c.*5'

The flattering vocal lines of this skilful setting of three Whitman songs by a leading Finnish composer have a sensuous beauty. The style owes much to the Second Viennese School, showing a Webernian sensitivity to precise vocal shading and nuance. Swooping leaps over a wide range are especially abundant; they are rewarding to sing and encourage the voice to bloom luxuriantly. Despite economy of means, the effect is never clinical. The songs are very short indeed but they give the singer ample opportunity to display a glowing palette of colours and to exhibit range and suppleness. The extremely detailed and rhythmically varied piano figurations often suggest orchestral colourings.

## 1. Twilight

Whitman's slow-moving evocation of summer is most rapturously captured by the meticulously crafted and expansive vocal lines of this song (marked 'Adagio rubato e espressivo'). The end of the first phrase hangs in the air on a pause on E. The inflections and accents are carefully planned for maximum effect.

Towards the middle of the song the line drops down gently and is marked 'quasi parlando'. The pitch is so close to that of natural speech, however, that this is easy to execute. The low B which ends the phrase must float gently without a rich vibrato. A glorious climax follows in the spectacular 7th leaps down from long, high notes which are vocally satisfying and much simpler to achieve than might appear. Segerstam's writing for the voice is particularly sympathetic. Consonants are used to aid smooth entries at the extremities of register; a mere 'ah' and 'oh' are used just when the singer needs to feel unrestricted. The echo, which sounds a little lower, is expertly judged. Fragments of text are exquisitely poised for simplicity and clarity. The phrases become gradually shorter and the song dies away on the word 'oblivion' at a pitch which makes for an unforced and gently accented delivery. There are absolutely no problems of breathing as phrases are of a reasonable length. The whole piece is perfectly tailored for immediate vocal comfort so that the singer is free to concentrate on tone quality and musical accuracy.

## 2. Lingering Last Drops

This tiny song contains many subtle variations of tempo, creating an impression of great flexibility and spontaneity. The piano begins a light, dancing 3/8 rhythm, which is taken up without embellishment by the singer before the style, obeying the natural contours of the text, becomes more relaxed and like recitative. Clear diction is extremely important to point the subtle nuances of the text. One particularly significant phrase is marked 'legato possibile' to obviate any possible interruption of the line when negotiating the 't' and 'f' sounds of 'drift'. The low parenthesis 'was the answer' is sung so softly and moves so swiftly in parlando that there should be no difficulty in placing it, even for a young voice.

There are a few unusual rhythmic groupings in the second half of the song, but none too troublesome for even an inexperienced performer. The singer should dwell on 'linger'd' and 'lagg'd' to heighten their alliterative effect; since the notes are separated by heavy accents, an interruption will not spoil the line. In the rather long penultimate phrase it is best to breathe after 'last'. A *tenuto* high A flat on 'here' needs to be placed with care, but it is accented and there is no need to be tentative. Once the note is attacked, the tone can be relaxed. Ideally there should be no further breath until a brief rest in the final phrase. The rhythms neatly fit the natural flow of the text as the song comes to an almost conversational, offhand close.

## 3. An Ended Day

The jagged rhythms of the flourishes in the dramatic piano introduction subside into extremely soft, high chords and there is a sudden stillness. The voice enters unaccompanied. The tempo is very slow and considerable control will be needed to ensure a cool and pure sound that is suitably unflurried. The uneven divisions of the beat must be smooth and seamless. A whole series of dramatic contrasts is contained within the four short phrases of this atmospheric and gripping song. A strong declamatory style and clear enunciation are required to convey the mood of triumph which is ritualistic and relentless in its swiftly gathering intensity. The piano part is written on three staves when the excitement is at its height. The big crescendos on the long notes will need much practice; they must be accurately timed to make their full impact. The 'ffp' marking must be closely followed so that the subsequent swells sound even more thrilling. The high B flat on the 'ju' of 'jubilate' should be a joy to sing and to hear.

Dotted rhythms must be brought out clearly. The tone must be kept in tune throughout the length of the final notes which ring out above the agitated fury of the piano. The last note ends with a *sffz* kick which should be achieved by the support muscles to protect the throat.

This intensely moving and succinct cycle shows a most expert understanding of the voice and is equally suited to soprano or tenor. It is best to perform it at the beginning of the second half of a recital as it immediately catches the listener's attention and creates its own atmosphere without any kind of preparation. The work would blend well with English Romantic and Austro-German expressionist music.

# At the Edge of Time
## (1982)

### Brian Elias (born 1948)
### Text by Mervyn Peake

T IV; M VI
Tenor
Duration *c.*12′28″

The composer's beautifully bold handwriting instantly encourages the performer. The refinement and delicacy characteristic of his music is at once apparent. Such meticulous details of nuance and accent and flexible and subtle rhythms demand dedication from the singer, who will be amply rewarded. Bar-lines are omitted in the third song and again at the very end of the cycle, but conventional notation is otherwise used. The musical idiom is atonal, but constant repetition of intervals and pitch cells are a good means of orientation for singers worried by intonation problems. The dramatic scope is very wide indeed. This is a superb vehicle for a tenor of high musicianship and powerful presence.

As might be expected from this composer, every moment is carefully judged for vocal practicability. Despite its musical difficulties, the piece is extremely well written to show off the quality of the voice to best advantage without causing strain. The very forceful penultimate song is followed by one which uses a more restricted tessitura so that the cycle is ended with complete control and clarity. Such consideration towards the singer is always welcome. There is nothing more unnerving than finding the most demanding and insecure moment in the final bars of a piece; the slightest lapse of poise or concentration could spoil the whole effect of the work and there would be no time to recover. *At the Edge of Time* is a most substantial and much needed addition to the tenor repertory. The piano writing is sensitive and well integrated with the vocal line.

## 1. And I thought you beside me

The graceful, flowing lines lie mostly in the middle range, allowing full opportunity for a comfortable, clear and well-focused sound. The rapt atmosphere is captured at the start and the music later branches out into more dramatic interjections (there is an effective downward portamento on 'belied me') with a strong sense of urgency in the last section. Accents and *tenuto* marks point the texts and the phrasing is fastidiously thought out. The piano continues after the voice is suspended on a low D and fades to nothing; the final tempo must not flag. The next song follows *attacca*.

## 2. That lance of light

This song rushes along at a tremendous pace. The intonation must never be allowed to become vague under the stress. A clear, well-defined tone is very important. Much is to be gained by practising this song slowly at first to make sure that no detail is overlooked. Percussive syllables are used to highlight the imagery (Example 1). The piano

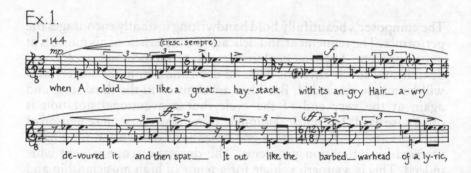

Ex.1.

part is also elaborate. The solo introduction and the ending contain many low trills. In the central part of the song, spiked rhythms and constantly changing dynamics provide ideal support and propulsion for the singer. The extremely loud, high passages may prove strenuous.

The singer should ensure that accents do not provoke forcing or split notes. Good control of the diaphragm will be necessary, especially for the consonants. The grace notes help to clarify syllables, and on the whole words are expertly set with careful regard for projection.

The last two phrases are fascinating and nicely contrasted. In the first, a sinewy line with a melisma on 'honey', the intonation of the close chromatic intervals may need special attention. Sprechstimme is used in the last phrase (notated with crosses through the note-stems), for 'Hissed at the impact'. It is an excellent idea to arrive at the 'ss' early to enhance the effect. The 'd' should be placed directly on the next beat, as should the 'ct' of 'impact'. It should be easy to find a suitably rasping tone colour at such a low pitch (reiterated low Ds), but there is a danger that too much breathiness will jar the larynx. The pitch should bend slightly at the end of notes so that they do not sound at all like normal singing. This exciting, flamboyant and colourful song requires considerable stamina.

### 3. Conceit

The third song, by contrast, is cool and contemplative. The voice part is very brief, but highly evocative. As the notes lie close together the tone should be pure. For the glissando from 'taken' up to 'wing' (followed by a 'diminuendo al niente' on the last note), it is helpful to use the two consecutive liquid sounds 'n' and 'w', joining them seamlessly together. It could otherwise prove difficult to start the word 'wing' securely enough for the sound to float out with ease. If the singer wishes, the 'ng' of 'wing' can be sustained at the very end. A dramatic chordal solo passage on the piano forms the second half of this song and gives the singer a welcome rest.

### 4. In crazy balance

This short but striking song is marked 'Appassionato' and it again takes the singer into a dramatic high tessitura. The projection of sound must be forceful and relentless. The chords in the piano are stark and dissonant. The vocal line scoops down momentarily to a lower note just before the crucial high note in each phrase (as in Example 2)

Ex.2.

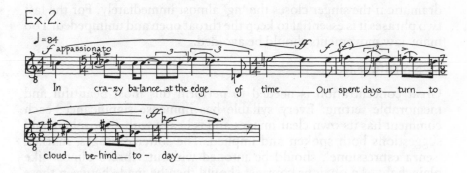

allowing the singer to flex and relax the voice and arrive at the top refreshed. Such considerate vocal writing is typical of Elias; the device prevents the voice from growing tired. The widely arching lines are generally rewarding to sing, and the glissando sweep up on the word 'rages' is particularly gratifying. Enunciation has to be well timed; swift consonants prevent the singer from squeezing the tone, which should remain free and open, with plenty of resonance.

### 5. Swallow the sky

The intensity reaches its height in the grand scale of this song. Sharply reiterated and accented high notes may seem somewhat strenuous at first; it is probably advisable to practise the piece quite softly. The voice opens the song, unaccompanied in a declamatory style. A double grace note emphasises the word 'munch'. The tone must be kept straight to penetrate the sound of the piano when it has entered. Sprechstimme is again used for the second syllable of 'torture'. The sound can fall away naturally, using the portamento as marked. The singer should not be afraid to let go of the note. The immediate rising up afterwards is most effective, aided by another slide across an awkward semitone on 'gorge'. The tessitura is consistently high and may prove tiring at first. The singer must stop practising as soon as the throat begins to feel tired. It is wise to sing the music an octave lower while learning the notes. Much work on support muscles may be needed as a preliminary training for the long, high-flying passages. Only if the muscles are working properly will it be possible to allow the throat to relax and to preserve sufficient energy. The flow of air must be well controlled. Such taxing moments can lead to unnecessary straining and result in a gusty, unclear tone which has less carrying power.

The highest note – a *fortissimo* B flat – is made easier by the preceding grace note; there is no need to linger on it. It is more effective to clip the sound off early on the 'p' of 'hump' and to separate the syllables of 'hump-backed'. The *sforzando* on 'thing' is even more dramatic if the singer closes the 'ng' almost immediately. For the last two phrases it is essential to keep the throat open and unimpeded. Too many jaw movements should be avoided.

## 6. No Difference

Great concentration is needed to perform this most beautiful and memorable setting. Every syllable has immense significance; each comment has its own clear images and is heavy with atmosphere and suggestions both spoken and implied. The softer passages, marked 'senza espressione', should be intoned without vibrato almost like plainchant. An obvious contrast should then be made between these and the phrases that have warmer and more colourful resonances. The singer should focus intently on details in the text and take care to obey the composer's carefully thought-out markings. Like the first song, this one lies comfortably within a middle compass. It is therefore possible for the singer to control the end of the cycle perfectly, holding the audience's rapt attention as the sounds die away. The pitch of the singer's last fading note is ideal.

This most distinguished and precisely conceived work will form a fine centrepiece to a programme. A song cycle by Debussy would make a good companion piece and 20th-century English songs of more traditional style (by, for example, Warlock, Finzi and Vaughan Williams) are also compatible. Examples of Viennese late romanticism, such as songs by Mahler and Strauss would be less appropriate. *At the Edge of*

*Time* certainly requires a high degree of accomplishment, and it is not suitable for a tenor whose voice is insecure in the top range. A weighty, dramatic voice is exciting in this music, but a youthful suppleness and a well-placed high register have to be the first priorities. One cannot pretend that the music is easy, but the vocal part is written with consideration for practicability, and rigorous practice will be rewarded. Audiences should find the cycle powerful and memorable.

## In the Temple of a Bird's Wing
### (1956 and 1965)

### Elisabeth Lutyens (1906–83)
### Text by Teresa Tanner

T IV; M VI
Baritone
Duration *c.* 10'

Lutyens, a much loved and mourned pioneer of the English avant garde, wrote a large amount of vocal works, all of which display the finest sensibility to vocal timbre and tessitura. Her vocal writing is virtuosic and wide ranging but smooth and comfortable to execute once the initial musical difficulties are overcome. As would be expected from the self-acknowledged innovator of British serial music, the melodic and rhythmic patterns are for the most part strictly controlled. The result, however, should be flexible and mellifluous. The cycle comes from what many regard as a particularly rich period in Lutyens's prolific output; it includes the cycles *The Valley of Hatsu-se* and *Akapotik Rose* for soprano and instruments and, most notably of all, the cycle *And suddenly it's Evening* for tenor and instrumental ensemble.

*In the Temple of a Bird's Wing* is splendidly crafted and assured and it deserves much wider recognition. It is a rewarding vehicle for a dedicated and musically gifted singer. Control of vibrato in the higher register and precise tuning are essential. It may take some time to become accustomed to the unevenly divided beats and complex rhythms so that the lines spring along spontaneously without inhibition. The phrases are often fragmented, but this must not be allowed to impede the continuous flow of the music and the singer should avoid taking too many breaths which might create an impression of panic. The rests of punctuation are to be gently placed within the natural lie of the words and a feeling of continuity must predominate. The accompaniment is well integrated with the vocal part, sharing many of its features, and makes much use of arpeggiated chords.

## 1. In the temple of a bird's wing

The title song is marked 'quasi fanfare' and its solo piano introduction is suitably vigorous and extrovert. As the voice enters the tempo slows down and the singer launches a series of curving, melismatic lines, dense with detailed expression and subtle dynamic markings which require scrupulous attention. The composer's natural empathy with the voice makes her expert in judging phrase lengths. At all times she shows an acute awareness of the finer vocal nuances suggested by specific words and sounds. A characteristic feature of Lutyens's vocal writing is her precise notation and setting of final syllables: an extra grace note or small note is often tied to the main one. The appearance of this on the page leads to greater clarity from the outset. A large number of 'ing' endings in this first song may need to be studied. The 'ng' sound must not be allowed to constrict the throat suddenly and impede resonance; the tongue should relax quickly after making the sound. Acciaccaturas within melismas must be clearly and precisely articulated. The tone should not be allowed to spread, for such refined and elegant vocal writing demands a pure and controlled sound. Word-painting, another typical feature in Lutyens's music, is evident at 'Bees are piping' and 'sky blown grasses sweeping'. The mood throughout should be poetic and enticingly sensual.

## 2. Drowning heaven rests her lullaby in earth

Atmospheric trills on the piano create a world of exotic sound for a vocal line that leaps more spectacularly than that of the first song. A sweeping, downward glissando makes the opening 'Drowning' simple to accomplish. The word 'weeping' dips low in the voice and the line then springs up again for the more exuberant declarations. The word 'teeth', emphasised and accented on a high E, is most effectively biting. Sibilant consonants convey sensuous images which are reflected in gently caressing phrases. The final phrase, in which a high E is sustained on the words 'blue on them', will require much control as there is a crescendo to *forte* and then back to *ppp* on a pause. The final 'm' is immensely helpful and can be started early for a smooth elision. This brief song is most colourful.

### 3. It seems the minutes creep

The singer is in more sombre mood and paints vivid images of a rain-swept autumn landscape. The tone can be warm and firm at first as the lines slide smoothly along. Darker vocal colours are appropriate. A sudden *pianissimo* pause on 'rain' is made easier by a well-rolled 'r'. Subtle rhythmic variations and divisions of the beat must be clearly differentiated. As the scene becomes starker and the text contains images of dying, the singer should not use vibrato, especially in the *pianissimo* phrases. The minor 7th upward leap which occurs twice at the very end will need to be placed carefully. The throat should not be tightened too soon in readiness for the final 'd' of 'dead'.

### 4. The moon, seen in the night

The voice floats dreamily with delicate phrases of magical beauty. The seemingly angular minor 7ths, for example on 'scythes high' and 'pyramid', must not be exaggerated. Each one is propelled by a helpfully percussive consonant and this is enough to make a clear attack without pushing. As Lutyens knows, such leaps are enjoyable to sing for they allow the voice to stretch comfortably with increased suppleness and elasticity. The subsequent lower *sotto voce* phrase should almost be hummed to help the vocal cords to relax. The lines arch excitingly and should be extremely satisfying to perform. The stimulating effect that such phrases have on the singer's physical well-being encourage full and correct use of the voice. The final paragraph is especially rewarding in this way once the problems of pitch have been overcome (Example 1). A dexterous aim is an absolute necessity and the intervals must be clearly defined within the well-controlled dynamics.

Ex. 1.

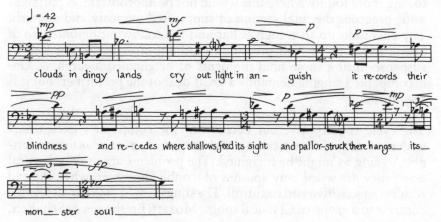

### 5. These birds were skeletons

This is a most fascinating song. Short, often sparsely textured fragments on the piano and the wealth of rhythmic detail in the voice part create a tense and agitated atmosphere. The singer will need to spend some time practising the fast rhythms in isolation so that their execution is precise. Musically this is the most difficult piece in the cycle as much movement is contained within a very short space of time. The performance could sound confused if not enough care is taken to make even the smallest detail spring out naturally from the rhythm of the words. The text is a little difficult, and extra practice will be needed to articulate it with assurance. A flexible, mercurial effect should eventually be achieved. The song whirls by so quickly that the singer must be careful not to cast it off thoughtlessly, although there should be a feeling of fleeting spontaneity in the delivery. The singer's last phrase is a potential danger point: a fast, widely arching setting of 'rapturous panic', the last syllable of which falls on a staccato note at the end of a short glissando up a minor 9th to high F. The piano follows this with a poignant postlude which repeats the opening material of the cycle.

### 6. How can I ask differently the current of the night

The final song, a masterstroke, is a completely unaccompanied epilogue of haunting lyricism and understated but deeply felt emotion. The vocal material is closely aligned in rhythmic character and pitch range to that of the two piano solo passages which open the work and precede this song. The voice, now ruthlessly exposed, must remain poised and concentrated with accurate placing and centring of notes. A caressingly soft dynamic pervades the solo throughout, except for the rise to an impassioned *forte* on high F which is immediately repeated *pianissimo*. The high tessitura must not tempt the performer to sing more loudly where this would not be appropriate. A parlando aside precedes the final section of suppressed intensity and anguish. The glissando up to a high E flat and the following *diminuendo al niente* needs to be well prepared. Nothing must break the web of suspense during these final moments of heightened awareness. Unaccompanied singing demands a great deal of the performer, but it is rewarding.

The cycle is not easy, but because of the composer's exceptional understanding of the voice's natural properties, it is not as uncomfortable to sing as might be imagined. The problems are mainly musical ones; they are worth any amount of trouble, however, when the end result is so sensitive and beautiful. The songs would make an agreeable contrast to a group of Classical songs: Mozart, Beethoven or Schubert.

Some Schoenberg or Berg pieces would complement them well, as would the songs of Debussy, a great favourite of the composer. Very typically English music might perhaps be less well suited to Lutyens's cosmopolitan and sophisticated idiom.

# Poems of Tagore I
## (1970)
### Naresh Sohal (born 1939)
### Text by Rabindranath Tagore

T V; M III
Soprano
Duration c.7'

The fascinating originality of this Indian composer's work gives his short scena strong and immediate appeal. The vocal writing inevitably shows the influence of an Eastern tradition and upbringing. The full vibrato of Western singing is inappropriate here and is not to the composer's personal taste, as I know from working with him. It requires some skill to avoid using a full vibrato on the lower notes. A knife-edge quality is desired, and it can be achieved very easily with a gentle, forward attack; the singer must not be afraid of what may at first seem a thin sound. A finely drawn tone has to be found for the accurate placing of quarter-tones (which Sohal notates with admirable clarity). The mood is gentle and the pace throughout is steady but for the occasional violent outbursts which punctuate the stillness. Rhythms are extremely straightforward but the words are set idiosyncratically, lending an added charm. The piano writing is mostly very simple. Various figurative devices create an effect of improvisation. The performance must be rapt and poised. The piece provides a most palatable introduction to the problems of singing quarter-tones without other causes of stress or distraction. The composer's experience as a professional copyist is obvious from the immaculate manuscript.

The first phrase already shows the distinctive trademarks of Sohal's exceptionally effective vocal writing: a gentle start, a descending glissando, the first quarter-tone of the piece and a supple line which often settles on sustained notes giving ample time to control the tone, keep it steady and carefully monitor its progress. The opportunity to check exactly the quality of each note increases the singer's awareness of the voice and sensitivity to the tiniest variation in tone and vibrato. The glissando down a quarter-tone and then back to the original note creates a lovely effect and is not as hard as it might seem. Another characteristic feature is a sudden sharp attack on a single staccato note which makes it stand out from the preceding long line. The word 'but' is a particularly good choice for directness and clarity. The subsequent lower glissando up and down a quarter-tone is comfortable to sing; it is easier if the sound is gently placed forward and not allowed to become breathy. Changes of dynamic marking are plentiful throughout and while some may seem merely pedantic, the result is most telling if they are closely observed. The use of Sprechstimme or half-whispered effects is also favoured by the composer. As these usually occur in unaccompanied passages there should be no danger of the forcing that can sometimes occur in fierce intensive whispering.

A particularly arresting idea is the use of suddenly exaggerated vibrato to heighten a special word. It works well because of the sharp contrast it makes to the pure and fine tone generally needed for the piece. This wide vibrato is graphically indicated above the note in question by a wavy line, like an uncoiled spring, which becomes gradually wider. When it is used as it is on the word 'laugh', where the dynamics rise from *subito pianissimo* to *forte*, the result can be very exciting. The huge downward surge, still on a crescendo, is quite difficult; it falls, undulating, from a high A to a low B and ends *molto sforzando*. The singer needs much physical energy. Such passages are normally followed by moments of quiet contemplation and sweet serenity. The vocal lines are comfortably wide ranging and mostly fall naturally in the best part of the voice for the clear tuning and placing which is so essential to this unusual idiom. Quarter-tones are in fact given alternative, 'normal' notes if too much difficulty is experienced. The method of notation is beautifully clear. As has become usual practice, a sharp sign has one less or one more vertical line according to whether a note is sharpened by one quarter or three. The notation of flats is more unusual but still easy to understand. A quarter-tone flat looks like an incomplete flat sign; a three-quarter-tone flat is marked by one of these signs together with an ordinary flat sign.

Achieving a perfectly poised quarter-tone for the last note of the phrase 'you will not believe them' is made more practicable by a smooth transition from the voiced 'th' to the vowel, with sufficient time to relate its pitch to the preceding middle C. Pitching and sustaining quarter-tones is an excellent and rewarding discipline. The singer need have no fear that such effects may be mistaken for out-of-tune singing. The sudden bend should be quite easily recognisable especially if nasal and head resonance is exploited to make sure that the natural overtones ring out.

For the delicate whirls of filigreed coloratura a fast articulation on the glottis (as used by Indian singers) helps to create the right effect and is also enjoyable to perform. Singers should not feel inhibited by using the throat in this way, provided that there is no forcing. The last section contains several very high notes which have to be punched out with as little air as possible. It is surprising how much easier this becomes when the articulation is dry and precise. A Western style of vibrato would spoil the atmosphere completely and must be avoided.

In the last phrase, marked 'ad lib' and 'molto espressivo', the word 'pain' has to be sung in the middle range (C sharp) on a crescendo –diminuendo with exaggerated, undulating vibrato. The tone is then straightened out once more and the sound fades away on a high A. These closing bars sound wonderful when they are sung without any vibrato at all.

The simple contours and steady pace of the vocal lines are most attractive and accessible. The flavour of the text is always evident in the music. The performer should aim for a calm demeanour and unruffled style of delivery, suddenly becoming stimulated at the isolated, very loud and dramatic passages which take the listener by surprise.

Poems of Tagore I is a piece of quite remarkable beauty and its effect, despite the myriad details and varying dynamics, is one of unadorned simplicity. The piano part is mostly unobtrusive, except for the tremolandos and improvisatory flourishes which highlight key moments. The music has an exceptionally strong appeal to all kinds of audience. It could be performed with other Tagore settings, such as those by Frank Bridge. Medieval or Renaissance songs are particularly well suited to Sohal's piece; the songs of Debussy and Ravel, because of their sensuousness, make an ideal complement.

## Ballad 2
### (1970)

### Bernard Rands (born 1935)
### Text by Gilbert Sorrentino

T V; M IV
Female voice
Duration *c.*9'

This exciting and amusing theatre piece was, like many works of the time, written for the incomparable and greatly missed Cathy Berberian. As the composer says in a note in the score, it is one of a series of ballads, each featuring a specific area of vocal technique and gesture. Rands quotes from the works of Brahms, Wolf, Berio, Satie and Cage.

The piece evokes the contrasting worlds of ballet, aerobics, circus performance and piano recital and even incorporates cabaret and silent-movie gestures, as well as various phobias. The theatrical range of the opportunities for a virtuoso interpreter is enormous. The structure of the piece is determined by the subject of the poem which describes in detail the form of 'a baffle for rats', an L-shaped concrete device put into the foundations of buildings to prevent rat infestation. This fascinating and compelling idea gives rise to an awareness of the relationship between the shape of the grand piano and the L shape of the baffle in the text. The singer is required to take up various positions on stage and the pianist's route to and from the platform is similarly outlined in the full and admirably clear instructions in the score.

Much detailed explanation is required to perform a theatrical piece such as this which offers so many choices to the performer. Any queries the performer may have are most lucidly dealt with by the composer in the excellent introductory notes. A complete glossary of symbols is provided along with meticulous and helpful instructions as to nuances of performance and gestures. There is also a lighting programme, which is not unduly complicated: two white spotlights and four coloured lights are needed. It is however possible, though not ideal, to give an effective performance without the lighting if budget considerations make this necessary. The composer intends the two performers to be independent of one another: the vocalist (the composer's term), is seemingly involved in a private rehearsal session, moving about and gesticulating as dictated in the instructions, while the pianist is in a fully formal public concert. The two should seem totally unaware of each other throughout. The composer makes detailed suggestions for the mode of attire of both performers to imply the foregoing contrast in situation and attitudes.

The only totally improvised passage for the singer should pose few problems. In a work of this kind it is extremely important for the composer to make all his intentions and ideas abundantly clear, and Rands does this particularly well. The score is beautifully presented in every aspect, giving it a distinctly appetising appearance that inspires confidence from the outset. A pleasure to perform, the piece is packed with interest for vocalist and audience alike.

The notation used will be familiar to those who know the works of Berio and others. Performers new to the idiom should not be put off by the avant-garde appearance of the score. Before practising this song the singer will need a certain amount of preparation to assimilate the symbols in the score. It would probably be advisable to divide the work into small sections for intensive study until the language becomes more familiar. Movements and gestures for the singer not given in the score are, as mentioned, most carefully annotated in the opening pages, but it is preferable to leave these until the piece is musically and vocally secure. They are eminently practical and straightforward and greatly enhance the atmosphere of the piece.

The opening bars are timed in periods of 10 seconds. This need not be done by stop-watch, although it is useful to practise such passages with a timing device as it is hard to judge lengths of time and there is usually a tendency to rush in less active passages; it is not difficult however to count roughly in seconds. In an amusing mime act the singer pretends to play the piano silently, as if accompanying herself. (She later closes the piano lid and plays with her fingers on the top of the case and lid; the rhythms and dynamics are complicated but great fun to play.) The voice part consists of sighs, whispers and a muffled yawn (all neatly defined) which progress into normal speech. Small arrows are used to suggest the curvature of the sound and notes are otherwise unpitched. The space–time notation gives the performer freedom and flexibility. Rands makes clever use of syllables, as for example when the voice makes a glissando up on the 'm' of 'simple' and down on the 'l'. Helpful and succinct written instructions for changes of mood and gesture are given in the score.

The singer will need much practice to co-ordinate the mock keyboard playing with the vocalising on this first page. The whole passage is performed seated. It must be stressed that the many staccato passages have to be articulated without taking too many breaths. It is precisely the sort of singing where careless production can result in a tired throat. Anything that hurts or feels uncomfortable is wrong. The clusters of syllables that occur in brackets are to be repeated ad lib in varying order so that they come out naturally. The glossary of symbols should always be consulted; everything is to be found there, including special signs for putting the hand over the mouth and tongue clicking, as well as more familiar ones, such as the vertical cross for bocca chiusa. The tense muttering in the quotation from Berio's *Sequenza III* works particularly well (Example 1).

Ex. 1.

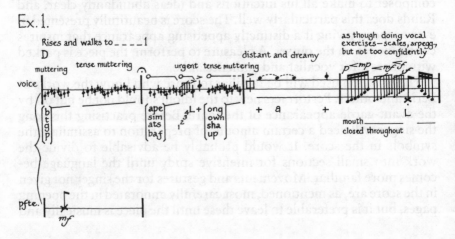

The dental tremolo used in this piece (another feature found in Berio's music), is somewhat of a misnomer. An oscillating, loose jaw is called for so that the chosen vowel pulsates, repeating rapidly as in a trill. It is not the teeth that wobble, merely the jaw. Inevitably, other sounds will have to occur to aid articulation of the tremolo, and maintain the regular jaw movement: namely the two impure consonants 'w' (when doing a tremolo 'a', 'aw' or 'oo') and 'y' (for 'ee', 'eh', 'ay', etc). It is certainly a fascinating device and excellent for loosening up taut muscles. Most singers have a tendency to tighten tongue, lower jaw and neck muscles under duress and this is an ideal way to free them and produce a naturally warbling, bird-like effect. The high-pitched humming is particularly hazardous. The singer should be careful to keep the back of the throat relaxed and open, as if yawning.

In the voice part normal singing occurs with numerous speaking, shouting, laughing, whispering, and murmuring effects. No matter what quality of sound is required, all should be treated like actual singing with full support and delicate placing. One careless push can cause a coughing spasm, as many know from experience. It is always important not to let more air escape than is necessary and this requires considerable strength and control of muscles. The medium-sized vocal range is extremely undemanding for the most part. After the avant-garde beginning, the music suddenly changes to cabaret style, with 'oompahs' in the piano, for the quotation from Satie's *Ludions* no. 1. Passages of the extended vocal technique already described are interspersed with quotations from the lieder repertory, such as a glorious burst of Brahms's *Mainacht*. Some extremely loud attacks on 'L' may be difficult to achieve without strain. The sound should be placed well forward and the nasal and labial resonances used for maximum penetration. The tip of the tongue should be curled forward between the teeth to keep the sound open. During this section the singer performs a number of actions including singing into the piano and hitting the strings. She is then required to take up the formal attitude of a lieder singer ready for the excerpts from Brahms and Wolf. These direct quotations are most enjoyably placed amid flurries of silent-movie or circus music, accompanied by appropriate gestures and movements.

The amusing chanting of instructions for an aerobics class is followed by a piercing shriek of 'RATS' (after rolling the 'r' the singer should not press too hard on the vowel). There is a frenzied run up to the exuberant waltz from Wolf's *Abschied* and the piano finishes with great élan. The effect of this piece, despite the frequent quotations, is wholly original and delightful. Of course a great deal depends on the charisma and artistry of the performer, and she must stamp her own personality indelibly on the occasion. The rewards are great, even if the newcomer to this kind of writing finds the hard preliminary work daunting.

It would be interesting to compile a programme with groups of songs by the quoted composers. It is a mistake to include the whole of Berio's *Sequenza*, however, and just one of the *Quattro canzoni popolari* could perhaps be sung instead. The works by Cage, Satie, Brahms and Wolf which Rands quotes, would all complement *Ballad II*. It is probably best to begin with Brahms and end with Wolf, or perhaps with some cabaret songs. An extremely diverting evening could be built round this skilful piece, which ought to be very popular with singers of presence and vocal versatility who wish to have a chance to display these qualities. Audiences respond most warmly to its wide-ranging appeal.

## *Music as Climate*
### (1984)

### Paul Robinson (born 1949)
### Text by John Ash

T V; M IV
Bass/baritone
Duration *c.*5′

Although *Music as Climate* is written for bass and piano, it is best sung by a baritone. The many high notes which have to be articulated so quickly would put it out of range of most actual basses, unless falsetto is used. With shades of American-influenced minimalism, note patterns are constantly repeated. The pitches are frequently doubled in the piano, thus relieving much of the potential strain on the singer. The whole effect is most fascinating and agreeable, even to the first-time listener. The poem is full of fetching images and musical allusions which make it a perfect vehicle for a setting of this kind; pretentiousness is skilfully avoided. It is perhaps courting danger to open with the lines 'Despite or because of all the wrong notes, the desired effect was in the end achieved'. Unschooled audiences may be tempted to snigger, but perhaps this lightly ironic beginning is meant to focus attention and prepare the listener for the more expansive descriptions that follow. The language fluctuates naturally between full-blown expressionism and stark practicality, the two perfectly balanced. The consonants are exceptionally well used for clarity of attack and colour; vocal practicalities are turned into felicitous, interpretative touches, often delicately understated. Vocal style is mainly non-expressionistic in contrast to some parts of the text.

Much vocal and rhythmic dexterity is needed to articulate the words at the fast pace: the piece is marked 'Vietato dondolarsi' which can be loosely translated as 'No Dawdling!' Robinson alternates between conventional and space–time notation where the singer is free to make phrases flexible and natural without having to rush. In the absence of specific guidelines, the singer may let the words, and the presence or absence of such features as liquid consonants and explosive sounds, dictate the flow of phrases, together with the word-painting implicit in the texts. Dynamic markings are extremely sparse, indicating that a bland, very clear, quasi-monotonous delivery may be appropriate, punctuated by sudden *sforzandos*. Syllables of the text are occasionally isolated for special effects throughout the piece; always enjoyable for the performer, these are easy to execute. The singer sometimes has to point *sforzandos* across natural beats and he should be careful not to force out breath and jar the voice. Acciaccaturas are often employed to give an extra kick to a word. The 't' of 'effect' is used explosively (since 't' is a silent sound, a vowel 'e' as in 'faster' will have to be employed because the notes are pitched). The 'd' of 'end' is likewise repeated, but as 'd' is an explosive vocal in strict elocutionary terms, the tone quality is already there at the moment of articulation. (This also applies to 'b' and 'g'.)

The voice opens strongly with reiterations of the word 'Despite' – the perfect way to make a positive vocal start. When the staccato reiterations occur on the 'au' vowel of 'aura', a glottal stop is obviously required. If done clearly and directly (drily, without air), this works perfectly well and does not harm the larynx. If the sound starts in the forward position, no pushing is needed for clarity. The attack is cut cleanly every time and is not at all fatiguing. It is a good idea to breathe out first. Accents off the beat may cause some problems. The underlay of syllables for 'great naturalness' needs to be clarified. As there are not enough notes to go round, it has to be 'great na-tchral-ness', which runs quite easily. A steadying of the tempo coincides with a rise in tessitura and a general stretching of the range. A high F and a low A both occur in the same phrase, but the setting is always well judged for comfort and practicability: very high notes come either as part of a melisma or with a useful projecting consonant, as in 'plan' and 'reels'. Pitches here may need some care, although key notes are doubled cunningly in the accompaniment just where needed. The lowest note is a soft G. The following phrase has a crescendo from *forte* to *fortissimo* with a *rallentando* in a climax which gives a bigger voice a chance to shine.

The original tempo resumes at the very high, *mezzo-forte* phrase which includes a high A flat, a sustained G and many repeated Es. The music is relentless, apart from a helpful scoop down and up on 'beyond' which provides a welcome moment of rest for the voice. It would be wise to practise this phrase an octave lower or in falsetto until pitch is secure and the articulation of the text is running smoothly and easily. A great deal of vocal damage is done by sight-singing such passages full voice. There is even a danger that the rough, imprecise effect of early attempts may develop into a habit of careless singing, something that no performer ought to risk. This strenuous movement is followed by ordinary speaking and the voice can drop to its most comfortable range for the short phrases such as 'bus timetables' and 'steamed spinach'.

The piano part now becomes more complex and active; the tempo winds down accordingly to accommodate the extra detail in the passage beginning 'a courtly dance'. Robinson's writing is delightfully apt and expertly tailored for singer and pianist. Gracefully lilting triple rhythms can be allowed to swing naturally. Another satirical twist in the text is mirrored in the music (Example 1); this phrase may need

Ex.1.

special concentration since here the piano part is not so helpful. The setting of 'down in a rush' is also a nice touch, as the rhythm suddenly hurries along with the words. The triple rhythms rise and become more arching and legato ready to change into Scotch snaps on 'quartz watch'. Springboard syllables are again used expertly. The free section of spatial notation now begins. The singer should not be put off by the appearance of such passages for they give him a wonderful freedom and the chance to tailor phrases for individual nuances, convey subtle ideas too difficult to be notated exactly, and to evolve his own interpretation unfettered by rigid rhythms. The accompaniment is limited to sparse, sustained chords; the inside of the piano is used for interesting acoustic effects. Here the performer has the opportunity to sing cantabile in contrast to the neat, precise, rather thin tone suitable for the rapid articulations of the outer sections. The range is extremely wide and intervals will need careful tuning. Word-setting is exemplary in its sensitivity to syllables and their vocalisations. A high E flat on 'd' of 'divisions' must not be pushed too hard, and neck and jaw muscles should relax immediately after. A descending melisma on 'full' is particularly gratifying.

The final section of the piece reverts to strict tempo, though which tempo is not actually made clear. Presumably it is the last slightly slower one, since there are many notes to fit in. Singers with a good coloratura technique will need it here. The 'legato' marking indicates that repeated demisemiquaver melismas should not be articulated; intrusive 'h's are most unsuitable. Notes should be joined together in groups of little 'whirls' which run along the palate easily and naturally without gripping the throat. The effect should be hypnotic, so mouth and jaw should be kept still. This is the most complex passage for the singer, although there are plenty of repetitions and the piano helps with pitch. The syllables are rather subtly and unexpectedly distributed across beats to create flexibility within the *perpetuum mobile* of the whole. The music starts to point appropriate consonants, leading up to a repetition of 'd's, as at the very beginning; it resolves on to the same major 3rd and returns to the more stable key of the opening centred on F major. As the texture gradually thins out, phrases become fragmented and the piece comes to a natural, delicate close. It dies out very softly, still up to tempo.

I am greatly indebted to my colleague, the tenor John Potter, for drawing my attention to this amusing and touching piece. It is the perfect vehicle for a young singer wanting to spread his wings a little. The piece should have a wide appeal, especially and most importantly to a young audience. Companion pieces in a programme should therefore be chosen with similar intent. *Music as Climate* could be slipped into a 'light music' programme including folksongs, cabaret songs, show songs or ballads. It could be sung as a most refreshing and striking contrast in a Classical programme, perhaps better with French and English rather than Austro-German music. It would be even more suitable, because of its obvious stylistic influence, to juxtapose it with various kinds of American music, both popular and classical.

## *Songs in Praise of Krishna*
(1970)

### George Rochberg (born 1918)
**Translation from the Bengali, edited by Edward C. Dimock Jr. and Denise Levertov**

T V; M IV
Soprano
Duration 35'

This ambitious and masterly cycle of 14 songs is, as the composer says, operatic in concept; it runs the whole gamut of emotions, portraying the love story of the beautiful girl Radha and the god Krishna of ancient Indian legend. It is a rewarding vehicle for a gifted performer as there is every opportunity to display the widest variety of technique and dramatic colouring and mood, without putting any strain on the voice. The musical idiom is highly individual, richly chromatic and yet not difficult. The warm romanticism mixes with strong Asian influence in a fascinating blend of styles that is most appealing and successful. The composer's numerous and meticulous instructions are immensely helpful to the performer. Rochberg obviously understands the vocal mechanism extremely well, and, despite the length of the cycle, he succeeds in maintaining tension and interest throughout. Most songs are quite brief, except for the opening song and those towards the end. The performance is quite a marathon for the singer, but it repays every effort and is sure to make a thrilling effect. An extrovert performer will particularly relish the challenge. The fact that the voice pitches are doubled or discreetly cued throughout in the piano part is a tremendous bonus; this eases many of the worst difficulties, except in the case of the last and most demanding song.

The three characters who speak through the mouth of the soprano soloist are the two lovers and an old woman messenger, whose task it is to mediate with Radha on Krishna's behalf. The different styles of vocal delivery are of dazzling variety and should prove exceptionally stimulating to the performer. The piano part comments on, underlines and links the texts; it is flexible and full of character. As the composer has said, some of the songs are like recitatives, some are arias or ariosos and others are straightforward songs with piano and voice as equal partners. The voice is used lyrically and with exceptional sensitivity to the softer colourings, and even the dramatic climaxes avoid undue stress and strain. The love music is passionately sensual, tender and erotic; only Krishna's contributions are in a more restrained and distant vein. The contrasts are always perfectly judged.

## 1. Hymn to Krishna (I)

The first piece opens with a parlando recitative, half-sung and half-spoken. The singer must let the lines flow naturally, almost as if chanting rather dolefully. The ends of phrases are shaded downwards with slight glissandos which create a perfect crooning sound. There is no glossary, but certain conventions of notation of this kind are now standard practice and the singer may thus make certain assumptions with regard to their meaning. The composer marks 'very thin voice' for the *poco adagio* passage. It is a good idea to think of a forward, almost reedy and rather starved sound without vibrato. The notes ring out properly if placed forward. The Asian mood is anyway more appropriately caught by keeping vibrato to a minimum. The *mezza voce* phrase beginning 'The hope of my life' can be covered and made more distant in contrast to the reedy sound; all these lines are unaccompanied so the dynamics can be very soft. Long and short stresses are carefully differentiated by rhythmic nuance. Extra care must be taken to ensure that the text is clear, particularly in the high passages. The piano weaves a flute-like monody in between the vocal lines, sometimes with long cadenzas to mark the singer's transitions of mood.

Quarter-tones occur in a half-sung passage. Again there is no glossary, but they are clearly notated (Example 1).

The composer's directions as to expression make his requirements

Ex.1.

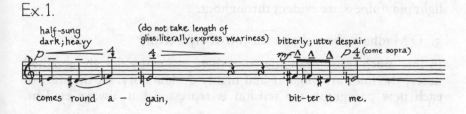

abundantly plain. Ample time is given to place the quarter-tones; they are directly preceded or succeeded by glissandos and so there is just a fleeting moment in which to enjoy the effect. The quarter-tones are later placed without a slide to follow and the singer must be careful to limit vibrato. In such speech-like settings quarter-tones are perfectly appropriate to convey natural cadences and inflections in the voice at the ends of phrases. They are fascinating to listen to and, if placed as they are here within the voice's natural speaking range, not as difficult to sing as they might seem.

## 2. Hymn to Krishna (II)

This more straightforward song carries an air of flexibility. The voice part is graceful and smoothly undulating; the piano follows the voice with simple chords and unisons of both rhythm and pitch. The high, floating *pianissimo* on 'looking' may need to be practised with some care. Dynamics are most subtly graded and varied and of the utmost importance. The high climax to the song may pose a problem of stamina. The phrase must be sustained very smoothly through to the final long F sharp on 'itself'. This last crescendo is not ideally comfortable and requires good breath control, but the relentless accents on each note do help.

## 3. Her Slender Body

Krishna here is 'quietly ecstatic' and talks in tiny fragments at the normal pace of speech. The occasional high notes must not be over-dramatised. It may be difficult at first to achieve the right parlando effect. The feeling of suppressed intensity must not be exaggerated; the notes have to be poised perfectly and naturally. The recitative ends very softly, *sotto voce*, testing the singer to the full and creating a most original atmosphere.

## 4. As the Mirror to my Hand

The abundance of wide intervals and flattering portamentos makes this a delicious piece to sing. It should spring lightly along, providing enjoyment through the athleticism of the melodies which lie naturally and easily in the voice. Each sudden *pianissimo* will need careful attention to achieve the desired effect. An irrepressible vitality and light playfulness are evident throughout.

## 5. O Madhava, how shall I tell you of my Terror?

In this much more dramatic song there are many fiercely accented notes; the lines are angular and highly declamatory. At the start of each new paragraph the tension is repressed but always evident, culminating in an almost unbearably breathless effect. Individual words are vividly painted and all details of the text are heightened by the composer's sensitive use of the subtlest expressive markings which make his intentions clear. Both tempo and mood fluctuate constantly in this dramatic arioso. The decorative melisma on 'dark' at the end is marked 'poco non vibrato' to make sure the singer's tone has an Eastern quality. The final passage gently releases the tension of the preceding terror-struck outbursts.

### 6. Lord of my Heart

The song is highly passionate, sensual and extrovert. The effect of the ravishing sudden diminuendo on the ecstatic, high G which slides up to G sharp is subtle and hypnotic and as erotic as the quotation from Debussy in the piece by John Casken. The composer's instructions are as explicit as ever: 'sultry, a suggestion of coyness mixed with simple acceptance', inviting the singer to use her interpretative imagination and respond to the challenge. The music becomes exultant and wildly impassioned; although the line rises high in the voice it always leaps down again and therefore does not tire the singer. The sudden *pianissimo* on 'flow'rs' on high A is much easier if the singer lingers over the 'l' and makes no attempt to pronounce the triphthong; 'ah-oo-ers' should be blended to make 'ahs'.

### 7. I Brought Honey

This is a bitter outpouring of rage and feelings of betrayal. The first line is deceptively simple until at the highly effective quarter-tone on 'sweetness' the mood suddenly twists into one of anger and suffering (Example 2). The lines of the furious *allegro* section are wide ranging.

Ex.2.

The word 'smoulders' is highlighted by another significant quarter-tone. When the fast tempo returns later the suppressed *pianissimo* tone should have a breathless, almost spitting sound. The ending is wilder still and very loud; the mood of desperation is uncontrolled. A superbly arching final phrase makes a striking impact.

## 8. My Mind is not on Housework

The composer instructs that the delivery should be generally distracted, erratic and unstable. This is another recitative without barlines which progresses in a series of declamations, punctuated by cascades of piano figures which need not be exactly synchronised with the voice. Radha reflects vehemently on her fate and what she has lost. For the low A flat on 'woods' the *sffz* helps to propel the singer into the note before there is time to be tentative. Moods and timbres change rapidly and this is a real test of the singer's flair and adaptability. She imitates the flute with delicate melismas as before. The 'cold, surreal' passage describing the effect of Krishna's flute is truly chilling, and the violent ending is meant to shock the listener. The singer should throw caution to the winds when negotiating the final hocketing on 'sea' and toss away the grace note with abandoned relish (Example 3). The tension must not be allowed to flag.

Ex. 3.

## 9. I Place Beauty Spots

Relief is provided by the graceful but halting appearance of the old woman as messenger. Her shortness of breath is depicted in the music. The singer should not exaggerate to the point of caricature as the music speaks for itself. The vocal lines are sparse but precisely detailed. The sudden lustful, joyous outburst at the end is somewhat unexpected.

## 10. Shining One

The old woman speaks again. This tender, beautiful song (marked 'lucid, radiant') is intended to have a seductive and winning effect on the disillusioned Radha. Sensuous images and sounds in the text can be fully enjoyed. The atmosphere must be rapt and persuasively wooing with as sweet a tone as possible.

## 11. My Moon-faced One

Krishna speaks again, remotely and clearly in soft, gentle fragments of vocalising, as in the third song. The scena is subtle and fleeting and the atmosphere may be difficult to capture since the dynamics are so delicate. Purity of voice is essential; there must be no breathiness or full vibrato. The sound on the high notes must be a mere thread, trailing into silence. This tiny song probably requires a higher degree of technical control than any of the others.

## 12. Beloved, what more shall I say to you

Radha is in warm and loving mood. The piano is again more closely linked to the voice and often in unison. The supple and satisfying lines are beautifully contoured; glissandos make the effect even more mellifluous. Contentment gives way to bitter reflections of loss and loneliness. A difficult, soaring line may be hard to enunciate without constriction. The throat should be kept well open always, especially for the high B flat on 'see'.

## 13. Let the Earth of my Body

A swinging, one-in-a-bar waltz feeling is asked for in this exuberant song of passion and sheer sensuality. The images of the text are highly erotic; the woman glories in them as she sings without constraint. The final bravura cadenza is stunning and lies wonderfully well in the voice (Example 4); broad, sweeping intervals such as these are always spectacular.

Ex.4.

## 14. O my Friend, my Sorrow is Unending

The final lament is an extremely poignant and apt ending to the drama. Long, keening phrases follow one another. Intervals of the 7th and 9th are abundant as the voice part reaches up only to drop again in a series of gently plaintive cries which become stronger and then subside. Then follows the final anguished outburst: 'Cruel Kama pierces me with his arrows'. The fierce, angular and forceful lines recall the eighth song. The violent high B flat should be searing in its passion. Voice and piano then alternate flute-like figures with reiterated ostinatos, which the composer asks the performers to treat as upbeat grace notes. The scene dissolves into quiet contemplation and a feeling of unreality, as the flute sounds gradually disappear into the distance. It would be appropriate to sing the final phrases without vibrato in a crystal-clear and bleak style.

A major cycle of such substantial proportions can hold its own at the end of a concert. Its exotic atmosphere could blend well with contrasting items influenced by the East, for example Frank Bridge's settings of Tagore. Russian music would make a good foil. It would be interesting to put the short *Poems of Tagore I* by Naresh Sohal in the same programme. A really pithy 20th-century programme could feature Rochberg's cycle in the first half and after the interval Messiaen's gigantic *Harawi* which is exotic in a different way. The piece requires a singer of real stamina with a strong stage presence. The audience should be fascinated by the work's vibrant colours, shifts of atmosphere and enchanting vocal effects.

# *Celebration of Divine Love*
## (1961)
### Malcolm Williamson (born 1931)
### Text by James McAuley

T V; M IV
High voice
Duration *c*.22′

Malcolm Williamson's most exciting (and neglected) song cycle is a tremendous *tour de force* for both singer and pianist. (The composer himself is a formidable player.) The visionary and fervently religious text is matched by music of the greatest variety of mood and texture, full of character and dynamic rhythms. Although the work runs continuously, its many subsections are clearly defined and the interest never flags. The influence of Messiaen may be traced in Williamson's style, especially in rhythmic features, characteristic harmonies, and the powerful conviction with which the general feeling of spiritual exaltation is sustained. The listener is carried along by the natural flow of pace and drama. Words and music are always well integrated, giving both singer and pianist ample opportunity to display their talents. Rhythmic vitality and drive are counter-balanced by expansive cantabile passages. As might be surmised, the cycle puts the singer's stamina to considerable tests and the initial practice sessions should be set well apart to prevent fatigue. Short concentrated periods of study, split up into sections, are better than repeatedly singing through from start to finish. Many details of rapid rhythmic and syllabic articulation will prove admirable exercises in their own right. The broad sweep of the phrases extends vocal technique considerably in an expansion of resources which will exhilarate and reward the singer. The overall effect is one of infectious vitality and musicality.

After a rhetorical, introductory outburst from the pianist, the singer undertakes a lengthy and gripping unaccompanied passage, to which the additive rhythms contribute swing and flexibility (Example 1).

This particularly crucial and difficult passage contains the most complicated vocal rhythms in the whole work. There are fine examples for word-painting and the singer must project the series of colourful images with complete clarity. Tone should be bright and true, with a feeling of disciplined pliability and always plenty of presence. The word 'tree' at the end of a phrase may prove awkward at first, but a rolled 'r' should help. All melismas should be sung legato.

The following *andante* section is relentless, its impetus provided by constant staccato quavers in the piano, while the voice moves smoothly (often with stresses across the bar-lines) in a fairly low register. Young voices may find it difficult to penetrate the texture and the accompanist should be especially sensitive here, since the right-hand chords rise above the vocal line. The graphic word-painting continues, as for example in 'creaking carts lurching'. The short rests which punctuate the line must not always be used as an excuse to take full breaths as this might result in gustiness and impair the clarity.

There is always enough air remaining in the lungs to effect short phrases and these are often much easier to control without the encumbrance of too much breath. The intensity gradually increases. Dynamics must be carefully graded and although there is nothing marked after the initial *piano* in this passage, a slow crescendo is surely implied. The vocal melodies have a portentous, ceremonial air. A recitative-like phrase brings this rhythmic passage to an abrupt end with a strong but simple declamation accompanied by harp-like arpeggios. The darker images in the text give rise to music of greater rhythmic complexity and correspondingly darker colours in the voice. The double-dotted rhythms are in unison with the piano's left hand. Details of style will need special practice: staccatos and accents, as well as the rapid succession of percussive syllables. All the composer's markings must be heeded scrupulously. The phrases flow more smoothly and the section comes to an end with a particularly grateful cadence with the piano's final left-hand chord before the opening piano solo passage is repeated.

In the next *allegretto* section the shadings in the music give maximum verbal clarity and attack. Sibilant consonants contribute to the heightened excitement. Phrases of arpeggios dart up and down in an exhilarating way. The double-dotted rhythms of the *andante ritmico* passage coincide with a sense of foreboding in dramatic music which is not at all difficult for the singer. The work's most exquisite moment then occurs: an introductory phrase sets the stage for a voice from the darkness and the singer is given full rein in the rewardingly spectacular and ravishing *pianissimo* phrase (Example 2). There could hardly be a

Ex. 2.

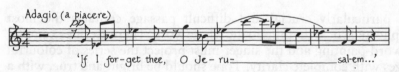

'If I for-get thee, O Je-ru——————sal-em...'

better way to approach a high C: as part of a smooth, arching melisma which floats upward on an open vowel. This is highly characteristic of the composer's understanding and love of the human voice. Williamson's cycle, and this passage in particular, may be more comfortable for a soprano than a tenor.

In the *lento* section the singer can control legato with ease, aided by particularly well-designed word-setting with grace notes to clarify syllables. The verbal details must never be allowed to disturb the long, shining phrases that follow. The composer again shows his sensitivity to a singer's needs in the perfectly placed, gently flowing unaccompanied line after the piano's bravura outburst. This memorable passage comes to a radiant, ecstatic close as the voice gradually descends, surrounded by warm E major chords.

The next Allegro trips along spontaneously and creates the problem of fast articulation which allows very little time to breathe. Syncopations point the text as the music builds up, again incorporating the composer's favourite arpeggiated melismas which are a joy to sing. It is somewhat difficult to punch out the words 'there Holy Poverty with Joy resorts' clearly at this moment of high tension. The consonants can be used to maintain the intensity if they are placed forward. There is a slackening of pace to *Andante lento* for another dramatic recitative. Its tessitura is well judged for clear diction and in general this is a particularly impressive passage for the voice. The piano gives discreet support with occasional chords and flourishes. The vocal lines become broader and expand so that the singer's full range can be exploited in a strenuous series of high, sustained *forte* Fs in a climactic outburst. The tone needs good support from beneath to avoid the temptation to clench the throat and thus tire the voice. The throat must be kept relaxed despite the need for clear enunciation. After this the voice suddenly drops down for a short, tongue-twisting phrase at a frenetic pace in unison with the piano.

A smooth tender song in 3/4, marked 'andante con moto', provides contrast in its simplicity. The mood becomes more exalted at the words 'For He shall come at last for whom we yearn'. The sudden subsequent fading to a rapt *piano* is most moving and potentially problematic for the female voice. It requires some skill to keep the sound well forward and thus avoid trouble. The 'mm' in 'communing' provides a welcome chance to sustain a smooth line. It would be a great pity to spoil this special moment. The warm cantabile line rises to a spontaneous 'Rejoice' on an augmented 4th from B flat to E. Two rather longer phrases must be carefully studied to grade the climax properly. 'Who knows what wanderer' are not easy words for a soprano, in particular, to sing loud at the top of the stave as the 'w's involve so much lip movement, but the effect is vibrant. A fragment of a welcome melisma curves up to high A. Pitches for the final declamation on the augmented 4th are found in the piano's reiterated *fortissimo* chords which precede it. Other pitch problems may occur in this work but help is usually available in the piano part and the music has a strongly harmonic orientation.

This major work cannot fail to make a lasting impression and it should be placed centrally in a programme, perhaps at the end of the first half. It is also suitable for a church recital. Care should be taken not to spoil its impact by including anything else too weighty. To introduce the work, a group of Purcell songs and arias would set the mood ideally, as would the lieder of Mendelssohn or Schumann. As the audience has to concentrate for a long span, they will need a break after the performance of this cycle. Something in complete contrast should be sung after the interval: French songs – Poulenc, for instance – or shorter songs from the English romantic period. Any delicate and fragmentary piece, such as settings of Japanese poetry, would be perfect. It would be fascinating to juxtapose *Celebration of Divine Love* with some of Hugo Wolf's settings of religious texts. If the music is all to be from the 20th century, an intriguing contrast would be provided by an extremely sparse work, such as the David Bedford work in this book and perhaps the John Cage items. Recognition of this important and satisfying work is long overdue.

# *Eight Shaker Songs*
## (1985)

### Lyell Cresswell (born 1944)
#### 19th-century Shaker texts

T V; M IV
High voice
Duration *c*.15′

The work of this New Zealand composer is full of boldness and originality. His use of the voice is highly imaginative and sometimes strenuous, but when the awkward corners are mastered, the results are stunning. Cresswell's style exuberantly defies classification, but it has an Ivesian iconoclasm. The music is entertaining and easily accessible. This cycle will refresh and refurbish the repertory of any singer, and particularly one in quest of more unusual works which are not too difficult. Voice and piano roles tend to be stark and simple with overt religious fervour. The third song is more virtuosic and spectacular; the sixth requires stamina and vocal resourcefulness in the spoken passages as well as those which are sung; and in the final 'Vision Song' the articulation of the fast note groupings is rather demanding. All the songs are brief and exceptionally well contrasted. A most exhilarating vehicle for the performer, this work will rouse the audience.

## 1. The Bugle

The bugle is depicted in the piano by a repeated F sharp while octaves are pressed down silently to produce harmonics and a G sharp clashes against it in jagged rhythms. The voice enters singing leaping 'Oho' fanfares in spiky, repetitive patterns of notes (Example 1). A primitive,

ritual tone without vibrato is appropriate. The sound should have a cutting edge, almost as if the singer were shrieking; this is not at all dangerous if the tone remains clear. The repeated high B flats should be squeezed out separately but not attacked violently each time.

## 2. Song of Humility

The composer states that in this song precise synchronisation of voice and piano is not necessary. The accompaniment, which is pedalled throughout, moves slowly and dreamily; a loud sudden attack occasionally penetrates the hypnotic flow. The voice's floating *pianissimo* phrases drift flexibly over the piano texture. The profusion of liquid consonants (especially C) facilitates legato singing. The song should be performed freely and with ease, particularly since the singer is not fettered by strict co-ordination with the piano accompaniment. The ideas in the text seem to arise spontaneously with natural and uncalculated emotion. In contrast to the first song, the tone is warm and more open. Tuning must be exact, as there are unexpected close chromatic intervals. There is perhaps scope for a subtle crooning to emphasise the legato; this would certainly seem stylistically apt. A classical drawing-room style of presentation is to be avoided at all costs.

## 3. Dismission of the Devil

In this extremely exacting song, the wild abandon of the thunderous repeated chords on the piano contributes to the general din that celebrates the dispatch of the Devil. The singer must adopt an uninhi-

233

bited and lively approach to the scooping glissandos and highly decorative lines.

Chromatic intervals and rhythmic details require careful study. The pacing depends on how fast the singer can articulate the repetitions of 'good riddance' in the rather troublesome semiquaver sextuplets. It is effective to keep the short fast notes well forward; an almost glottal attack on each note, though not standard singing practice, is highly appropriate to the raw energy and possessed atmosphere of this song. A somewhat primitive delivery (though this should not be overplayed) will enhance the impact.

### 4. Verdant Groves

The plain lines which weave a slow counterpoint between voice and piano, provide an immediate contrast to the previous song. The voice has just two deceptively simple phrases, which move softly up and down in close chromatic steps; they require a pure and particularly sweet tone. The volume increases to *mezzo-forte* for the highest point which centres on a high G. It is quite difficult for a soprano to keep an open tone while clearly enunciating such words as 'here' and 'sweet'. With its touching simplicity and grace, this song is an ideal central point for the work.

### 5. Funeral Hymn

This is the most ambitious and taxing song and it demands considerable stamina and power at a very high range. It is a most impassioned dirge, with divergent moods, and it requires relentless commitment throughout.

The song builds up slowly with great dramatic effect, rising to its first climax on a high G sharp on 'away'. The dynamics must be finely graded to maintain the momentum; the audience's attention must be held through the rests in between phrases. The lowest section may present some problems. The intensity must be sustained and a younger singer's voice may sometimes be less secure in this lower region. Diaphragm and stomach muscles will be needed to support the sound and to avoid any possible strain on the throat. An unwavering, even tone is essential and this may require much practice. An aura of the blues pervades the long triplets of the next section which can be swung slightly in the style of jazz or spirituals.

The final verse rises to the highest pitch of emotion as the slow-moving *fortissimo* lines encompass a procession of searing high Cs. These passages are not as impracticable as they may seem at first. Once the throat is open, the notes remain close together and can be joined smoothly. The lines must not be disturbed by jaw and tongue movements and the effect should be thrilling. The obviously strenuous passages which gradually build up through this extended song should make the listener respond to and become directly involved in the singer's physical exertion. The song makes a superb breathing exercise. The most difficult ending is that of the word, 'sting' on a long, high B flat. The 'ng' should be sung quickly to avoid pinching the throat. If the singer imagines a yawning position throughout these last phrases, there is less danger of losing stamina at the last hurdle. Some special training of support muscles before singing this song will prove an advantage and is strongly advocated.

## 6. Keep the Fire a-burning

The toccata-like piano part creates a feeling of urgency. Although relative pitches of notes are suggested around a central single line, a singing tone is to be avoided and the singer actually shouts. The ornamental melismas in Sprechstimme will need to be treated with care (Example 2); to come across clearly they should be articulated

Ex.2

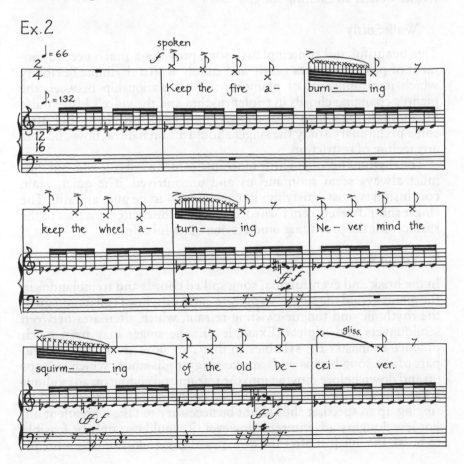

drily (as in Indian singing), directly on the throat. Air must be strictly controlled: the less breath the better. The singer should aim for a metallic timbre and make the most of percussive consonants (for example, 'burning' and 'squirming') for rhythmic clarity. The second part of the song, which is sung rather than spoken, continues the wild exaltation of the first. The venomous ejaculations are fast moving and biting. If the air is forced, the singer will feel discomfort. The final phrase is hurled out, spoken once again, with rapid articulation of the last melisma on 'Believer'. Each singer will have to work hard to find his or her individual way of achieving comfort and security. It is a good idea to space out practice sessions to avoid becoming tired before everything is properly assimilated. A small amount of strain or stress is inevitable (as with learning a new Bach aria, for instance), but it is important that the singer does not neglect work on support muscles which may well need to be exercised particularly for this piece as any slackness will be ruthlessly exposed. This is therefore a most instructive as well as an exciting song.

## 7. Walk Softly

This beautiful and contemplative song provides a much needed moment of peace. It moves gently and calmly with a rhythmic flexibility which is reminiscent of plainchant. The relationship between the piano's changing chords in triplet rhythm and the voice's faster pulse in common time, also with triplets, may cause problems, but after some preliminary study the singer should attain natural flow and lose any feeling of restriction.

The rhythms become a little more intricate towards the end, but they must always seem spontaneous and uncontrived. The quiet, plain conclusion is most satisfying; its execution must be pure and still. The singer should never seem rushed, even when the excitement rises to the surface, for the prevailing mood is one of joyful calm.

## 8. Vision Song

In the brisk and eventful final song spiked chords and tremolandos in the piano herald the singer's *a piacere* entry on a low D glissando up to the rhythmic and tongue-twisting refrain, which alternates between semiquavers and triplets (Example 3). The singer may need much practice to master the syllables so that they flow neatly. The second part of the song begins with an even bigger glissando, which swoops up and down before moving into the refrain and ending on an exultant B flat. The main problem is finding the right moment to breathe. When singing up to speed, it should not be necessary to take a breath at all. For less doughty adventurers, however, it would certainly be feasible to break the line just after the downward glissando and take a breath

Ex.3.

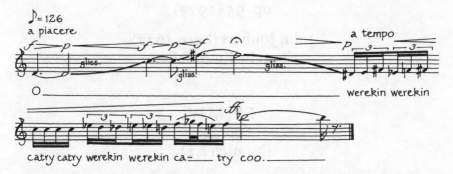

immediately before the 'tempo' mark. The singer should make an exaggerated slide ending with a kick, so that the dramatic impetus is not lost. If a breath has to be taken then it is best to do so boldly rather than surreptitiously. Boundless exuberant confidence is of prime importance to bring the work to a triumphant close.

This song cycle is particularly stimulating and unusual. Such pieces are greatly needed in the concert hall. There is no doubt that it is most effective at the end of a recital, perhaps after songs by Charles Ives or other American composers. To start the concert Paul Cooper's *From The Sacred Heart* (Chester), a wonderfully effective set of Gospel songs, and less strenuous than the Cresswell, would be ideal. Cresswell's cycle should not be performed beside works of a polite drawing-room nature or conventional lieder and art songs. The first half of the programme, however, could consist of more traditional fare so that the piece makes the wildest of contrasts after the interval.

# The Turning Wheel
## op. 95 (1979)

### John Joubert (born 1927)
### Text by Ruth Dallas

T V; M IV
Soprano
Duration *c*.23′

Joubert's substantial and moving cycle alternates between mellifluously comfortable vocal writing and passages of forceful energy. The latter are somewhat taxing for the soprano voice because of the number of words that are sung loud at the top of the stave. A certain amount of skill will be needed to prevent vibrato from obscuring the texts. It is wise to practise the piece at well-spaced intervals, gradually getting the lines to sit more easily in the voice and keeping enunciation crisp and efficient so that there are no delays in reaching the vowel sounds. Some moments in the fourth song are apt to stick in the throat at first; the sixth song, however, is by far the most demanding and will need individual work at a softer volume to avoid exhaustion. The limpid lines of the final song provide welcome relief. The musical idiom is mainly traditional; the textures are rich and colourful and often teasingly chromatic, to the extent that some pitch orientations need special care. Rhythmic co-ordination, too, will take some time to become smooth, but the result should be very exciting. The cycle is well constructed for balance and variety and is an impressive and characteristic achievement from this excellent and thoughtful composer.

The piano writing is bold and extrovert for the most part, with very tightly controlled rhythms. So much of the music is intense that the singer must be very careful not to force accented notes or syllables in her enthusiasm. It may not be perceptible to the listener if breathiness creeps into the voice in dramatic moments, but the singer could eventually suffer strain because of it.

### 1. Headlands in Summer

The agile and springy vocal line makes it necessary for the singer to concentrate on the subtleties of intonation and close chromatic intervals. There are quite a few foxing moments to trap the unwary. Tuning is absolutely vital so that the lines are clean and clearly defined within the surging impulse of the rhythms. There is ample opportunity for characterisation of the images in the text. The wide variety of dynamics will repay close observation. The quiet section beginning 'Holding the ripening flower' is particularly beautiful; its effect is made simply and with a pure tone, using consonants for their sensuous qualities. The tumbling melisma on 'fall' must be tossed off in one legato whirl. Apart from intonation problems, the song makes an untroubled start to the cycle.

## 2. Autumn Jig

This perky, folklike song is not as easy as it might seem at first. Much control and dexterity of rhythm in the placing of rests and consonants will be needed. The song must of course seem to flow with complete effortlessness, but this will only be achieved by meticulous attention to every interval and careful grading of tone quality through phrases, especially those with crescendos and diminuendos. In such fast-moving, lively music, breaths should be kept to a minimum. It is permissible to take a breath after 'day' in the penultimate phrase (an opportunity for a particularly rustic lilt in the music will be lost if one is taken after 'bride'), but it should eventually be possible to take the whole phrase in one; this is certainly desirable. The clipped staccato on the first 'skip and hop' must be neatly timed, with the 'p's exactly in the gaps so that rhythmic control is preserved.

## 3. Narcissus

This delightful recitative-like scene is most original. A poised, floating *pianissimo* sound must be sustained through most of the opening section, but consonants must be brought out with especial clarity to enhance the feeling of rapt concentration. The lie of the lines (in the middle of the voice, centring on B and moving no higher than E) means that a good technique will be needed to keep them running smoothly without sticking, especially at such a soft volume. The contrasting, fast middle section, accompanied by shimmering tremolandos on the piano, must have a trumpet-like brightness in the voice for its fanfare-like lines. The *rallentando* must be skilfully gauged for the return to the slow music. This time the bird's call is depicted in the vocal line and the effect is most arresting (Example 1). The perfect 4th must be scrupulously tuned. The whole closing section, as it winds down to a hushed *ppp*, must be expertly controlled and the quality of sound must be flawlessly pure.

Ex. 1.

### 4. The Remarkables, Queenstown

This turbulent and majestic song evokes another image from the New Zealand landscape. Jagged rhythms in the piano hammer out the introduction. The singer's first two phrases contain very fast crescendos from *piano* to *fortissimo* as the wheel gains momentum. The forceful syllables must be handled carefully and perfectly timed. Many of the lines leap around excitingly over a wide range; some start high and then drop later, which is more comfortable for the voice than the other way round. Tremendous urgency is maintained to the very end. It must be noted that in the last half the vocal dynamics are surprisingly light. The piano provides an exciting series of broken chords and scurrying triplet figures. Singer and pianist will have to work extremely hard to achieve co-ordination. Balance may be a problem near the end when the vocal line drops lower into the piano texture.

### 5. Meditation in Winter

Very careful counting is needed for this song as the piano's two hands move a semiquaver apart, making it rather difficult to follow the beat. Above this, the voice floats in a finely wrought line which is not at all easy to pitch. It focuses on the register break (top F to F sharp), a particularly vulnerable area with regard to intonation. It is also a little difficult to enunciate such words as 'With sand-paper leaf' at that pitch. It may be some time before this feels comfortable or the singer finds it possible to clarify words without feeling constricted in the throat. A singer with a really good technique will have the advantage here. Throughout much of the song a good legato has to be sustained through phrases which contain juxtapositions of explosive consonants ('bright fruit', 'fade from') which may disturb the line if care is not taken. A separately articulated style is, of course, more appropriate for the 'Footsteps from the street' section.

The phrase 'I ponder a common thing' again centres around the break area; it will be awkward at first and somewhat tiring. The singer may need to take more breaths to avoid tautness. The leap up to the loud 'wak'ning' works very well although the singer must be careful not to squeeze the staccato 'ng' ending too tightly. The final *pianissimo* phrase must be brought off coolly and deftly, making its point by understatement.

## 6. The Sea

The driving 12/8 rhythms of the piano part cross the singer's 4/4, testing both skill and musicianship. The soprano's line is again high, and it is a good idea to bear in mind that too full a vibrato may blur the pitches. A more instrumental technique is ideal with a bright and resonant sound that is precise and easily manoeuvrable. Small breaths have to be taken strictly in time, as in Bach arias. This will prove an excellent training exercise in muscular control and dynamic energy; the voice must be supported to avoid the kind of exhaustion that results from gripping neck muscles instead. This exciting song is potentially hazardous.

## 7. Song in Spring

The ending of the cycle is most poignant, starting with smooth, low lines which gradually gather in intensity. There is much detail to be observed in dynamics and accents. As the activity increases, there are some final hurdles to be negotiated: for instance it is not easy to project 'Cried that I could pipe' and 'Hurrying like ants' clearly as they both start on high G. In the longer phrases near the end the singer must put some thought into deciding where to breathe (Example 2): it is feasible

Ex. 2.

to take a breath after 'ran' or 'old', but neither is ideal. The very last phrase is potentially dangerous. The singer will need much stamina to negotiate it in one breath, especially as it ends on a high G on 'spring'. (It is unfortunate that this word, so often found in songs, should be such a particularly uncomfortable one to sing high. The 'ng' sound is always a problem; the triple consonant start is also difficult, although rolling the 'r', is helpful.)

This cycle is a clear example of a work whose quality deserves the extra effort that it is undoubtedly necessary for it to feel vocally secure. Its musical and dramatic effect is undeniable and it is a most important addition to the repertory. It should be placed at the end of the first half of a recital. Preceding items should be chosen to warm up the voice. Some French music (Debussy or Poulenc, in particular) would lift the voice well and prepare it for placing syllables forward with precision. German pieces are perhaps less suitable, whereas early Italian music would be excellent, as indeed would Handel's arias. The second half could include another work in English, perhaps a piece which flows in a continuous span by contrast, but it should not be too long. John McCabe's *Requiem Sequence* (Novello) would be a good choice. As a complete change of style, songs by Cage or Ives could be used to round off the evening.

## *Sun, Moon and Stars*
### (1978)

### Elizabeth Maconchy (born 1907)
### Text by Thomas Traherne

T V; M IV
Soprano
Duration *c*.10'

Elizabeth Maconchy's enchanting and lyrical short cycle of four perfectly contrasted songs is written with complete mastery and integration of style. Tone colours and placing of the voice are heard very keenly. The text is beautifully set to make the voice glow with bright resonance. The writing shows craftsmanship, control and delightful spontaneity. The piano writing is warmly sonorous in a clear texture, ideally complementing the voice. The cycle is especially suited to a young singer with an easy ability to make high sounds float out into space, although a warmth of tone is needed rather than a boyish quality. Audiences are bound to fall under the spell so subtly woven by this most distinguished composer at the height of her powers.

### 1. Sun, Moon and Stars

Rhetorical phrases on the piano prepare the way for the clear and telling entry of the voice. A visionary atmosphere is set, with a sense of heightened spirituality and wonder. The first two phrases, though recitative-like in their rhythmic variability, must not be allowed to blur the slow pulse already set up except in the *tenuto* on the word 'beautiful'. The tone should glow naturally on words such as 'rare' and 'delightful', and the singer should take full advantage of liquid consonants. A new, slightly slower tempo begins as the wonders unfold. The vocal lines move gracefully up and down. It is easily possible to make a full, resonant sound on the low notes for the word 'mine'. The lines are then inverted so that the phrases end on high notes, climbing with a rapt, characteristic *piano* on the word 'stars'. The approach to it – an upward leap of a 9th – is ideal, allowing the singer to poise the note. Another exhilarating high note is flung into the air on 'mine' (high G) at the end of an exultant outburst. The recitation continues, alternating moods of quiet poetry and introspection with irrepressible shouts of joy. There is a decorative triplet high on this very word. The singer should allow the legato sound to ring out like a peal of bells.

The final section of the song, marked 'Più mosso, semplice', is calmer and inwardly radiant. Clarity of line is all important here. As the music rises to a climax, the singer must decide whether to breathe after the word 'so' or after the more difficult 'cream' (Example 1).

Ex. 1.

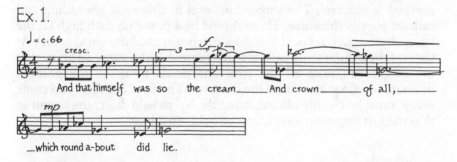

Rolling the 'r' acts as a lever but some practice is needed to find the right sound on the 'ee' vowel without constricting the throat, especially as there are more percussive syllables to follow. It is easier not to disturb the line by breathing during these more strenuous moments. Maintaining the legato through 'And crown' with another 9th leap is especially difficult. It is perhaps advisable not to take another breath until after the word 'all'. The last few words must be delivered in a most simple and unaffected manner so that the song ends gently and serenely in preparation for the excitement to follow.

## 2. The Hill

This thrilling song sweeps along with relentless impetus and seems hardly to stop. An exuberant rhythm of eight quavers to the bar (grouped irregularly as $3 + 2 + 3$) is set up but this is occasionally interrupted by passages of 5/8 (divided $3 + 2$). This movement is thus a real test of composure and rhythmic control. It will need to be practised many times, but as it is such a short song and moves at such a breathtaking pace, the singer should have great fun grappling with its problems. A natural swing is eventually achieved and the singer will become less selfconscious and apprehensive about counting. At the initial stages it is a great help to mark the vocal part with the symbols commonly used by conductors: a triangle for 3-quaver groups and a 'downbow' sign for 2 quavers. This makes it easier to keep track of the piano part while singing long notes. Piano and voice have to be as one as the slightest hesitation will destroy the bouncing rhythms. There are few rallying points; the voice's duplets within the triple beat have a slight braking effect and provide a chance for the performers to come together. It is tempting to rush but this would result in chaos. The composer intends the song to dance along with a one-in-a-bar feeling throughout. The performers should choose a speed at which the voice's opening coloratura runs naturally. The 'echo tone' (composer's marking) of the repeat of the opening call which sounds an octave down, must be clearly poised. The opening and closing virtuoso passages for the singer, which centre on recurring, shining high Gs, are marked 'a piacere'. The singer can revel in this most rewarding and radiant part of the voice. There should be a pause on each high G; the strict rhythm in the vocal line does not begin until the word 'soul'. At the end the exhilarating cadenza-like flourish fades away ad lib so that the singer can take all the time she needs to make the gradual diminuendo float away into the distance. The final delicate 'and come away' must be cleanly placed, using the 'w' to help direct the sound so that the last lingering long C can be held effectively.

## 3. Solitude

A very clear tone is needed for this series of passionate statements. Tone must not be allowed to spread and blur the line even when it dips low in the voice. Once again the suppleness of the vocal writing is greatly to be admired and it makes the music enjoyable to sing. Wide intervals help to keep the voice relaxed and secure. The singer may need to take care with the quintuplets and pitch too may cause problems. Melismas on key words heighten their dramatic effect, for example 'woeful', 'skies' and 'shined'. It is helpful to take a quick breath immediately after 'shined' so that the singer is not rushed while poising the difficult notes of the second part of the phrase. To clarify the verbal sense and preserve continuity, the singer should think through the following rest. After leaning on the word 'yield' it is possible to snatch a breath without spoiling the line.

In the final section the mood suddenly changes on the word 'felicity'. The outburst is anguished and the agony should be conveyed with great impact right up to the final echo on 'O where'. The composer again uses the term 'echo tone' to indicate a lessening of vibrato, thus creating an almost sepulchral, distant effect. The last note is marked 'morendo'. The final E flat may prove difficult at first. It is helped greatly by the subtle accent on the preceding G flat, which provides a welcome springboard for a straight thread of sound which can easily be controlled. The singer moves into the fourth song without a break, accompanied by the piano which continues in the same harmony. There is just time to take a good breath before moving into the soft serene legato opening of the last song.

## 4. Clothed with the Stars

The pitch of this very short epilogue is extremely wide ranging and the piece requires intense control and concentration. Only the two short decorative triplet whirls which accentuate important notes deviate from the slow, inexorable tread of the music. A shimmering quality is required for the frequent high notes; the entire song should glow brightly in a mood of intimacy. The second phrase ('Till you are clothed with the stars') should ideally be sung without a breath, but it requires a very solid technique to avoid wavering on the final moments of the long high A. The effort involved in singing a long phrase makes the support muscles work so hard that the next phrase is thereby also improved. A perfectly co-ordinated beginning, with good technical control, gives the singer a satisfying sense of security. The last phrase should also be spun out in one breath as only the smallest amount of air is needed to sing the final *pianissimo* word 'jewels'. The triplet swirl and initial consonant help to place the sound, but the singer must avoid pinching the tone. The 'l' can be used to keep a forward sound.

The lyricism of this fine addition to the English song repertory is most alluring. The superb texts are set in an assured way that enhances the natural resonances of the words. The piece will be excellent in a varied recital of British music. It is succinct and therefore fits well between longer items without being swamped. The singer may prefer to begin with something bright and extrovert, so that the voice is well warmed up and prepared to sustain a steady tone through Maconchy's long and voluptuous phrases. Some Purcell arias would make a good start to the programme.

# *Peripheral Visions*
## (1984)
## George Nicholson (born 1949)

T V; M IV–V
Soprano
Duration *c.5'*

It is a pleasure to find a lighthearted work which is satisfying on many different levels and is unerringly tasteful; its humour is never misjudged or heavy. Nicholson's piece is delightful, and both a joy and a challenge to sing. As well as the usual devices found in a song written in a contemporary idiom there are a few special effects: breathiness and inhaling audibly, for example. These are clearly indicated in the music.

The cycle is not strictly English, as the third song is in French. One cannot but suspect that this poem is described as anonymous to conceal the author's identity rather than because the author is not known to the composer.

The vocal part contains the most agreeable effects which work perfectly in agile and pliable lines of many contrasts. The piano part is also highly detailed and has a great deal of character. Its sharply delineated lines are more often percussive than cantabile, with strongly defined rhythms and a Webernian concentration of varied dynamics within short spans, as in the voice part. The pitches are certainly not easy for the singer to learn, although quite a number of subtle cues come from the accompaniment. The straightforward accessibility of the words is a great boon. The general concept of the piece makes it immediately enticing on first perusal. The singer should not be deterred by the detailed work which is necessary to achieve a deft, seemingly effortless and accurate performance. The brevity of the work means that the task will anyway not seem too irksome.

## 1. Abroad and at Home (Jonathan Swift)

The musical treatment of this forthright and mordantly amusing tale of 'Thomas who was cudgel'd' by his wife is highly appropriate. The words are set clearly and boldly. The voice is only lightly supported by the piano until the suitably noisy and violent ending.

The beginning is marked 'Declamato' and gives the singer a good, uninhibited start. Hard, accented staccato notes emphasise the strong vocal line. There is no need to breathe before the word 'life' on an accented, *fortissimo* low B flat: there is a crescendo through the gap just before it and the rest is there to throw the word sharply into relief and to increase its impact. Breathing before the low note is in fact likely to make it disappointingly gusty and forced. A clear tone is always more penetrating.

A contrasting, slower passage, marked 'calmo e amabile' gives interpretative scope. The crescendo and diminuendo must be keenly observed. Words such as 'squabble' and 'rabble' are ideal for rhythmic precision and bounce. The phrase 'and the rabble' is picked out in a delicate *pianissimo marcato* sound which requires some skill and as little air as possible. The 'pomposo' marking for the next phrase is helpful to add colour to the interpretation, as is the glissando up a 7th, immediately followed by a *pianissimo* downward 9th. The singer should enjoy the athleticism and supple lightness of feeling, finishing with a firm though still very soft tone on the held note at the end of the phrase. The triplets of the 'pianissimo cantabile e legatissimo' line can be casually swung as a foil for the crisper passages. This is particularly apt in the small phrase that is almost spoken, where a half-crooning effect is needed. It is perhaps more practicable to close the diphthongs on 'wise' and 'counsel' early and also the final 'l' of 'counsel'. The sound then closely resembles a natural spoken delivery. The following *cantabile* phrase can be exaggerated a little to make a contrast.

The singer must pay attention to such subtle details as the *fortepiano* on 'three' (which is highly effective on this middle B flat), and the variety of accents. Care must be taken to place the final consonant of 'challenge' exactly on the beat to allow time to continue *fortissimo* while keeping within the rhythm. To make the following crescendo easier, it is probably advisable to snatch a very short breath in the rest. The 'n' of 'morning' should be percussive rather than liquid to make the sound precise and to accent the note as marked. Closing on to 'ng' on such an awkward note (high F) can sometimes be uncomfortable. The singer should not allow the sound to become throaty or set too far back and the 'ng' should be enunciated as swiftly and neatly as possible.

A slight risk of constriction could also mar the extremely loud final paragraph. A steely sound on 'Three duels' is most appropriate and the tone should be kept incisive and straight. In the diminuendo and crescendo on 'home' the 'm' should be explosive. The hard, clipped staccatos for 'and was cudgel'd' will benefit from a dry, airless sound, as will the deftly placed final words 'by his wife', marked 'preciso'.

## 2. I passed by his garden (Lewis Carroll)

The rhythmic lilt of this very brief song must be maintained despite the steady tempo. The vocal style should be deceptively sweet and smooth until sudden small rhythmic and dynamic shocks begin to occur and sly details punctuate the even flow. As in the previous song, the staccato phrases should be clear and straight in tone, without breathiness. The singer should not take a breath in each rest. Crisp enunciation is essential, and the consonants of the text are again helpful. It is particularly important to avoid taking a breath after the word 'meat' as a bumpy restart might disrupt the poised return of the triple rhythms (Example 1). A glottal stop at the start of 'owl' is desirable.

The Pan-ther took pie-crust, and gra-vy, and meat,—While the Owl had the dish as its share of the treat.

Throughout this charming song, there are many consonants which provide a springboard for bouncing on to the next beat, and rhythms are beautifully judged to fit the words. It is always enjoyable to feel the syllables under perfect control, timed to arrive precisely at the right moment. The huge downward glissando on 'growl' is exhilarating. A sudden decrescendo on the word is followed by a crescendo to *fff* on the slide down to low B. A rolled 'r' will encourage both a good tone and an appropriate snarling effect. The singer should not be tempted to strain on the low note; diaphragm control will help produce a stronger sound. The most unusual vocal effect occurs on the last few words, 'eating the owl', which have to be mouthed silently with much relish.

### 3. J'ai peur (Anon.)

The French language facilitates the precise forward placing of short syllables. Glissandos are again used well. The composer's brief instructions and markings of mood aid the interpreter. A wealth of detail is packed into this tiny fragment. No pitch is determined at the end of the first downward glissando on 'chaud', so the tone may be allowed to croon a little, arriving at a more spoken sound to accord with the 'parlando' marking. The breathiness asked for on 'Dans la glace' is not too difficult to achieve for such a short while; a little push can be allowed on each note to mark the separate short staccatos. A high E is a good choice of note for a wan and ghostly sound without vibrato. In the quarter-tones the singer should bend the note smoothly down and then up again. A ghostly, thin sound will help to achieve clarity. Much concentration is needed to stop the note from going too far and the intervals becoming semitones. The notes should be kept very close together and virtually no air should be used.

In the next phrase there is a comfortable glissando up a 9th to help the voice to relax after the admittedly strenuous task of controlling the quarter-tones without vibrato. The earlier quarter-tone on D, 'whisky chaud', is made easier by using the Scottish pronunciation of 'wh' and a long hissed 's', together with a lingering 'ch' ('sh'), all of which impel the tone directly forward so that it can be dropped carefully into place. It is difficult to articulate the written-out, very loud rhythmic trills on high B flat and A on the word 'moi'. The sound must be cutting and clear, and the fast notes should run evenly. It is inadvisable to alter the shape of the mouth or throat once the open vowel has been launched; the tongue should not be used to articulate the separate notes. Intonation at such a high pitch is sometimes difficult to clarify, which is perhaps why the composer has asked for 'quasi vibrato'. The 'audible inhalation' comes as a short gasp. It is unaccompanied and so there is no need to exaggerate. The singer must find a way to make a good sound without gulping in too much air or jarring the voice. It is safer not to take another breath before the next entry.

The last two notes are in Sprechstimme, both with trills, and the last one fades away to nothing. This is an especially striking and original effect and quite difficult at first. The safest way to achieve it is to allow a gentle pressure on the larynx to produce a slight rattle (the natural vibration of the vocal cords without air). This vividly conveys the croaking effect of the feared 'flu'. Very soft dynamics can be controlled down to the finest thread at the end.

## 4. Call (Incident at Weekend Party) (D. B. Wyndham Lewis)

The brief, heavily ironic finale has a mock march for its main theme. The vocal lines are much more conventional than in the other songs. The ending is very gentle and expressionless as the song fades to nothing. It is unaccompanied and requires a pure tone and precise timing.

Though brief, this cycle parades a large selection of vocal effects, each of which is used with expertise. It is tremendous fun to be presented with unusual tasks when the end result is so satisfying and effective. A singer with a youthful, clear-toned and flexible voice is ideal and too heavy a vibrato would be unsuitable. *Peripheral Visions* is highly enjoyable for both performers. Despite some intricacies, the general effect is fresh and immediate and its conciseness is a virtue. The piece would be a good complement to a more romantic song cycle. French music would also go well in the programme.

## *Beata l'alma*
### (1966)

## David Blake (born 1936)
### Text by Herbert Read

## T V; M V
### High voice
### Duration *c.*12′

*Beata l'alma* is an important addition to the vocal repertory and it deserves to be heard more often. It makes considerable demands on the singer and the piano part is also a *tour de force* (the composer is an excellent player). Some very high passages contain awkward strings of syllables and they may be more easily and smoothly negotiated by a tenor. Diction could certainly be a problem at first. A good deal of preliminary work is needed for the piece to fall naturally into place, but the effort is well rewarded. Many special, expressive effects and changes of vocal timbre have to be mastered with patience, and the practice sessions should not be too lengthy because of the risk of tiring the voice. The work is through-composed in one long span. A piano solo divides the two poems of the text, and there are several sub-sections where the music varies greatly in character.

The fact that this is a 12-note composition should not lead anyone to suppose that it makes a purely academic impression. It is fascinating to observe the variety that can be achieved within such a disciplined framework. Passages of tremendous dramatic power contrast with phrases of sheer lyricism, and there is scope for myriad tone colours and unusual vocal highlights.

After an atmospheric introduction on the piano, the voice's first task is to state clearly and simply the twelve notes of the series in soft semibreves, each marked with a pause. It is very important to keep the tone pure so that the centre of every pitch is unmistakable. The length of the notes is determined by the singer, and optional breath marks are provided after every short group. Some of the notes may be sung legato, particularly the lovely glowing sweep up a 7th on 'its lapse' (the 'l' can be used to place the note perfectly), but too expressive a tone quality is to be avoided at this early stage. The high A will bloom naturally and must not be pushed. Almost immediately the singer begins a strong declamatory phrase, ending in hissing, staccato semi-quavers on 'voiceless bodies', contrasted by the soft, melting legato of the following fragment. It is not particularly easy to sing the word 'echoes' smoothly and some practice will be necessary to iron out any bumps after the 'k' attack. The simplest phrases do tend to require a good technique and vocal security.

A lively, fast tempo may present some difficulties in the enunciation, especially in the higher tessitura, although it will certainly be easy to colour the word 'screech' appropriately. The rhythmic bite of this passage should be emphasised. Breaths must be dexterously timed. In particular, the many percussive sounds in the text, such as 'ghoulish stumps' or 'opaque filth', may at first cause some stress and breathless-ness. The word 'filth' is snarled in a heavily accented Sprechstimme (Example 1). It is most dramatic if the singer flings out this note with

Ex. 1.

abandon. A slight *ritenuto* gives time to recover before the music hurtles back, *fortissimo*, to tempo. The writing becomes more virtuosic, with some thrilling high notes, and all dynamics should be carefully observed. The word-setting is exemplary in its expressive-ness.

The pace must not be allowed to slacken during this hectic passage, and when the dynamics become gentler this should not be a reason for letting the tempo sag. A high B flat on 'woeful' is a joy to sing, helped by the careful placing of the 'w'. The long, staccato triplet on 'flutter-ings' is delightfully practical and works with ease. It will take some time for the smoother, recitative-like passage for the voice, with little accompaniment, to flow naturally with accurate pitching. Any grop-ing or smudging is painfully obvious, and nor should the singer adopt a cold, clinical approach. If the low register is secure the slow climb down to a low A on 'ease' is greatly preferable to the upper octave suggested as an *ossia*. To negotiate this difficult vowel change the tone must be covered and rounded, and spacious rather than thin. The timing of the breath after this is crucial as it prepares for a leap up a major 7th. The approach is ideal for a poised and relaxed arrival on the upper note. The word 'why' has to be sustained for some length and the note (C in the middle register) thus has to be launched perfectly. The driving, rhythmic writing makes a brief return and the piano is as always an equal and dynamic partner.

By complete contrast, the final stanza of the first poem is free and flexible without strict rhythm; the phrases undulate naturally, almost as if they were improvised. A flourish of grace notes arches up to a high G, and the mood is warmly expressive and contemplative for a short while. The piano gives the merest support with single pizzicatos. The final three phrases require detailed attention for exact observance of the expressive features. The *sfp* on 'bones' can be exaggerated without risk of throwing the note off balance. In the subsequent intense phrase it is best if a breath is not taken until after the word 'ferns'. The *subito pianissimo* will be more easily achieved if air is kept to a minimum. The last, unearthly sounding succession of high legato *pianissimo* notes is at once the most difficult and the most electrifying moment in the whole work (Example 2). The voice, without any vibrato, should send shivers down the spine.

Ex.2.

The shorter second part of the cantata brings a gentler mood and a more relaxed vocal style which is mostly radiant and cantabile. The long phrases take the singer to the limit of capacity; they should float, with good support, and no explosive consonants should be allowed to interrupt the flow. The accented 'love ends in hate' is a temporary contrast and it should be well brought out. A most unusual passage suddenly employs free notation for the voice part. The singer chooses the pace and spacing of syllables according to the natural stresses of the words, in a monotonous (*senza espressione*) timbre, uniformly *mezzo-forte*. The pianist remains in normal strict notation throughout, but provision is made for an adjustment if necessary (by holding a chord and adding extra repeated notes) so that the parts coincide neatly at the end. It is good for the singer to practise the discipline of avoiding any rhythmic unisons with the accompaniment and deliberately interweaving with it.

An ecstatic swoop at 'Art ends' up a 9th on to a high B needs a pure, open sound without any suspicion of pinching, especially for the 'nds'; it is safer to delay these consonants until after the note has finished, if the acoustics will allow a slight overhang to cover the gap. (This piece of cheating is justified by its guarantee of more safety and vocal beauty.) The soft high spans of the final phrases are strenuous for the performer, even more so if support muscles slacken and not enough energy is conserved. Considerable physical strength and fitness is needed to hold everything in place so that the sound can float out freely. The range plunges up and down luxuriantly but very gently and poise must be maintained. The final, almost parlando casual phrase is most effective in its simplicity; it must be delivered emotionlessly as instructed.

Blake's compelling work gives the performers full scope to exhibit their powers and range. Its perfect length makes it an ideal recital item. Stylistically *Beata l'alma* suits Austro-German lieder of all periods; it would make a strong and interesting contrast to more conventionally romantic English music. Some technical work will be needed to master some of the more difficult sections, but the singer will learn a great deal and benefit from stretching the technique.

## *Cantata II – Three Lovescapes*
### (1967)

### Jonathan Harvey (born 1939)
#### Text by F. T. Prince

T V; M V
High voice
Duration *c*.15′

Jonathan Harvey's substantial settings of Prince's visionary texts are an important addition to the repertory. Romantic and full-blooded in vocal style, they contain strikingly modern vocal features which are spectacular and practicable at the same time. The songs were originally written for the touching artistry of the late Annon Lee Silver, a Canadian soprano; they need a voice of warmth, flexibility and wide expressive range and an interpreter of open-hearted assurance who is able to communicate directly and unaffectedly with the audience. The scope of the work is immensely satisfying for both pianist and singer. This is one of the most outstanding works from the earlier period of Harvey's versatile output. The musical idiom achieves a perfect fusion of Romantic and contemporary elements; the influence of the Second Viennese School is strongly evident.

## 1. Handfast Point

The opening is marked 'Andante delicato e espressivo' and in the light transparent textures of the piano staccato is used for extra clarity. The voice part features gently dropping, reiterated semitones. The lines are almost hesitant at first but they expand excitingly as the song develops. The sudden *pianissimo* after the crescendo on 'breeze' is ideally set: the final 'z' guarantees a perfect placing of the word 'touches' which is staccato as well as *pianissimo*. The vocal lines become smoother and more luxuriant as the piano's textures grow more complex. Details in the text are subtly highlighted by brief rests and fleeting changes in dynamics. The concentration of 'ee' vowels on high F sharp may make it difficult for the singer to keep the tone warm and open. The 'k' of 'kiss' must not be allowed to jar the sound but should be enunciated quickly and not too forcibly. After this warm-blooded moment the music becomes more fragmentary, both in voice and piano, until much more decorative and extended vocal melismas begin to emerge. Short rests are aptly used to delightfully expressive effect, but the singer should not take a breath in each one. The kicking of the little grace notes is particularly attractive. The final line ('Through the dry grass', sung *pianissimo* on E) will be most effective if sung with as little vibrato as possible. This exquisite song is full of interest.

## 2. Monologue of the Sibyl of Cumae

The extended dramatic scena gives the artist ample opportunity to show her or his mettle. A wide range of pitch and dynamic variation is covered; unpitched speech and Sprechstimme are used to heighten the intensity of the drama. The vocal part veers from smooth, closely-knit phrases of a small intervallic range to the most extreme examples of wide angular leaps, spectacular mood changes and wildly diverging dynamics.

An ominously suppressed beginning, focused in the middle range, points towards a sudden surge of passion and vocal tension. Explosive staccato notes at the ends of phrases can be made to cause a sharp shock. The colourful and evocative consonants enhance the vocal timbre throughout. The thrillingly high passage at 'Capes and beaches laugh and clap their hands' must be delivered with panache despite the somewhat awkward placing of the word 'clap' on high C. The singer should not prepare for the final 'p' too soon or try to make too full a sound. The percussive slap of the explosive consonants encourages a clear, trumpet-like delivery and preserves rhythmic vitality. Although it is marked 'fortissimo', this phrase must not be forced; at such a high pitch, the sound is naturally piercing. The singer is allowed to rest immediately after this strenuous phrase as attention is focused on the pianist; the role of the piano is most important throughout. The subsequent Sprechstimme passage is splendidly conceived; the line is pitched on or just above a normal speaking range and moves at a pace that allows an almost natural style of delivery. Pitches must however be carefully plotted. The phrase should be sung in one breath. The singer can bounce off the final soft 's' ('z') of 'sorrows' on to the accented word 'flash'. All consonants should be emphasised in strict rhythm; support muscles should be employed fully as in normal singing so that no energy is wasted. Spoken effects must always be firmly projected. Nothing is more disappointing than a sudden lapse into unsupported vocalising with no sense of physical involvement. The piano figurations sound more hectic and improvised in whirling groups. The voice soars above them, scooping up and down in a series of exhilarating lines whose wide intervals must be studied with care. The succession of triplets on 'scurrying music' is especially problematic; the notes should be sung smoothly without undue pushing. Although the appearance of the leaping staccato phrases which eventually reach up to a high C (with an *ossia* B flat) is daunting at first, the vocal part is in fact satisfying and enjoyable to sing, especially when the line cascades spectacularly down from the top. As the melodies continue to dip and soar it is important to control vibrato. With such exciting vocal writing, there is no need for the singer to use added expressive devices. The words are full of suggestive resonances and the images are most clearly conveyed by means of a pure and translucent tone (Example 1 overleaf).

In the *più lento* passage the lines are less angular and stay in the middle range. (Tempo indications are not abundant and it is often left to the performers to choose speeds which are comfortable and musically and dramatically viable.) The soft tone should not become too warm as the marking is 'desolate'. A plain quality of sound without vibrato is very effective. The singer must pay scrupulous attention to the accents and subtle nuances, as the paragraph rises to a more passionate and intricate expansion; the line drops to low B and then suddenly snaps off. The spoken passage works comfortably: since the piano part is low pitched there is no need for strong declamation. It

Ex. 1.

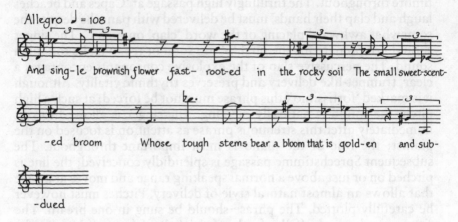

always sounds convincing when the singer makes the most of sibilants by clipping words short.

Light and buoyant lines at a rather high tessitura lead up to a much more taxing melismatic passage containing more high C's, which should not prove too strenuous as long as a good pace is sustained. In the delightfully mellifluous phrases glissandos are used to create vocal comfort and the lines now become more decorative. One high C is held for five beats, but the composer is then sensitive enough to allow the singer to drop immediately down a major 7th to rest the voice and increase its flexibility. Most of the phrases in this central passage show Harvey's flair for sympathetic vocal writing. Lines which swoop up and down, especially those with glissandos, always exercise the voice in a healthy way and make it supple.

The ending shows a deft touch in the sweeping phrase with the *piano* staccato notes on 'our disgrace'. The delivery tends to sound more precise if the singer has little breath to spare. The close of the song brings a return of the Sprechstimme, this time on a monotone F. A strange chanting effect is required, but difficulty arises when the notes at the end of the phrases have to be held. When a pitch is sustained it sounds as if it is sung, and in Sprechstimme the singer must in some way create a distinctive tone without singing. A hint of breath can be added to the voice, or the note can be bent slightly off pitch to inflect it in a more natural way. The actual written pitch of the note must be touched first.

## 3. Dark Night

The last song is as substantial as the first two. Both singer and pianist will need considerable resources of energy and concentration to sustain the intensity through such broad spans of musical argument. It is a challenging exercise, particularly for those recitalists who are somewhat unwilling to stretch themselves and often choose undemanding miniatures rather than more expansive pieces.

Grace notes embellish the low and sombre phrases of the opening paragraph. At the words 'O happy chance' a light staccato and dexterously poised sound interrupts the dark, smooth lines. Many of the short rests that punctuate the phrases improve vocal clarity, emphasis and aim; they are not intended to be breathing places, although several small, almost imperceptible breaths can be taken instead of one large one, supplying both rhythmic and physical needs. It is good to acquire the habit of taking small sips of air without gasping. After many fragmentary phrases the vocal line finally expands on to a long and loud high B flat, leaving the voice well lubricated for the following delicate, very soft, single attacks. The long crescendo on F on the word 'night' is helped by its approach note which is a 7th lower. The singer should be sure to join the two notes seamlessly so that the F is well focused from the start. The diphthong should not be closed early and the ending should be swift. The following phrases are also rather high and it may be difficult to enunciate the words clearly as there are some fast successions of consonants ('than the dawn of', for instance) but the singer should be able to avoid sounding strained. The next section is much more relaxing for the singer as it is low and soft. The *pianissimo* sound floats directly up from its bocca chiusa base, the foundation of well-tuned vocalising. The text is again a great help: many long liquid consonants can be sung through even when the marking is 'ppp'. The phrase starts with the word 'lulled', which is ideal as the singer can use the tip of the tongue and its position close to the lips and teeth to place the entry on the most delicate thread of sound.

The singer must be conscious of the music's pace throughout the song: a steady tread, sometimes solemn, sometimes incorporating sudden flights of lighter inspiration and flexibility. The music must never sound amorphous or unrhythmic. Unfortunately this can often result from too much concentration on detailed rhythmic and dynamic subtleties which interrupts the flow. The almost breathless quality of the fragmentary sections of the song gives it great atmosphere and poignancy, and the final few pages are particularly moving. The text is split further into single syllables in a series of sobs and sighs; each note needs to be plotted with meticulous care and the dynamic markings must be followed with the utmost sensibility (Example 2). The slightest tremor or patch of unfocused sound would be disastrous. The *molto tranquillo* phrase is ecstatic and ethereal; as the notes drop gently and tenderly into place the last phrase curves exquisitely, twisting and arching to a final glissando down a 7th. The rapt finish can thus be perfectly controlled.

Ex. 2.

This powerful and deeply felt cycle makes considerable demands on performers and listeners. It is best placed before the interval, perhaps after a group of songs by Beethoven, Schubert or Wolf. Some early Schoenberg or Webern pieces would complement it perfectly in the second half; the recital should be rounded off with some light relief in the form of shorter songs in English.

## A Penny for a Song
### (1981)

### Nicola LeFanu (born 1947)

### T V; M V
### Soprano
### Duration c.15'

Nicola LeFanu's set of 10 miniatures shows great economy of style. The texts are taken from *The Penguin Book of Irish Verse* and *The Penguin Book of Japanese Verse*; the tenth poem is from *All That's Past* by Walter de la Mare. The work contains many challenges to the singer, and the piano part too is demanding. The first item is a piano solo which appears twice more between songs. The vocal line is fairly complex rhythmically and covers a wide span, but it shows the composer's natural flair and feeling for what is comfortable to sing and rewardingly spectacular. A great deal of variety of vocal nuance and inflection is employed. The singer is given a satisfying range of different modes of delivery to negotiate with ample opportunity to show her control and flexibility and to examine closely the purity of her tone. The sparse textures and delicate rhythmic flourishes of the accompaniment are wholly in keeping with the Japanese flavour of the texts, some of which are Haikus.

The first fragment of song which follows the opening piano solo is unaccompanied. A basically simple and steady line is decorated by uneven groupings which ought to sound improvised. The voice scoops down very low indeed, only to spring up again; such wide leaps are gratifying to sing and limber up the voice beautifully, banishing any initial tentativeness or tightness. The setting of the text is apt. In the phrases 'winter snarls' and 'the seas moan' the low A's should be touched lightly and not pushed; the transitional 'z' sounds help to make the singing smooth. As the still tranquil line becomes even more fragmented, the bar of 14 quavers in the time of 12 has to be gently shaped without accents, as in natural, unforced speech rhythm. The song suddenly becomes more intense and there are exhilarating and wide-ranging leaps in the final section. The legato must nonetheless be preserved, even when widely spaced notes are accented individually. The slow-moving consonants of such words as 'birds', 'wings' and 'freeze' make continuity easier. The fast and decorative hocketing on the word 'cries' should be sung with abandon, as in yodelling (Example 1). It is appropriate to keep a precise edge to the voice and make a more stark sound with little vibrato for the quiet ending; it is very important that the delicate setting of 'the world is ice' is sung very softly.

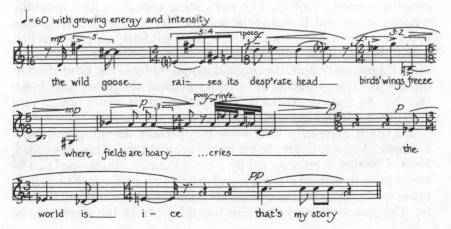

The second vocal fragment is a complete contrast as the sounds are sustained and each phrase ends on a long note. A most skilfully written echo occurs on the word 'ebbing' as the piano immediately quietens to *pianissimo* each time. The effect should be unearthly; it is best without vibrato at that pitch (D on the treble stave) and a thin tone will be heard clearly. At the word 'moonpath' on a lovely arching 10th down from high G to E flat the composer gives the instruction to open lips gradually on the 'moon'. This works perfectly and is flattering to the voice. The atmosphere of this short song is created by its delicate understatement.

The third song is more lively. On the word 'stretching' the singer reaches down a tenth from E flat to middle C. The intervals widen progressively and the last in the first section is a 12th. There is always a luxuriant feeling in negotiating such leaps and vocal suppleness is thereby greatly improved. As in the first song, uneven groupings of notes (in this case semiquaver quintuplets) are used for decoration and emphasis. The intervals will need to be tuned carefully so that the exhilarating effect of all the downward leaps can be fully exploited. A *forte* climax is reached in the middle, but otherwise the dynamics are gentle. The singer should poise herself carefully for the last leap of a 12th at the end which leaves her suspended for much longer on the higher note before descending.

The fourth fragment is quite delightful and very brief indeed. The piano writing heightens the atmosphere with delicate tracery in fast-moving and very quiet semiquavers. The composer makes a special note stressing that *pianissimo* must not be too quiet in this song. The voice's tiny fragments must come out clearly and simply while the piano fills in the detail.

The high piano part (written mainly in the treble clef) sets up a fascinating rhythm in the fifth song. Uneven groupings of semiquavers (reminiscent of Messiaen) alternate with straightforward bars in 6/8, creating a nervous effect. The voice must appear to flow naturally without stress and the singer should not let her necessarily intense concentration be too obvious. The vocal line is fairly simple in the first half of the song. When the tempo slows momentarily, the line becomes more fragmentary until the original tempo returns. The echo effect at the end is rather difficult to interpret because the music goes by so swiftly; the final unexpected 'kiss him' must be deftly poised in a suitably unaffected manner (Example 2).

The sixth extremely brief song is especially arresting and quite virtuosic. A misty, filigree line is traced gently by the piano; the veiled, blurred quality is emphasised by a continuous, sustained pedal. The singer joins in with an elaborate and delicate counterpoint at a slightly faster speed. The vocal line demands good breath control and flexibility. The composer marks suitable breathing places, but there must be

Ex.2.

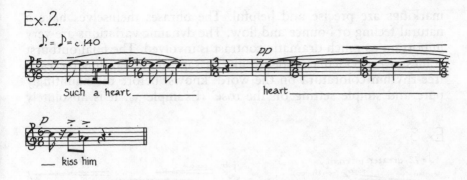

no bumpy entries. The line should flow in a natural, introspective manner, as if the singer were embellishing her thoughts. Singer and pianist come together for the second half of the piece and the voice is now so low in pitch that from time to time it changes smoothly to ordinary speech without undue histrionics. The vocal part slows down at the end as it grows even quieter and then the piano (now very low in the bass) continues the filigree thread of sound, as at the beginning. The ending is barely perceptible, so that the song appears not to end at all, but to continue in the mind after the last sounds have died away.

The opening brilliant piano solo is repeated, followed by a distinctive miniature about cicadas. Subtle rhythms in spiky, staccato phrases, are exactly tailored to the words. A deft, light touch is needed from both performers. Enchanting details in the music point the syllables and heighten accuracy of timing and enunciation. The tone must be kept straight and piercing to suit the text; for the final *dolce* phrase the sound should be slightly warmer. In the lovely phrase arching up to a flattering long high G on 'grows' it is quite hard to sing the last two words 'steeper' and 'still' with a full, round tone; the singer will need to practise this carefully to avoid shrillness.

In the eighth song the composer asks that the quotation in the piano part from Chopin's Prelude op. 28 no. 2 should be played at its original tempo. The singer must gently but firmly control the plain, almost static low vocal line over the piano's legato left-hand melody. This tiny song is a poignant and apt tribute to the memory of Seymour Shifrin.

As a complete contrast, the following fragment of song is loud and turbulent at the start. The vocal part leaps athletically around a wide range. The delicate poise of the downbeat ending on 'silent clouds of stars' is unexpected.

The last short piano refrain leads directly to the final song which, like the first, is unaccompanied and requires some careful preliminary work from the singer. The song opens with dipping, high carillons of sound and gradually increases in drama and presence. Some extremely intricate melismatic phrases may pose problems, but the composer's

markings are precise and helpful. The phrases themselves have a
natural feeling of bounce and flow. The dynamic variations are very
important as much dramatic contrast is involved. The final outburst
comes in a spectacular, cadenza-like passage full of dazzling pieces of
free-rhythm coloratura on the word 'knows' before the hauntingly
pure and simple setting of 'the rose' (Example 3). It is absolutely

Ex. 3.

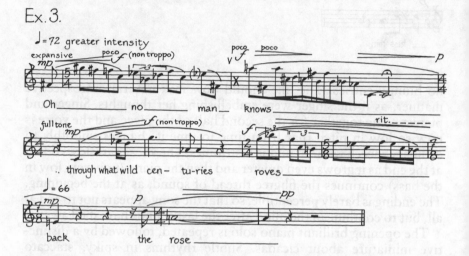

essential that the singer should maintain intensity at the highest level to
the very end as any tiredness or lack of vocal strength at this stage
would be apparent to the listener. The song gives the singer a perfect
chance to show control and artistry. The basic feeling should be of
deep commitment and inner control and concentration; the loud
passages should not be too flamboyant, but must radiate a sense of
harnessed exultation. As the composer says in her excellent introductory programme note '(the songs) are echoes of a world that is always
there if we stop to listen for it'.

This exquisite set of interlocking songs would make an appealing
recital item, preferably contrasted with a major Romantic cycle of a
more expansive nature and surrounded by songs which use the voice in
a more conventional manner, such as the earlier works of Fauré. It is
unwise to juxtapose it with another modern work unless the style is
completely different, as for example in pieces by Cage and Ives. There
are some taxing moments in the cycle, but there is a lightness of touch
throughout which is most refreshing for an audience.

# *i am a little church*
## (1976)

### Malcolm Singer (born 1953)
### Text by e. e. cummings

T V; M V
Soprano
Duration *c*.7′

The high grading of this piece may seem surprising at first glance, but to perform such harmonically static music as this requires the highest skill. There is a real danger of the singer's throat seizing up through tension caused by having to repeat notes at a medium to high tessitura. (E is a particularly difficult note in this respect.) Vocal ease is not the composer's top priority in this most ingenious and delightful piece, but it is however fun to work out and audiences will be enchanted by it. The display of technical skill in using numerically-based systems to produce rhythms and pitches is typical of Malcolm Singer. Other pieces of 'systems music' by him are enjoyable in the same way, for example *A Singer's Complaint* for voice, piano and marimba, which contains some memorable musical and rhythmical jokes. *i am a little church* is one of the most successful settings of cummings's poetry that I have come across. Other composers have been daunted by the quirky originality and innately musical rhythms of the poems, but Singer has caught admirably the sparkle and bounce of this lovely poem; the asymmetrical and ever-shifting rhythms enhance rather than detract from the words. The atmosphere is most beautifully captured. The dynamic markings are sparse: there is a big crescendo in the introduction and a decrescendo to nothing in the piano at the very end. Otherwise, the fact that the voice part is *pianissimo* when low, together with the few markings that the composer does give, might indicate that the intensity may be allowed to rise to some extent with the register. This piece also features examples of minimalism, using repeating patterns, often on one note, in intricately controlled rhythms. The piano occasionally mirrors the vocal part, but otherwise it has plain octaves on the beat, which guide the singer. Such music exercises the performers' concentration and nerves. It is considerably harder than it appears, but the result is most appealing and justifies the trouble involved, especially as audiences are sure to find it fascinating and diverting.

The opening sextuplets across the beats fall naturally and lightly in

Ex.1.

i am a lit-tle church i am a lit-tle church i am a little church (no___ great___ ca- the-___ dral)

the voice (Example 1). The crescendo is the only substantial one in the piece, and it makes this phrase rather difficult for the singer. Having to breathe too often in this music can disturb the rhythmic steadiness. The singer must keep absolutely strict time. The tempo is moderate and there are moments of rest between phrases, allowing the singer to relax tongue and jaw muscles, which may have tightened. (They should not have done so, but the possibility must be recognised.) The slight *tenuto* on 'i' at the beginning of each line in the second paragraph is very important and must be leant on to set the rhythm rolling along. In the high *pianissimo* passages the singer should not use vibrato and should touch the notes gently. To push them will prove instantly exhausting and impossible to maintain. The singer should try to keep the line as undisturbed and as evenly placed as possible. Enunciation could be a slight problem at this tessitura. A thin, child-like clarity of tone is most useful. When the line moves slowly, the liquid consonants can help to keep the placing neat and precise, as for example in 'My life is the life of the reaper'. The low *pianissimo* A is sung with a very gentle head voice. The merest thread of sound will come through as the voice is unaccompanied. Some of the longer phrases are barely manageable and they therefore make useful exercises for increasing lung capacity. They may have to be subdivided for a singer whose breathing technique is not strong. It is always possible to snatch a quick breath before an explosive consonant when there would anyway be a slight bump, as in the phrase 'clumsily striving', for instance. There is a similar possibility after an explosive aspirate such as the 'f' in 'grief'. The ensuing glottal stop must arrive directly on the beat. The rhythms are mostly subdivided into triplets, some of them tied, and it is helpful to practise by drumming fingers on a table-top. A case could be made for using a metronome as it will certainly improve the singer's rhythmic discipline.

In the opening passage of the middle section of the work, the vocal line rises and demands extra care; the range of pitch is wider than in the rest of the song (Example 2). It is difficult to know when to breathe. It is probably best to wait until after 'death', but an alternative would be to separate the 'f' of 'of' and to inhale quickly in the guise of a glottal stop on 'unceasing'. This is preferable to breathing according to the sense of the words, which would upset the rhythmic flow.

Ex. 2.

The line leaps up on 'resurrection'. There is a welcome drop down after the sustained Fs, which could prove tiring at first. The singer's rapt concentration throughout should hold the listener's acute attention. The opening chant starts up again: 'i am a little church, i am a little church'. The next phrase is probably the most problematic with regard to intonation as it lies at the register break. E, F sharp and F natural are reiterated in succession; they must sound as poised and unfaltering as possible in this drawn-out version of the opening lines. The singer should breathe after 'world', placing the 'd' on the beat. As before, a lower passage brings relief, allowing the vocal cords to relax. The small crescendo is important in the very smooth transition from 'grow' to 'longest'. The staccato note on 'now' is exceptionally short, in context, as is the 'ver' of 'forever'. A breath may be taken comfortably after 'spire', or between 'Him' and 'whose'. The line climbs up in major 3rds in the impressive last phrase. A quick breath can be taken before 'His', since an 'h' can conveniently conceal the difference between an inward or outward breath. The piano finally fades to 'niente' on plain octaves.

The overall impression created by the performance must be hypnotic and powerful in its understatement. This demands much of the performer in poise, control and the ability to maintain a calm atmosphere. The piece will exert great fascination and is a rewarding one to prepare. It represents something a little different from the normal concert item and is most refreshing.

The singer will need to be well exercised before singing *i am a little church*, but not tired by too long a preceding item. Early Italian arias or Baroque music are appropriate for this purpose. Romantic music may provide too sharp a contrast, although some new music of a more emotional or expressionistic nature would be excellent. A wide-ranging cycle by Debussy or a group of Poulenc's songs would go very well indeed with this music. The piece makes a very good ending to a concert, or it could be followed by the Barry Seaman work discussed in this book. More settings of poems by e. e. cummings would also be appropriate.

# Ia Orana, Gauguin
## (1978)

### John Casken (born 1949)
### Text by John Casken

T VI; M V
Soprano
Duration 14'

This is one of the most exciting and powerful songs it has been my pleasure to perform. It repays every bit of the considerable effort needed to master the composer's detailed markings and frequently innovative vocal devices. The whole soprano range is used with tremendous skill, making the cycle a marvellous vehicle for a singer of commitment and high standard of musicianship. Many of the technical feats are used with great originality and they illustrate superbly the extremely effective conception.

The cycle has great exuberance and an inherent impetus. It must be timed carefully and not allowed to drag; there are many opportunities for the use of rubato. As might be imagined from the text, the atmosphere of the music is exotic and colourful. The idiom has many features of French impressionism and in fact at the highpoint of the work there is a quote from Debussy's *Cinq poèmes de Baudelaire*. The composer's own evocative text is an amalgamation of French and English, employing much alliteration and the technical and visual images and terms of painting. It is a most vivid and arresting poem with a host of syllables which are especially singable and suggestive of striking vocal effects. The text and music are closely blended in the true lied tradition, yet allowing much more flexibility in phrase lengths. The singer often pauses to dwell on a bocca chiusa or a gentle reiteration of nasal French consonants and gradual elisions from one syllable to another, the effect of which is atmospheric and delicate.

The composer has succeeded in creating an individual and totally idiomatic piano style which suits and illustrates the words perfectly. The part is virtuosic in its own right, whirling and darting with passages of pointillism interspersed with blocks of extremely sonorous and sensuous chords. The effect is decidedly French with strong overtones of more exotic climes. Much is made of faster and slower repetitions of notes. Many now standardised features of 20th-century notation are used. The composer's intent is always clear and a succinct set of instructions conveys all that is necessary.

There is no point in concealing that a good deal of vocal skill will be required. A light, flexible voice will have the advantage in the *pianissimo* passages and, more especially, in singing the quarter-tones. A more vibrant and dramatic quality is however needed for some key moments and when the vocal line drops to low or medium range. A wise composer starts the singer off with a bold, positive entry which immediately brings confidence and focuses attention: the loud, repeated F on an 'a' vowel with a glottal start achieves this perfectly. The composer askes for the singer not to roll the 'r' on the opening word 'Arrows' but instead to use a prolonged version of the 'r' of a West Country or an American accent. In the fragments of French words the singer should always exploit the nasal timbre to the full. (The 'n' in such words as 'cylindres' should not be pronounced.)

Rhythmic co-ordination in the opening passage and in similar recurring paragraphs throughout the piece may cause problems. It needs to be conscientiously worked out and practised until it becomes secure. (The grace notes in the piano part precede the beat.) In the slightly slower 'Time-weary' passage the final syllables of 'weary' go from a specifically notated rolled 'r' to Sprechstimme and then into unvoiced explosive consonants. In the glissando on the Sprechstimme note the sound should croon downwards quite quickly, blending into a more spoken sound at the end. The composer asks for single grace notes to be unusually slow and smooth. Space–time notation recurs frequently in between more strictly notated paragraphs. Phonetics are clearly indexed in the score. It is not easy to manage a perfect transition from 'm' to 'w' (sung 'oo') on the high F with a fairly long diminuendo. The next, lower passage is exceptionally practicable. It produces a booming bell-like sonority, helped by the syllables of the text: 'Breton bourdons'. Again 'r's are to be rolled and they impel the sound comfortably forward. The percussive 'd's and 'b's are similarly useful. The echo effect of the repeated accents on notes without initial consonants can be articulated with some exaggeration. Nonetheless the natural ringing sound must predominate. The whirling flourishes of grace notes must be rapid and join the longer notes they precede. The breathing in this passage has to be well planned to avoid accents which are not marked. All markings of interpretation and dynamic must be observed with great care.

At the word 'Douleurs' the *fortissimo* G which descends with ad lib pauses to low C sharp is wonderfully relaxing vocally. The most successful vocal composers know exactly when the voice needs to rest and Casken provides respite between strenuous passages throughout the piece. There are more intricate, strictly rhythmic passages to negotiate before the voice dissolves again on to longer drawn-out (spatially notated) monotones which elide from one nasal French vowel to another. In the glissando on 'going' the singer must be sure to catch the 'ng' sound in a place which allows nasal resonance to continue through the following sounds. This will seem a very long phrase. Much stamina is needed for the long A flat at the end of the word 'cloisonné'. The preceding melisma with an *accelerando* may prove awkward as the singer has to alight on the high note with great abandon and spontaneity.

The section beginning 'Bold patchwork quilt' is fascinating in its most telling use of explosive consonant groups ('patch' and 'blocks', for example) which are heightened by some rather difficult rhythmic relationships with the piano. The rests must be counted very carefully. There is no need to take breaths in them all; the percussive consonants are must easier with less air. This passage has wonderful bite and impetus but the singer must be careful not to lose momentum. It will take some time to learn the music accurately. Tension is now rising and louder passages are more dramatic than ever. The Sprechstimme marking of 'triangular' almost converts it into a shout. The singer should aim for a dry sound which is not breathy.

The first quarter-tone appears somewhat hazardously on an 'n' sung very softly at the end of a phrase, as are the other quarter-tones. The singer has to bend the note rather eerily to make the necessary, small thread-like and absolutely straight sound. The tongue is pressed firmly up behind the teeth and the sound should not be pushed outwards. This is probably the most difficult note to sing in the whole piece. Fortunately, relief comes immediately in another liberating high G on an open 'o' vowel.

The composer's frequent use of repeated notes gives the singer a good opportunity to enjoy her own resonance and recapture it. The work's highest note, a ravishing B flat, is approached most gracefully in a freely notated passage. The singer has time to poise and place the note using the 'fl' of 'fleurs' to impel her into a good sound which drops at just the right moment during a gentle diminuendo. The following quarter-tone has to be inflected downwards from a high F, creating an unearthly effect. The choice of pitch is excellent for achieving a 'white', thin sound. Quarter-tones tend to be marked 'senza vibrato' which enables them to stand out in sharp relief to the preceding warmer notes. This wonderfully sensuous section ends with a most gratifying climb up to a shining high A flat on 'fleurs'. The quarter-tone on a continuous 'm' bending down from the note is followed by another which moves upwards from middle G at a particularly good tessitura for clarity of pitch without vibrato. In the cadenza passage where the piano repeats a set figuration it is a good idea for singer and pianist to decide how many repetitions there will be before the voice enters each time. As the piano is also very free in rhythm, a distinct signal may be useful to cue the singer in again. This should not be too conspicuous: a glance upwards would suffice. On the word 'where' a held C (an octave above middle C) drops down the quarter-tone. If the sound is kept forward a particularly reedy and distinctive resonance comes through at that pitch. The following *pianissimo* with normal vibrato on F sharp must stand out.

The singer has to hold a very long C on an 'a' vowel with a gradual crescendo. A sympathetic pianist will not delay too much and will make full use of the 'poco a poco più mosso' marking. There follows a lovely atmospheric passage on repeated Cs. In these faster quarter-tones there is no more than the gentlest inflection away from the main note. The oriental feeling of the acciaccaturas which punctuate the line on the word 'going' is unmistakable. The piano flourishes must be well co-ordinated and paced for mutual comfort. There is more use of prolonged nasal sounds as the word 'going' ingeniously changes to 'Gauguin'.

The thrilling climax arrives suddenly and unexpectedly, bursting out of a strict rhythmic passage which impetuously breaks its bounds as the voice soars decoratively up to a wildly impassioned high A. This in turn becomes an exuberant *fortissimo* shriek on the words 'sun-youth'. The singer should not be afraid to let her voice go really high with an open and resonant sound which is not too shrill. The joyous shout of welcome, 'Ia Orana, Gauguin', is ad lib and it must not lose momentum. By this time the singer, after the excitement and stress of the build-up, should feel as if she were at the summit of a mountain and suddenly indestructible. Loud bell-like calls ring out and the tension is not allowed to slacken until that most entrancing moment when the music sensuously dissolves into the quotation from Debussy. The preceding passage must be timed perfectly to make the sudden transition absolutely spellbinding. The melting glissando on 'd'aurore', with its subtle diminuendo, has to be poised with great skill and control to leave enough strength for the warm crescendo as the piano rises voluptuously (Example 1).

Ex.1.

The last climactic *fortissimo* B flat is exhilarating and cannot possibly pose problems since the voice has already been so well exercised. The singer only needs to open the throat and let the sound ring out, impelled by the release of the tongue after the 'l' of 'Couleurs'. The almost unbearable excitement winds down with the lowering of the pitch. The coda has to be sung firmly and simply. The slightly muffled bell-chime effects must be clear in rhythm; the grace notes provide a gentle swing towards them. The final 'n' can be held for as long as is comfortable. An uninhibited performer will create an irresistible and remarkable effect with such highly passionate and colourful material, but this cannot be achieved without a considerable amount of technical and musical discipline.

The songs of Debussy are obvious companions to this rich and memorable piece: the Baudelaire songs are possibly too long, but the *Chansons de Bilitis* would be ideal in mood and length. Songs of an Italianate vocal idiom, such as those of Mozart or Handel, would form a good opening group, as would songs influenced by folk music. Works of a Germanic nature are less suitable. Lighter works, including cabaret songs, would make a good finish to the programme. After such a full-blooded outburst, something less demanding is certainly advisable.

## *Enitharmon*
### (1973, revised 1984/5)

### Gwyn Pritchard (born 1948)
#### Text by William Blake

T VI; M IV
Mezzo-soprano
Duration *c.*7′

*Enitharmon* is an extremely appealing and sensitive example of a style of vocal writing which was pioneered in the 1960s by Berio and others. Proportional notation is employed and the composer's guidelines in the front of the score give clear answers to most of the questions that might arise from a first perusal of the music. Close study of this introductory page is essential and it ought to prove reassuring to anyone unacquainted with such notational methods and symbols. The performers are allowed considerable freedom, and some further guidance for newcomers may be necessary. The composer's attractively neat calligraphy is an added bonus, but the text seems very small in comparison with the notes and bolder lettering would have been helpful. It is advisable for the prospective performer to write out the words in capitals (perhaps underlining with a brightly coloured pen) as initial learning sessions will otherwise be held up unnecessarily. There is also the question of visibility during stage performance under artificial lighting. Practicalities must take priority, for even small handicaps can inhibit the singer's involvement in the stimulating process of working on such a piece in detail.

Nevertheless, the lyricism of the vocal lines and the slightly exotic and very beautiful harp-like sonorities of the sparse piano accompaniment make it an excellent choice for an unusual concert item. A considerable number of effects use the inside of the piano. The harmonic range is deliberately limited, and the singer can check pitches in relation to the frequently repeated chords. Good breath control will be a great advantage as some of the phrase lengths indicated by the composer may seem something of a tall order. Extra breathing places are marked and can be used if necessary, but a few more may still be needed in order to observe the louder dynamic markings where breath tends to be used up more quickly.

A well-judged tessitura and excellent aural sense, including careful setting of phonetics, make this a gratifying work to sing and hear. One or two more unusual effects, such as half-voiced whispering and making sounds on an inhalation, may require special preparation to avoid vocal discomfort. The inward gasps are in fact so well placed that they provide 'official' breathing-space at the right moment. As the composer states, it is very important for the performer to be able to switch flexibly from an extrovert, declamatory style to a more inward, contemplative manner where appropriate. An intense focus on the smallest details is also necessary for the piece to make its fullest effect. Dullness could easily result from too bland an interpretation and the singer must be sure to generate an inner energy which avoids rigidity and to achieve – through a secure familiarity with the music – an improvisatory effect (the composer's aim) in the final version. Exact coincidence of voice and piano is not required, except in a few places which are indicated by a dotted line between the two parts.

Consonants which require special emphasis are underlined, but as they invariably coincide with written accents or staccato endings, this tends to happen naturally. The composer's method of isolating the actual sounds to be sung from the rest of the word and of setting under one note the final consonants of one word together with the beginning of the next can confuse the eye at first, but it does make for very clear enunciation. The syllabic distribution of the text is further complicated by some gradual transitions, often in diphthongs, for which the sign is a wavy line. The pitch must not be allowed to waver and it is merely a verbal device. It is particularly important to keep a legato sound flowing through the melismas and not to lose this through concentrating on the many verbal details which may at first prove distracting.

The composer suggests that the first ligature should last about nine seconds and others can be worked out in proportion to this. By a swift calculation it will be seen that each page of the score should take roughly 30 seconds to perform. As soon as the notes are beginning to fall into place, it is useful to practise each page separately with a stop-watch to ascertain the basic timing, but this must not become a strait-jacket. The distribution of syllables and frequent use of separated consonants is a little unexpected. All queries are fully catered for in the introduction, but it might be wise to add some personal reminders *in situ* to aid initial progress through the score. There are quite a number of points to remember.

In the opening pages a flutter-tongue effect on a rolled 'r' is particularly successful, and grace notes and accents are well-judged. In the singer's first phrase the 'z' sound in 'seize' must not be closed too tightly or it will be impossible to maintain a uniform *forte* sound for the accented repeat of the words 'the golden sun'. It may be necessary to take a breath before 'sun' because the dynamic is generally loud. This is a better solution to the problem than to allow the tone to deteriorate and to become strained or lacking in substance which would cause a crucial lapse of tension at a particularly exciting moment. The alternative of breathing after 'sun' will spoil the small crescendo through 'sun' to 'bears'. All such details must be carefully preserved.

The next opportunity to take a breath is after any one of the repeated staccato Cs on 'so' (Example 1). As the earlier ones are more

Ex.1.

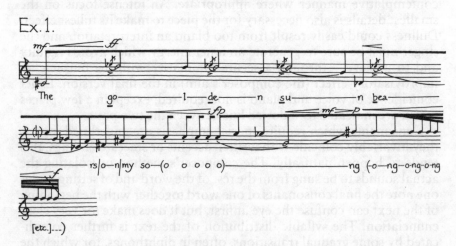

widely spaced they allow the singer more time to refuel to carry her through the strenuous *accelerando* to *forte* on the repeated F sharp on 'song'. The 'ong-ong-ong' provides an excellent exercise for the muscles of the soft palate. The singer must make sure to keep the throat well open and to let the tongue, rather than the jaw do most of the work. If not, an uncomfortable choking feeling will result and the tone will be muffled and well below the necessary level of volume. This whole phrase is one of the most difficult in the work, but once the individual points are mastered, it should fall into place quite easily.

The following phrase begins *ppp* on a high E on the word 'And'. This may seem daunting, but the piano's rippling accompaniment figures at *mezzo-forte* should provide a reassuring cover for any nervous beginnings. The voice is not audible until the following crescendo has gained strength and it is presumably intended to seem as if the sound has come from nowhere. The very soft dynamic marking should perhaps not be taken at its face value. It is important not to waste air in a tentative entry as this phrase rises to *forte* and breath must be conserved. The long decorative phrase on 'spheres of harmony' is sung *piano*, unaccompanied, and it requires special care and security of pitch. The vocal writing is beautifully supple and idiomatic throughout the piece and the effect of the more contemplative moments such as this should be very fine. The glissando up a 7th on a rolled 'r' of 'round' will be easy to sing; the use of other rolled 'r's in the same sentence is particularly well judged. On the last word, 'king', the singer must gradually close on to the 'ng' during an upward glissando and continue through another slow glissando down a semitone. From experience I know that much energy and muscular support are needed to sustain a high-lying 'ng' over a long span and without it, there is a tendency to clutch at the throat. If the singer learns to use the lower support muscles, a most useful habit will be acquired. Many singers do not engage their bodies fully when supporting consonants.

A vocal line of more evenly spaced notes has to be co-ordinated at regular intervals with the piano's patterns of short notes. The left-hand chords are pedalled and the composer must intend to create a smooth sound, punctuated by sharp accents. The vocal lines are very long, and as good opportunities for taking breaths do not readily present themselves emergency action may have to be taken. Accented notes in the voice are marked 'fpp', so the singer can instantly drop to a light sound and save energy. Even so she will be fortunate to sing through to the end of the first 'sing unceasing' without taking another breath. The best place to snatch one is in between the two words, but an accent on restarting must be avoided. A seamless impression must be retained, even though a good breath will be needed before the words are repeated in parenthesis. Sustaining the 'n' and 'ng' sounds will help to keep the tone pure and free from breathiness. When the singer is stretched to the limit of lung capacity, the awareness of the importance of control of every moment of each note becomes more acute, and a more disciplined approach invariably results.

Pritchard uses the helpful glissando and staccato effects throughout the work, but the most difficult tasks occur towards the middle in the two phrases of pitched speech which contain audible inhalations and exhalations on parts of the words 'solemn' and 'silent'. For the half-voiced stage whisper required by the composer the singer will need to place extra breath on the sound (Example 2).

Ex.2.

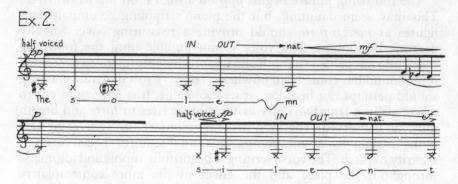

I must confess that I find the inhalation on 'l' in both cases impossible to effect cleanly without the pitch jumping up, but such dangerous moments are not loud and are virtually unaccompanied so it is advisable not to try too hard. Despite the composer's stipulation that exact pitches be followed, he recognises that it is not possible to pitch an 's'. The inhaled 'l's present a similar problem and an unpitched gasping sound may be the best that can be achieved. It is uncomfortable to take more air in than is required. A firmly practical attitude must be adopted, even if it involves simplifying what is written. The singer should, with a few trial sessions, evolve a way of performing the whispered phrases that does not throw the voice off balance for the rest of the piece, which continues in lyrical vein. If the most dramatically effective and comfortable solution is to drop the voice to natural pitch without worrying too much about the exact notes, then this should be sufficient. (It is certainly inadvisable to spend time agonising over something which may be a slight miscalculation. I would even be tempted to ignore the 'in' and 'out' markings altogether, if they cause unwonted stress. The voice has to remain clear and poised for the remaining pages and it would be a pity to spoil them through tiredness.) Fortunately the only other passage that is not sung is one of rapid and unpitched *pianissimo* muttering of the text and this is simple enough.

A low phrase beginning at 'Now my left hand I stretch', loosens the voice for the fast grace notes which work very well. The singer may need to take extra breaths, or perhaps some licence with pacing may be allowed so that her breath capacity is not exceeded. At the exciting, loud high As on 'terrible' the piano writing becomes extremely intricate and fast-moving. This is the highpoint of the work and it is potentially strenuous for the voice. Full advantage must be taken of the extra breathing places provided and of the chance to reduce volume immediately when marked to conserve strength for the climactic notes. The sudden diminuendo will come as a relief from the effort of holding the high notes for so long, something which is difficult for singers with heavier voices.

The work closes with music of dream-like raptness and delicacy. The vocal phrases gently unfold in a long span over a wide range and thus require the most immaculate control of tone quality within the legato sound. There is a danger of slowing down too much and thereby allowing interest to flag. The final long middle C on 'death' may have to end a little sooner than marked. It is never worth risking loss of quality in order to sustain the note to the end. It is extremely important to keep the music moving and to maintain an underlying rhythmic energy throughout. So much freedom of timing puts a heavy weight of responsibility on the performers, and the personal charisma of the individual can make an enormous difference to the work's impact.

*Enitharmon* is an excellent choice for an experienced and technically sound singer who is seeking a more adventurous outlet for her artistry. The considerable amount of detailed preparatory work needed to polish almost every phrase may seem overwhelming but once this early work is done, an exceptionally secure and disciplined performance should result. This is one of the advantages of a notational system that demands an analytical approach to practising. Works written in conventional notation can sometimes be so invitingly easy to read through that the newcomer acquires the habit of singing straight through without stopping. Small details overlooked the first time may be neglected over and over again, and careless slips left uncorrected may become more deeply engrained and hard to eradicate. Slipshod performances of what is thought to be simple music are, unfortunately, quite common. There can be no misjudgments of that kind here. The piece is technically demanding but the effort of such intense concentration should command an audience's attention and respect, and the world of sound it creates is sensuous and stimulating to the ear.

It is best to sing *Enitharmon* at the beginning of the second half of a recital when the singer is thoroughly warmed up and the voice is fully stretched. It would be a good idea to allow the singer to rest afterwards during a piano solo, or instead to perform some simple songs in a lighter vein which do not have long phrases. Some show songs with concentration on verbal details (such as those of Coward, Porter and

Rodgers) or songs from the Berlin cabaret era of Eisler, Weill and Schoenberg would be an ideal contrast. Folksong settings are appropriate for similar reasons.

# Acknowledgments and publishers' addresses

William Alwyn: *Mirages*. Alfred Lengnick & Co Ltd, Purley Oaks Studios, 421a Brighton Road, South Croydon, Surrey, CR2 6YR, by whose kind permission the examples are reproduced.

Milton Babbitt: *Three Theatrical Songs*. Peters Edition Ltd, 10–12 Baches Street, London, N1 6DN.

Alison Bauld: *Dear Emily*. Novello and Co Ltd, Fairfield Road, Borough Green, Sevenoaks, Kent, TN15 8DT.

Robert Beaser: *The Seven Deadly Sins*. European American Music, PO Box 850, Valley Forge, PA 19482.

John Beckwith: *Five Lyrics of the T'ang Dynasty*. Berandol Music Ltd, 110a Sackville Street, Toronto, M5A 3E7, Canada, by whose kind permission the example is reproduced.

David Bedford: *Come in here child*. Universal Edition (London) Ltd, 2/3 Fareham Street, Dean Street, London, W1V 4DU, by whose kind permission the example is reproduced.

Richard Rodney Bennett: *A Garland for Marjory Fleming*. Novello and Co Ltd (see under Alison Bauld), by whose kind permission the example is reproduced.

Leonard Bernstein: *I Hate Music!*. Warner Brothers Music Ltd, 17 Berners Street, London, W1P 3DD and Warner Brothers Music, 9000 Sunset Boulevard, Penthouse, Los Angeles, CA 90069, by whose kind permission the examples are reproduced. (Copyright 1934 by M. Witmark & Sons, 1943 by Warner Brothers Inc)

David Blake: *Beata l'alma*. Novello and Co Ltd (see under Alison Bauld), by whose kind permission the examples are reproduced.

Alan Bush: *Voices of the Prophets*. Stainer & Bell Ltd, PO Box 110, 82 High Road, London, N2 9PW and Galaxy Music Corporation, 131 West 86th Street, New York, NY 10024, by whose kind permission the examples are reproduced.

John Cage: *The Wonderful Widow of Eighteen Springs* and *A Flower*. Peters Edition Ltd (see under Milton Babbitt), by whose kind permission the example is reproduced. (Copyright 1961 by Henmar Press Inc)

Ronald Caltabiano: *First Dream of Honeysuckle Petals Falling Alone*. Example reproduced by kind permission of Rosalie Calabrese Management, New York; score available from Ronald Caltabiano, 60 West 76th Street, New York, NY 10023.

Elliott Carter: *Three Poems of Robert Frost*. Associated Music Publishers Inc, 866 Third Avenue, New York, NY 10022.

John Casken: *Ia Orana, Gauguin*. Schott & Co Ltd, 48 Great Marlborough Street, London, WIV 2BN, by whose kind permission the example is reproduced.

Lyell Cresswell: *Eight Shaker Songs*. Lyell Cresswell, 8 Leslie Place, Edinburgh, EH4 1NQ, by whose kind permission the examples are reproduced.

Donald Crockett: *The Pensive Traveller*. Examples reproduced by kind permission of Serenissima Music Co, PO Box 982, Pasadena, CA 91102; score available from The Unicorn Music Co Inc, 170 NE 33rd Street, Fort Lauderdale, FL 33334.

Gordon Crosse: *Voice from the Tomb*. Oxford University Press, Walton Street, Oxford, OX2 6DP, by whose kind permission the examples are reproduced.

David Del Tredici: *Four Songs*. Boosey & Hawkes Music Publishers Ltd, 295 Regent Street, London, WIR 8JH, by whose kind permission the example is reproduced.

Brian Dennis: *The Exiled King*. Brian Dennis, by whose kind permission the examples are reproduced, c/o Royal Holloway and Bedford New College, Egham Hill, Egham, Surrey, TW20 0EX.

Peter Dickinson: *Extravaganzas*. Novello and Co Ltd (see under Alison Bauld), by whose kind permission the example is reproduced.

Ross Edwards: *The Hermit of Green Light*. Example reproduced by kind permission of Universal Edition (Australia) Pty Ltd; score available from Universal Edition (London) Ltd (see under David Bedford).

Brian Elias: *At the Edge of Time*. J. & W. Chester/Edition Wilhelm Hansen London Ltd, 7–9 Eagle Court, London, ECIM 5QD, by whose kind permission the examples are reproduced.

Corey Field: *Escape at Bedtime*. Vox Nova, PO Box 485, Wayne, PA 19087.

Irving Fine: *Mutability*. Novello and Co Ltd (see under Alison Bauld).

Harry Freedman: *Anerca*. Example reproduced by kind permission of Harry Freedman; score available from the Canadian Music Centre, Chalmers House, 20 St Joseph Street, Toronto, Ontario, M4Y 1J9, Canada.

Peter Racine Fricker: *Two Songs*. Examples reproduced by kind permission of Serenissima Music Co; score available from The Unicorn Music Co Inc (see under Donald Crockett).

Iain Hamilton: *Songs of Summer*. Example reproduced by kind permission of

Theodore Presser Co, Presser Place, Bryn Mawr, PA 19010; score available from Theodore Presser Co and Alfred A. Kalmus Ltd, 2/3 Fareham Street, Dean Street, London, W1V 4DU.

John Harbison: *Mirabai Songs*. Example reproduced by kind permission of G. Schirmer Inc; score available from Associated Music Publishers Inc (see under Elliott Carter).

Lou Harrison: *May Rain*. Hermes Beard Press, 7121 Viewpoint Road, Aptos, CA 95003.

Jonathan Harvey: *Cantata II – Three Lovescapes*. Novello and Co Ltd (see under Alison Bauld), by whose kind permission the examples are reproduced.

Paavo Heininen: *Love's Philosophy*. Paavo Heininen, by whose kind permission the example is reproduced, c/o Finnish Music Information Centre, Runeberginkatu 15A, SF 00100 Helsinki 10, Finland.

Hans Werner Henze: *Three Auden Songs*. Schott & Co Ltd (see under John Casken), by whose kind permission the example is reproduced. (Copyright 1984 by B. Schott's Soehne, Mainz.)

Robert Heppener: *Four Songs*. Donemus, Paulus Potterstraat 14, 1071 CZ Amsterdam, The Netherlands, by whose kind permission the examples are reproduced.

Trevor Hold: *Something Rich and Strange*. Basil Ramsey Ltd, 604 Rayleigh Road, Eastwood, Leigh-on-Sea, Essex, SS9 5HU, by whose kind permission the examples are reproduced.

Robin Holloway: *Wherever We May Be*. Boosey & Hawkes Music Publishers Ltd (see under David Del Tredici), by whose kind permission the examples are reproduced.

Elaine Hugh-Jones: *Six de la Mare Songs*. Elaine Hugh-Jones, 95 Church Road, Malvern Link, Worcestershire, WR14 1NQ, by whose kind permission the examples are reproduced.

Keith Humble: *Five Cabaret Songs*. Score available from Universal Edition (London) Ltd (see under David Bedford).

Karel Husa: *Twelve Moravian Songs*. Example reproduced by kind permission of G. Schirmer Inc; score available from Associated Music Publishers Inc (see under Elliott Carter).

John Joubert: *The Turning Wheel*. Novello and Co Ltd (see under Alison Bauld), by whose kind permission the examples are reproduced.

Earl Kim: *Letters found near a Suicide*. Example reproduced by kind permission of EMI Music Publishing Ltd; score available from International Music Publications, Southend Road, Woodford Green, Essex, IG8 8HN.

Peter Lawson: *Care Charmer Sleepe*. Peter Lawson, 13 Clifton Road, London, SE25, by whose kind permission the examples are reproduced.

Nicola LeFanu: *A Penny for a Song*. Novello and Co Ltd (see under Alison Bauld), by whose kind permission the examples are reproduced.

Elisabeth Lutyens: *In the Temple of a Bird's Wing*. Example reproduced by kind permission of the executors of the Elisabeth Lutyens Estate; score available from Universal Edition (London) Ltd (see under David Bedford).

Elizabeth Maconchy: *Sun, Moon and Stars*. J. & W. Chester/Edition Wilhelm Hansen London Ltd (see under Brian Elias), by whose kind permission the example is reproduced.

Daniël Manneke: *Five Songs on English Poems*. Donemus (see under Robert Heppener), by whose kind permission the examples are reproduced.

Donald Martino: *Three Songs*. E. C. Schirmer Music Co Inc, 138 Ipswich Street, Boston, MA 02215, by whose kind permission the examples are reproduced.

William Mathias: *A Vision of Time and Eternity*. Oxford University Press (see under Gordon Crosse), by whose kind permission the examples are reproduced.

Nicholas Maw: *The Voice of Love*. Boosey & Hawkes Music Publishers Ltd (see under David Del Tredici), by whose kind permission the examples are reproduced.

Thea Musgrave: *A Suite o' Bairnsangs*. J. & W. Chester/Edition Wilhelm Hansen London Ltd (see under Brian Elias), by whose kind permission the example is reproduced.

George Newson: *Four Songs*. George Newson, Chapel Cottage, Stone-in-Oxney, Tenterden, Kent, by whose kind permission the examples are reproduced.

George Nicholson: *Peripheral Visions*. Schott & Co Ltd (see under John Casken), by whose kind permission the example is reproduced.

Anthony Payne: *Evening Land*. J. & W. Chester/Edition Wilhelm Hansen London Ltd (see under Brian Elias), by whose kind permission the examples are reproduced.

Barbara Pentland: *Sung Songs nos. 4 and 5*. Examples reproduced by kind permission of Barbara Pentland; score available from Canadian Music Centre, Chalmers House, 20 St Joseph Street, Toronto, Ontario, M4Y 1J9, Canada.

Ronald Perera: *Five Summer Songs*. E. C. Schirmer Music Co Inc (see under Donald Martino), by whose kind permission the examples are reproduced.

André Previn: *Five Songs*. Edition Wilhelm Hansen/Chester Music New York Inc, 575 Eighth Avenue, New York, NY 10018, by whose kind permission the examples are reproduced.

Gwyn Pritchard: *Enitharmon*. Gwyn Pritchard, 55 Belmont Road, St Andrew's, Bristol, BS6 5AP, by whose kind permission the examples are reproduced.

Priaulx Rainier: *Three Greek Epigrams*. Schott & Co Ltd (see under John Casken), by whose kind permission the examples are reproduced.

Bernard Rands: *Ballad 2*. Universal Edition (London) Ltd (see under David Bedford), by whose kind permission the example is reproduced.

Karl Aage Rasmussen: *One and All*. Edition Wilhelm Hansen A/S, Gothersgade 9–11, DK-1123 Copenhagen K, Denmark; score available from Chester (see under Brian Elias)

Jeremy Dale Roberts: *Beautiful Lie the Dead*. Jeremy Dale Roberts, c/o Royal College of Music, Prince Consort Road, London, SW7 2BS.

Paul Robinson: *Music as Climate*. Paul Robinson, 23 Manor House Road, Wilsden, Bradford, BD15 0ED, by whose kind permission the example is reproduced.

George Rochberg: *Songs in Praise of Krishna*. Examples reproduced by kind permission of Theodore Presser Co; score available from Theodore Presser Co and Alfred A. Kalmus Ltd (see under Iain Hamilton), by whose kind permission the examples are reproduced.

Gunther Schuller: *Meditation*. Score available from International Music Publications (see under Earl Kim).

Barry Seaman: *Chamber Music Book I*. Example reproduced by kind permission of Barry Seaman; score available from Composers' Guild of Great Britain, 10 Stratford Place, London, W1N 9AE.

Leif Segerstam: *Three Leaves of Grass*. Josef Weinberger Ltd, 12–14 Mortimer Street, London, W1N 7RD.

Roger Sessions: *On the Beach at Fontana*. Example reproduced by kind permission of EMI Music Publishing Ltd; score available from International Music Publications (see under Earl Kim).

Malcolm Singer: *i am a little church*. Malcolm Singer, 33 Abdale Road, London, W12 7ER, by whose kind permission the examples are reproduced.

Roger Smalley: *Three Songs*. Faber Music Ltd, 3 Queen Square, London, WC1N 3AU.

Naresh Sohal: *Poems of Tagore I*. Novello and Co Ltd (see under Alison Bauld).

Richard Steinitz: *Songs from the Thousand and One Nights*. Richard Steinitz, by whose kind permission the example is reproduced, c/o Department of Music, The Polytechnic, Queensgate, Huddersfield, HD1 3DH.

John Tavener: *A Mini Song Cycle for Gina*. J. & W. Chester/Edition Wilhelm Hansen London Ltd (see under Brian Elias), by whose kind permission the example is reproduced.

Virgil Thomson: *Five Songs from William Blake*. Examples reproduced by kind permission of Theodore Presser Co; score available from Theodore Presser Co and Alfred A. Kalmus Ltd (see under Iain Hamilton).

Judith Weir: *Scotch Minstrelsy*. Novello and Co Ltd (see under Alison Bauld), by whose kind permission the examples are reproduced.

281

Malcolm Williamson: *Celebration of Divine Love*. Novello and Co Ltd (see under Alison Bauld), by whose kind permission the examples are reproduced.

James Wilson: *Bucolics*. James Wilson, 3 Grosvenor Terrace, Monkstown, Dublin, Eire, by whose kind permission the example is reproduced.

Hugh Wood: *Graves Songs Set II*. J. & W. Chester/Edition Wilhelm Hansen London Ltd (see Brian Elias), by whose kind permission the examples are reproduced.

If the reader has difficulty contacting publishers or composers, the national music information centres may be able to help.

British Music Information Centre, 10 Stratford Place, London, WIN 9AE.
Canadian Music Centre, Chalmers House, 20 St Joseph Street, Toronto, Ontario, M4Y 1J9.
American Music Center, 250 West 57th Street, Suite 626/7, New York, NY 10019.

Readers in America will find the Yesterday Music Service Inc (1430 Massachusetts Avenue, Room 318, Cambridge, MA 02138) particularly useful.

# Composer index